First World War
and Army of Occupation
War Diary
France, Belgium and Germany

9 DIVISION
South African Brigade
4 South African Infantry Regiment
1 July 1916 - 28 February 1918

WO95/1785

The Naval & Military Press Ltd
www.nmarchive.com
Published in association with The National Archives

Published by

The Naval & Military Press Ltd

Unit 10 Ridgewood Industrial Park,

Uckfield, East Sussex,

TN22 5QE England

Tel: +44 (0) 1825 749494

www.naval-military-press.com

www.nmarchive.com

This diary has been reprinted in facsimile from the original. Any imperfections are inevitably reproduced and the quality may fall short of modern type and cartographic standards.

Contents

Document type	Place/Title	Date From	Date To
Heading	9th (Scottish) Division 5th African Infy Bde. 4th 8th African Infy Regt. Jly-Dec 1916 Diaries For May-Jun 1916 Are Missing.		
War Diary	Grovetown	01/07/1916	02/07/1916
War Diary	Billon Valley	03/07/1916	05/07/1916
War Diary	German Trenches Montauban.	06/07/1916	11/07/1916
War Diary	Bernafay Wood Talus Boise Montauban	12/07/1916	14/07/1916
War Diary	Longueval & Delville Wood	14/07/1916	18/07/1916
War Diary	Talus Boise	19/07/1916	20/07/1916
War Diary	Happy-Valley	21/07/1916	23/07/1916
War Diary	Mouflers	24/07/1916	26/07/1916
War Diary	La Thieuloye	27/07/1916	27/07/1916
War Diary	Hermin	28/07/1916	15/08/1916
War Diary	Mesnil Bouche	16/08/1916	24/08/1916
War Diary	Trenches Berthonval No 1	25/08/1916	31/08/1916
War Diary	Camblain L'Abbe	01/09/1916	03/09/1916
War Diary	Estree Cauchie	04/09/1916	06/09/1916
War Diary	Carency In Support.	07/09/1916	16/09/1916
War Diary	Vimyridge-Carency Sector Trenches Carency I & Part II	17/09/1916	19/09/1916
War Diary	Vimyridge Carency Sector Front Line Trenches.	19/09/1916	24/09/1916
War Diary	Villers Brulin Camblain L'Abbe	25/09/1916	25/09/1916
War Diary	Ambrines	26/09/1916	05/10/1916
War Diary	Beauvoir	06/10/1916	07/10/1916
War Diary	Behencourt	08/10/1916	08/10/1916
War Diary	Mametz Wood	09/10/1916	09/10/1916
War Diary	In Front of High Wood	10/10/1916	11/10/1916
War Diary	Front Line N7 22.23	12/10/1916	12/10/1916
War Diary	High Wood & Trenches N W of Eaucourt L'Abbaye	12/10/1916	12/10/1916
War Diary	Trenches West of Eaucourt L'Abbaye	13/10/1916	13/10/1916
War Diary	Highwood S.W. edge	14/10/1916	14/10/1916
War Diary	High Wood	15/10/1916	19/10/1916
War Diary	Mametz Wood	20/10/1916	27/10/1916
War Diary	Millencourt	28/10/1916	28/10/1916
War Diary	Herissart	29/10/1916	29/10/1916
War Diary	Arras	30/10/1916	19/11/1916
War Diary	Arras Wanquetin	20/11/1916	20/11/1916
War Diary	Wanquentin	21/11/1916	03/12/1916
War Diary	Arras	04/12/1916	06/12/1916
War Diary	Arras J 2 Sub Sec.	07/12/1916	07/12/1916
War Diary	Arras	08/12/1916	08/12/1916
War Diary	Arras J.2	08/12/1916	08/12/1916
War Diary	Arras	09/12/1916	10/12/1916
War Diary	Arras J 2	10/12/1916	14/12/1916
War Diary	Arras J 2 to J 3	15/12/1916	15/12/1916
War Diary	J3	16/12/1916	18/12/1916
War Diary	Arras J III	19/12/1916	22/12/1916
War Diary	J III to J.1	23/12/1916	23/12/1916
War Diary	J 1	24/12/1916	31/12/1916
Heading	9th (Scottish) Division 8th African Infy Brigade 4th 8th African Infy Regt Jan-Dec 1917		

War Diary	Reserve Arras	01/01/1917	07/01/1917
War Diary	J 2	08/01/1917	12/01/1917
War Diary	Arras J 2	13/01/1917	13/01/1917
War Diary	J2	14/01/1917	15/01/1917
War Diary	J 3	16/01/1917	23/01/1917
War Diary	J I Sub-Section	24/01/1917	24/01/1917
War Diary	J I	25/01/1917	31/01/1917
War Diary	Arras	01/02/1917	08/02/1917
War Diary	J II Subsection	09/02/1917	09/02/1917
War Diary	J II	10/02/1917	10/02/1917
War Diary	No. 2 Section Right Sector	11/02/1917	16/02/1917
War Diary	No. 2 Section Right Sector To Reserve Arras	17/02/1917	17/02/1917
War Diary	Reserve B/n Arras.	18/02/1917	24/02/1917
War Diary	Right Sector Left Section	25/02/1917	04/03/1917
War Diary	Y. Hutments Near Etrun	05/03/1917	08/03/1917
War Diary	Y Huts	09/03/1917	10/03/1917
War Diary	Y. Huts Etrun	11/03/1917	12/03/1917
War Diary	Ostreville	13/03/1917	21/03/1917
War Diary	Penin	22/03/1917	24/03/1917
War Diary	Hermaville	25/03/1917	29/03/1917
War Diary	Y. Huts Etrun	30/03/1917	04/04/1917
War Diary	Y Huts	05/04/1917	06/04/1917
War Diary	Y Huts Etrun	07/04/1917	07/04/1917
War Diary	Y Huts	07/04/1917	07/04/1917
War Diary	J. Sector Front Line	08/04/1917	08/04/1917
War Diary	J. Sector.	08/04/1917	09/04/1917
War Diary	Railway Cutting 2nd Objective	10/04/1917	10/04/1917
War Diary	Railway Cutting	11/04/1917	11/04/1917
War Diary	Brown Line Cam. Trench	12/04/1917	12/04/1917
War Diary	Fampoux	12/04/1917	13/04/1917
War Diary	Physic Trench	13/04/1917	15/04/1917
War Diary	Arras	16/04/1917	16/04/1917
War Diary	Hutments ACQ.	17/04/1917	21/04/1917
War Diary	Monchy Breton	22/04/1917	27/04/1917
War Diary	Arras	28/04/1917	30/04/1917
Operation(al) Order(s)	1st South African Infantry Brigade, Instructions Regarding Forthcoming Operations This Issue All Previous Instructions.		
Operation(al) Order(s)	Operation Order 17/24. 4th S.A.I	12/04/1917	12/04/1917
Operation(al) Order(s)	4th. South African Infantry. Operation Order No. 17/18	03/04/1917	03/04/1917
Miscellaneous			
War Diary	Arras	01/05/1917	05/05/1917
War Diary	Black Line	06/05/1917	06/05/1917
War Diary	Green-Line	07/05/1917	11/05/1917
War Diary	Y Huts	11/05/1917	11/05/1917
War Diary	Y Huts Etrun	12/05/1917	12/05/1917
War Diary	Monchy Breton	13/05/1917	01/06/1917
War Diary	Arras	02/06/1917	17/06/1917
War Diary	Y. Huts	18/06/1917	20/06/1917
War Diary	Y Huts Etrun	21/06/1917	22/06/1917
War Diary	Y Huts	23/06/1917	30/06/1917
War Diary	Y. Huts Etrun	01/07/1917	01/07/1917
War Diary	Y. Huts	02/07/1917	05/07/1917
War Diary	Y. Huts Etrun	06/07/1917	06/07/1917
War Diary	Berneville	07/07/1917	27/07/1917
War Diary	Bertincourt	28/07/1917	28/07/1917

War Diary	Ytres	29/07/1917	03/08/1917
War Diary	Trescault Left Sub Sector	04/08/1917	09/08/1917
War Diary	Metz En Coutures	10/08/1917	17/08/1917
War Diary	Trescault Sub-Section	18/08/1917	28/08/1917
War Diary	Barastre Achiet Le Petit	29/08/1917	29/08/1917
War Diary	Achiet Le Petit.	30/08/1917	12/09/1917
War Diary	Watou Area 2 L	13/09/1917	13/09/1917
War Diary	Shrine Camp Watou Area	14/09/1917	14/09/1917
War Diary	Brandhoek	15/09/1917	17/09/1917
War Diary	Trenches	17/09/1917	17/09/1917
War Diary	Square Farm	17/09/1917	19/09/1917
War Diary	Low Farm	20/09/1917	20/09/1917
War Diary	Barry Farm	20/09/1917	21/09/1917
War Diary	O.G Line Y Truck	22/09/1917	22/09/1917
War Diary	Winnezeele	23/09/1917	27/09/1917
War Diary	Ledringham	28/09/1917	03/10/1917
War Diary	Houlle	04/10/1917	10/10/1917
War Diary	Brake Camp	11/10/1917	11/10/1917
War Diary	Reigersberg Camp	12/10/1917	26/10/1917
War Diary	Coudekerque-Branche	27/10/1917	28/10/1917
War Diary	La Panne	29/10/1917	31/10/1917
War Diary	La Panne Bains	01/11/1917	06/11/1917
War Diary	Coxyde Bains	07/11/1917	09/11/1917
War Diary	Middlesex Camp	10/11/1917	16/11/1917
War Diary	La Panne	17/11/1917	18/11/1917
War Diary	Chyvelde	19/11/1917	19/11/1917
War Diary	Teteghem	20/11/1917	20/11/1917
War Diary	Esquelbecq	21/11/1917	21/11/1917
War Diary	La Reicle	22/11/1917	22/11/1917
War Diary	Wardrecques	22/11/1917	23/11/1917
War Diary	Assinghem	24/11/1917	24/11/1917
War Diary	Renty	25/11/1917	30/11/1917
War Diary	Epes	01/12/1917	01/12/1917
War Diary	Anvin	02/12/1917	02/12/1917
War Diary	Peronne	03/12/1917	03/12/1917
War Diary	Don Camp	04/12/1917	04/12/1917
War Diary	Line	05/12/1917	10/12/1917
War Diary	L 2 Camp	11/12/1917	11/12/1917
War Diary	Line	12/12/1917	15/12/1917
War Diary	Support Line	16/12/1917	18/12/1917
War Diary	Line	19/12/1917	22/12/1917
War Diary	Hutments W.3.C.	23/12/1917	23/12/1917
War Diary	Hutments	24/12/1917	27/12/1917
War Diary	Line	28/12/1917	30/12/1917
War Diary	Support Line	31/12/1917	31/12/1917
Heading	9th (Scottish Division) South African Infy Bde 4th Sth African Infy Regt Jan-Feb 1918 To 66 Div 1918 Sept		
Heading	9th Div To African Bn. 4th Bde. To. African Inf Reg. Jan-Feb 1918		
War Diary	The 1st 2nd & 4th South African Infantry Battalions Were Formed Into South African Composite Battalion On 24th April 1918		
War Diary	Support Line	01/01/1918	03/01/1918
War Diary	Line	04/01/1918	07/01/1918
War Diary	Fins	08/01/1918	11/01/1918
War Diary	Moislains	12/01/1918	24/01/1918

War Diary	Rt Sub Sector Gouzeaucourt	25/01/1918	27/01/1918
War Diary	Support Map 57 C Q 23c63	29/01/1918	31/01/1918
War Diary	Arms Clothing and Equipment		
War Diary		01/02/1918	01/02/1918
War Diary	Suzanne	02/02/1918	28/02/1918

9TH (SCOTTISH) DIVISION
STH AFRICAN INFY BDE.

4TH STH AFRICAN INFY REGT.

JLY - DEC 1916

DIARIES FOR MAY -JUN 1916
ARE MISSING.

Instructions regarding War Diaries and Intelligence Summaries are contained in F. S. Regs., Part II. and the Staff Manual respectively. Title Pages will be prepared in manuscript.

WAR DIARY
or
INTELLIGENCE SUMMARY
(Erase heading not required.)

Army Form C. 2118

9

4th S. African Infantry — July 1916 — Vol 4

Place	Date	Hour	Summary of Events and Information	Remarks and references to Appendices
GROVETOWN	1/7/16		Battalion bivouacked at GROVETOWN. which is about a mile N.W of the Village of BRAY. ZERO of Z day for attack on MONTAUBAN was 7.30AM	
GROVETOWN	2/7/16		Battalion still bivouacked at GROVETOWN & completed fighting equipment. In the evening moved up to BILLON VALLEY & occupied dugouts on E side between Trigger Wood & Billon Wood	
BILLON VALLEY	3/7/16		Still in dugouts	
BILLON VALLEY	4/7/16		Still in dugouts	
BILLON VALLEY	5/7/16		In evening left Billon Valley & occupied trenches to South of MONTAUBAN, viz GLATZ REDOUBT - CASEMENT TRENCH - TRAIN ALLEY & vicinity, building strong points at GLATZ REDOUBT & TRAIN ALLEY. BATTALION Hqrs ~~in GLATZ REDOUBT~~ on road between MARICOURT & CASEMENT TRENCH	

1875 Wt. W593/826 1,000,000 4/15 J.B.C. & A. A.D.S.S./Forms/C. 2118.

Instructions regarding War Diaries and Intelligence Summaries are contained in F. S. Regs., Part II. and the Staff Manual respectively. Title Pages will be prepared in manuscript.

WAR DIARY
or
INTELLIGENCE SUMMARY
(Erase heading not required.)

4th S. African Infantry — July 1916

Place	Date	Hour	Summary of Events and Information	Remarks and references to Appendices
GERMAN TRENCHES MONTAUBAN	6/7/16		Still in same trenches as on 5th. Battalion HQrs moved into GLATZ REDOUBT. Took over & began consolidating BRIQUETTERIE TRENCH. Germans shelled the locality in evening. Lt OUGHTERSON killed.	
Do.	7/7/16		Still consolidating BRIQUETTERIE trench. Raining & trenches in bad condition. Still in same trenches. Heavily shelled at intervals	
Do	8/7/16		Still in ~~our~~ same trenches. Working in trenches in locality. Shelled all day.	
Do.	9/7/16		Still in same trenches. About 9 pm. A Coy moved forward ~~into~~ to S.W corner TRONES WOOD, ~~supported by~~ & a platoon of C Coy moved into sunken road EAST ~~SOUTH~~ of BRIQUETTERIE. A Coy joined up on right of MANCHESTER & dug in 50 yds from TRONES WOOD along its southern fringe	
Do.	10/7/16		A Coy about daybreak with some MANCHESTERS went through TRONES wood from SOUTH to NORTH, & found wood clear of enemy. Returned to ~~our~~ trench & enemy opened fire from wood also heavily shelled trench. Capt RUSSELL hit & died next morning. A Coy relieved at night & returned to GLATZ redoubt. ~~B & C~~ companies relieved by LIVERPOOLS & concentrated in GLATZ REDOUBT. ~~A~~ B & D occupied trenches in BERNAFAY WOOD. Lt SHENTON wounded.	

Instructions regarding War Diaries and Intelligence Summaries are contained in F. S. Regs., Part II. and the Staff Manual respectively. Title Pages will be prepared in manuscript.

WAR DIARY
or
INTELLIGENCE SUMMARY
(Erase heading not required.)

Army Form C. 2118

Place	Date	Hour	Summary of Events and Information — 4th S. African Infantry — July 1916	Remarks and references to Appendices
BERNAFAY WOOD TALUS BOISÉ MONTAUBAN	11/7/16		~~A Coy moved~~ A & C coys in vicinity of GLATZ REDOUBT all day, & heavily shelled. B & D coys heavily shelled in BERNAFAY WOOD. A coy moved up about 9 pm to BERNAFAY WOOD. Lt COLONEL F.A. JONES & Lt FRY killed	
	12/7/16		In evening A. B & D relieved, & together with C coy the battalion concentrated & bivouacked on ground west of TALUS BOISÉ & north of tramline	
	13/7/16		On evening of 13th the battalion occupied trenches close up to & south of MONTAUBAN. Heavily shelled with "tear" shells and H.E. Lt TAYLOR severely wounded - Lt FARRELL gassed.	
LONGUEVAL & DELVILLE WOOD	14/7/16		At 2 30 AM the battalion moved thro' MONTAUBAN ~~up~~ into the sunken road from BERNAFAY wood to LONGUEVAL halting short of the village. B & C coys moved at 7 A M into trench between LONGUEVAL & WATERLOT already occupied by 5th CAMERONS. At midday CAMERONS took WATERLOT ~~with [illegible] platoons of [illegible] coy~~ supported by two platoons each from B & C coys. B & C coys remained at Waterlot farm during day &	

1875 Wt. W593/826 1,000,000 4/15 J.B.C. & A. A.D.S.S./Forms/C. 2118.

Instructions regarding War Diaries and Intelligence Summaries are contained in F. S. Regs., Part II. and the Staff Manual respectively. Title Pages will be prepared in manuscript.

WAR DIARY
or
INTELLIGENCE SUMMARY

(Erase heading not required.)

Army Form C. 2118

4

4th S African Infantry — July 1916

Place	Date	Hour	Summary of Events and Information	Remarks and references to Appendices
LONGUEVAL & DELVILLE WOOD	14/7/16		in evening received orders to retire to trench from which attack was made. A & D Coys. went to support of troops in DELVILLE WOOD & were distributed there. LT THORBURN killed at Waterlot farm, & Lt KIRBY wounded	
	15/7/16		A Coy & D Coy still holding on to positions in N.E corner of Delville Wood in rough craters & hastily dug trenches very heavily shelled all day & counter attacked about dusk. At dawn B & C Coys were retired to communication trench near Longueval road & stayed there all day & night & very heavily shelled.	
	16/7/16		A & D Coys still holding on in same place, heavily shelled all day, counterattacked at dusk & at night improving trenches as much as possible. B & C Coys ~~about 11 & 12~~ moved during morning,	

1875 Wt. W593/826 1,000,000 4/15 J.B.C. & A. A.D.S.S./Forms/C. 2118

Instructions regarding War Diaries and Intelligence Summaries are contained in F. S. Regs., Part II. and the Staff Manual respectively. Title Pages will be prepared in manuscript.

Army Form C. 2118

WAR DIARY
or
INTELLIGENCE SUMMARY
(Erase heading not required.)

4th S. African Infantry — July 1916

Place	Date	Hour	Summary of Events and Information	Remarks and references to Appendices
LONGUEVAL & DELVILLE WOOD	16/7/16		through LONGUEVAL, into DELVILLE WOOD. B Coy at first occupied line from CAMERON REDOUBT to CEMETERY afterwards withdrawing to Cameron Redoubt after heavy loss from Maxim fire & occupied trench with Camerons in front of redoubt maintaining position till about ~~major~~ midnight when ordered by Col Dawson to return to trench by sunken road. C Coy occupied ground (on entering wood) to right rear of B Coy about 50 to 100 yds ~~west of BUCHANAN~~ north of cnr TANNERS Hdqrs. Later in day two platoons moved to left to occupy a trench ~~(west~~ near the German redoubt & west of Cameron redoubt. At dark C Coy ~~who~~ were ordered to withdraw to same trench as B Coy, but ½ Coy of C which had moved to left did not return to trench by sunken road till next morning. Lt Brown Killed – Lt Watkins wounded. Lt Young wounded.	

1875 Wt. W593/826 1,000,000 4/15 J.B.C. & A. A.D.S.S./Forms/C. 2118.

Army Form C. 2118

6/

WAR DIARY
or
INTELLIGENCE SUMMARY
(Erase heading not required.)

Instructions regarding War Diaries and Intelligence Summaries are contained in F. S. Regs., Part II. and the Staff Manual respectively. Title Pages will be prepared in manuscript.

4th S. African Infantry — July 1916

Place	Date	Hour	Summary of Events and Information	Remarks and references to Appendices
DELVILLE WOOD	17/7/16		A & D Coys maintained the same positions as on the 16th. The Germans heavily counterattacked at dawn, getting in some cases up to parapet, but were driven off. Heavily shelled all day & counterattacked at dusk. B & C remained all day and night in sunken trenches, very heavily shelled & had a good many casualties. Capt MARSHALL wounded. Lt GRIERSON gassed	
LONGUEVAL	18/7/16		A & D coys very heavily shelled all day & by this time almost all killed & wounded. A Coy attacked about 5 p.m. & the remains of A & D coys withdrawn to centre of wood & joined Col Thackeray's party. At 7 AM fifty men of "C" coy sent forward to reinforce 2nd Regt under Major Burges in wood. In afternoon remainder of C & all B coy moved forward to trenches on S. west	

Army Form C. 2118

Instructions regarding War Diaries and Intelligence Summaries are contained in F. S. Regs., Part II. and the Staff Manual respectively. Title Pages will be prepared in manuscript.

WAR DIARY
or
INTELLIGENCE SUMMARY
(Erase heading not required.)

4th S. African Infantry — July 1916

Place	Date	Hour	Summary of Events and Information	Remarks and references to Appendices
	18/7/16		edge of wood & in LONGUEVAL, & 25 men went to Buchanan Street & again moved forward from there. The few men remaining of B & C remained all night in these trenches. Lt Ross killed - Capt Brown wounded - Lt Bell killed - Lt Smith wounded - Maj McLeod wounded - Capt C[illegible]	[illegible]
TALUS BOISE	19/7/16		At 3.40 AM Major HUNT received orders from Lt-Col DAWSON to withdraw battalion to TALUS BOISÉ. This was done except the men of the battalion who were with Colonel THACKERAY. The battalion rendezvoused at TALUS BOISE 5 (five) Officers - Medical Officer & 134 O.R. In the afternoon another 9 men reported back making a total of 146 O.R. - Lt CHASE wounded - Lt NEWSON missing.	Capt GRADY wounded date not available
	20/7/16		All day bivouacked at TALUS BOISE	

Instructions regarding War Diaries and Intelligence Summaries are contained in F. S. Regs., Part II. and the Staff Manual respectively. Title Pages will be prepared in manuscript.

WAR DIARY
or
INTELLIGENCE SUMMARY
(Erase heading not required.)

Army Form C. 2118

Place	Date	Hour	4th S. African Infantry — Summary of Events and Information — July 1916	Remarks and references to Appendices
[HAPPY VALLE]Y - VALLEY	21/7/16		Battalion moved in afternoon to HAPPY VALLEY & bivouacked. Draft of 88 O.R. joined battalion	
	22/7/16		Still at HAPPY VALLEY. Draft of 59 O.R. joined battalion. Capt MITCHELL rejoined from 26th Bde.	
	23/7/16		Battalion moved from HAPPY VALLEY at 1-15 pm via MEAULTE to MERICOURT L'ABBE station, reaching station about 5 p.m. Entrained app at 12 midn. Dumped 13 hand carts at station.	
MOUFLERS	24/7/16		Train left MERICOURT L'ABBE about 2-30 a.m. Battalion detrained at HENGEST & marched to MOUFLERS where billeted by 10-20 a.m. app.	
	25/7/16		Still billeted at MOUFLERS. Men resting, washing & cleaning up. Rifles inspection in morning. Lt Charlton took over temporary command of A Coy.	

1875 Wt. W593/826 1,000,000 4/15 J.B.C. & A. A.D.S.S./Forms/C. 2118.

Instructions regarding War Diaries and Intelligence Summaries are contained in F. S. Regs., Part II. and the Staff Manual respectively. Title Pages will be prepared in manuscript.

WAR DIARY
or
INTELLIGENCE SUMMARY

(Erase heading not required.)

Army Form C. 2118.

4th S. African Infantry — July 1916

Place	Date	Hour	Summary of Events and Information	Remarks and references to Appendices
MOUFLERS	26/7/16		Transport moved at 6 A.M. Battalion moved at 7-20 a.m. Entrained at LONGPRE (LES CORPS SAINTS) by 9-30 A.M. & left 10-30 A.M. Detrained at BRIAS & marched to LA THIEULOYE where billeted.	
LA THIEULOYE	27/7/16		Battalion with transport moved at 2 p.m. Clear of village by 2-15 p.m. Billeted at HERMIN by 5.30 p.m. app.	
HERMIN	28/7/16		10-12 A.M. Parades under Coy arrangements, also Band, Signallers & LEWIS gunners under instruction same hours. Complete deficiency lists taken to complete Coys & details, also deficiencies in Lewis gun & Signalling equipment; all passed to Q^r M^r for indent. 30 O.R.s reported to O.C. 182nd Tunnelling Coy at MINGOVAL today for attachment.	
HERMIN	29/7/16		10-12 A.M. Parades under Coy arrangements, also Band, Signallers & LEWIS gunners under instructions same hours. Coys handed in new nominal rolls to orderly room. Draft of 50 O.R. joined battalion from 2nd [illegible] B. [illegible]	
HERMIN	30/7/16		Church Parades.	

1875 Wt. W593/826 1,000,000 4/15 J.B.C.& A. A.D.S.S./Forms/C. 2118.

Army Form C. 2118

10/

Instructions regarding War Diaries and Intelligence Summaries are contained in F. S. Regs., Part II. and the Staff Manual respectively. Title Pages will be prepared in manuscript.

WAR DIARY
or
INTELLIGENCE SUMMARY

(Erase heading not required.)

4th S. African Infantry — July 1916

Place	Date	Hour	Summary of Events and Information	Remarks and references to Appendices
HERMIN	31/7/16		Parades. 7·15 – 7·45 am Physical Drill; 10 – 12 noon Route Marching; 2·30 – 3·30 pm. Bayonet fighting } Under Coy. arrangements. Band – Signallers & Massan[illegible] out for instruction same hours.	
			Lt Dalgety took over temporary command of "D" Coy vice Capt Anderson.	
			Lt Lees assumed duties of Transport Officer vice Lt Dalgety.	

HERMIN
31–7–16

D. E. Hume
Major Commanding
4th South African Infy.

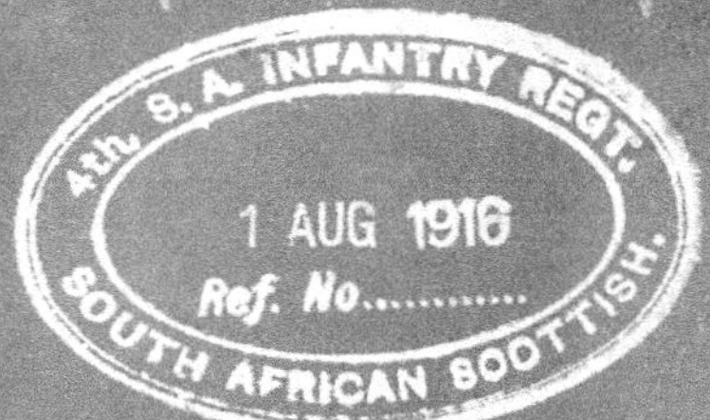

1875 Wt. W593/826 1,000,000 4/15 J.B.C. & A. A.D.S.S./Forms/C. 2118.

Instructions regarding War Diaries and Intelligence Summaries are contained in F. S. Regs., Part II. and the Staff Manual respectively. Title Pages will be prepared in manuscript.

WAR DIARY
or
INTELLIGENCE SUMMARY

(Erase heading not required.)

Page 1

Army Form C. 2118

4th S.A.R

4th South African Infantry — August - 1916 — Vol 5

Place	Date	Hour	Summary of Events and Information	Remarks and references to Appendices
HERMIN	1/8/16		Parades - By company arrangement. 7-15 to 7-45 a.m. Physical Drill 10 to 12 noon Parade 2-30 to 3-30 p.m. Parade. Battalion Strength (less attached) 16 officers 594 O.R. 10 men sent to train as signallers at Brigade	[illegible]
HERMIN	2/8/16		1 Bathing & disinfecting clothing of the battalion at FRESNICOURT under supervision of S.A. Field Ambulance. 2 Draft - 2 officers & 283 rank & file arrived at 6 p.m. The officers names are Capt MOWAT and Capt NORTON 3 Six O.R. sent to course at Cadet School ST OMER	
HERMIN	3/8/16		Parades. Physical Drill - Bombing - Bayonet fighting - Close order Drill & Lectures - [illegible] 7-15 to 7-45 All Coys 10 - 11 a.m. ✓ A. Coy - B. C & D Coys. 11 - 12 noon B Coy - A. C. & D Coys. 2-30 - 3-30 p.m. C. Coy A Coy B Coy D Coy Band - Signallers & Lewis gunners same hours.	
HERMIN	4/8/16		Parades - 7-15 - 7-45 A.M. Saluting Drill 10-30 A.M. C.O.s Parade - Battalion Drill & Ceremonial 2-30 p.m. R. Sgt. Major parade - Battalion. Smartening up. R.E. Instruction - 8 N.C.O.s attending Rejoined from Hospital - 32 O.R. Draft arrived - 1 - O.R	

1875 Wt. W593/826 1,000,000 4/15 J.B.C. & A. A.D.S.S./Forms/C. 2118.

Instructions regarding War Diaries and Intelligence Summaries are contained in F. S. Regs., Part II. and the Staff Manual respectively. Title Pages will be prepared in manuscript.

Page 2

Army Form C. 2118

WAR DIARY
or
INTELLIGENCE SUMMARY
(Erase heading not required.)

4th Regt. S.A.I. Aug. 1916

Place	Date	Hour	Summary of Events and Information	Remarks and references to Appendices
HERMIN	5/8/16		Parades. 7.15 to 7.45. AM - Physical Drill 9.30 to 10 A.M. A.B.C. Bayonet fighting: D Coy Bombing 1.30 p.m. Parade for Brigade inspection by G.O.C. 1st Army. 16 N.C.O.S training with R.E instructor. 12 Men detailed to Signallers. 12 men detailed to Lewis Guns - All for training	
HERMIN	6/8/16		Church parades.	
HERMIN	7/8/16		Parades - 7.15 to 7.45 - Saluting Drill. 10 A.M. "A" Bombing. "B" Bayonet fighting 10-12 C & D Coys - Route Marching - 11 A.M. "A" Bayonet fighting. "B" Bombing 2-30. pm. C.O's parade. Assault Formation. 4 pm. Cpls & L/Cpls to instruct in Guard Mounting. 16 N.C.O.s training with R.E. Instructor	

1875 Wt. W593/826 1,000,000 4/15 J.B.C. & A. A.D.S.S./Forms/C. 2118.

Instructions regarding War Diaries and Intelligence Summaries are contained in F. S. Regs., Part II. and the Staff Manual respectively. Title Pages will be prepared in manuscript.

WAR DIARY
or
INTELLIGENCE SUMMARY
(Erase heading not required.)

Army Form C. 2118

4th Regt. S.A.I. Aug. 1916

Place	Date	Hour	Summary of Events and Information	Remarks and references to Appendices
HERMIN	8/8/16		Physical Drill 7.15 to 7.45 am. All Coys.	
			10 A.M. C. Coy Bombing D Coy Bayonet fighting	
			11. A.M. D. Coy Bombing C Coy Bayonet fighting	
			10-12 noon A & B. Coys Route Marching	
			2.30 pm All Coys C.O.s parade	
			4-5 pm. Cpls & L/cpls for instruction in Guard mounting	
			~~A & C M G Coy held sports~~ ~~sent over pipe band~~.	
HERMIN	9/8/16		7.15 to 7.45 A.M. All Coys Physical Drill - 9-10.30 am. A Coy Bombing	
			9-10 am. B. Coy Gas Instruction 10-11 am C. Coy Gas instruction	
			10-11 am. D Coy Trench Practice 10.30-12 noon B. Coy Bombing	
			11-12 noon A Coy Coy Drill - C Coy Coy Drill - D Coy Gas instruction	
			2.30 to 3.30 pm. A. Coy. Gas Instruction - B & D Coys Coy Drill C Coy Trench instruction	
			4 to 5 pm. Cpls & L/cpls under a/R.S.M.	
			Promotions to Sgt & Cpl to replace ~~[illegible]~~ casualties put in orders	

1875 Wt. W593/826 1,000,000 4/15 J.B.C. & A. A.D.S.S./Forms/C. 2118.

Page 4 Army Form C. 2118.

WAR DIARY or INTELLIGENCE SUMMARY

Instructions regarding War Diaries and Intelligence Summaries are contained in F. S. Regs., Part II. and the Staff Manual respectively. Title Pages will be prepared in manuscript.

4th Regt. S. Afr. Infy (Erase heading not required.) Aug. 1916.

Place	Date	Hour	Summary of Events and Information	Remarks and references to Appendices
HERMIN	10/8/16		7-15 to 7-45 a.m. Squad drill by L/cpls. All Coys	
			9-10 a.m. ~~Laying~~ D. Coy Laying out trenches. 9-10.30 a.m. C. Coy Bombing	
			9-30 to 12 noon A. Coy Field Engineering 10 to 12 noon. B. Coy Route march	
			10-30 to 12 noon D Coy Bombing 11-12 noon C. Coy Laying out trenches	
			2-30-3-30 p.m. A. Coy Field Engineering. B Coy Assault formations	
			do C & D. Coys Route marching.	
			4 to 5 p.m. Sgts out for instruction.	
			Bde M. G. Coy Sports - our pipe band attended.	
HERMIN	11/8/16.		1 7-15 to 7-45. a.m. Squad drill by L/cpls. All Coys.	
			9-10 A.M. B Coy Gas practice 9-10-30 A.M. A Coy. Bombing	These parades broken
			9-30-12 noon C. Coy Field Engineering 10-11 A.M. Gas practice	off to line road
			11-12 noon Gas practice A Coy. 10-30-12 noon B Coy Bombing	King went through.
			11-12 D. Coy - Coy Drill. Afternoon parade cancelled to get ready working party	
			2 A working party of 300 O.R. under Capt MOWAT left at 4 p.m. to	
			relieve similar party of 26th Bde in BOIS HILEUX. (100 men each A.B.C. Coys)	
			Halting till dusk at ESTREE CAUCHIE.	
			His Majesty the King went through at 11-35 a.m.	

1875 Wt. W593/826 1,000,000 4/15 J.B.C. & A. A.D.S.S./Forms/C. 2118.

Army Form C. 2118

Instructions regarding War Diaries and Intelligence Summaries are contained in F. S. Regs., Part II. and the Staff Manual respectively. Title Pages will be prepared in manuscript.

WAR DIARY
or
INTELLIGENCE SUMMARY
(Erase heading not required.)

4th South African Infantry — August 1916

Place	Date	Hour	Summary of Events and Information	Remarks and references to Appendices
HERMIN	12/8/16		Details A.B & C Coys & D Coy.	
			7-15 to 7.45 a.m. Physical Drill	
			10-12 noon Route marching	
			2.30 p.m. D Coy refitting	
HERMIN	13/8/16		Church parades - Pres; C. of E., R.C.,	
HERMIN	14/8/16		1 Details A.B & C Coys & D Coy.	
			7-15 to 7-45 a.m. Physical Drill	
			10-11 a.m. Bayonet fighting	
			11-12 noon Fire Direction & Control	
			x 2-30 to 3-30 p.m. Route Marching	
			2 Band left 5 p.m. to play to 1st Regt at FREVILLIERS.	
			3 At 6-30 p.m. a Draft of 1 Officer (2/Lt. J. DAVIES) and 100 other ranks arrived. Draft included 26 LEWIS gunners & 9 signallers	
			4 Rained a little during the day.	
			5 LEWIS GUNNERS practising with ball cartridge at Range VHD.	

Instructions regarding War Diaries and Intelligence Summaries are contained in F. S. Regs., Part II. and the Staff Manual respectively. Title Pages will be prepared in manuscript.

Page 6

Army Form C. 2118

WAR DIARY
or
INTELLIGENCE SUMMARY
(Erase heading not required.)

4th South African Infantry — August, 1916.

Place	Date	Hour	Summary of Events and Information	Remarks and references to Appendices
HERMIN	15/8/16		7.15 to 7.45 All Coys - Physical Drill.	
			10 - 11 a.m. All Coys. Company Drill	
			3.45 p.m. The battalion paraded with transport ready to move.	
			3.50 p.m. The battalion moved via Fauchin Ligny to MESNIL BOUCHÉ	
			6.15 p.m. The battalion billeted in its new quarters.	
			The medical officer inspected billets at Hermin on leaving reported same clean. The new billets at Mesnil Bouché not too clean. There were seven men fell out on line of march (4 drunk · 3 medical reasons) but all rejoined at the halt.	
MESNIL BOUCHE	16/8/16		7.15 to 7.45 A.M. All Coys Physical Drill	
			10-11 a.m. All Coys Bayonet fighting	
			11-12 noon All Coys Attack practice	
			2.30 to 3.30 p.m. All Coys Route Marching.	
MESNIL BOUCHE	17/8/16		7-15 to 7.45 a.m. All Coys Physical Drill	
			10-11 am A.B.C. Coys Rapid Loading	
			11-12 a.m. D Coy do.	
			2.30-4 p.m. All Coys. Route Marching	
			By 12 noon. The whole working party of 300 men under Capt Mount returned from BOIS DES AILEUX & billetted. They had no casualties whilst absent.	

Instructions regarding War Diaries and Intelligence Summaries are contained in F. S. Regs., Part II. and the Staff Manual respectively. Title Pages will be prepared in manuscript.

WAR DIARY
or
INTELLIGENCE SUMMARY
(Erase heading not required.)

Page 7.

Army Form C. 2118

4th Regt. S. Afr. Infy — August 1916.

Place	Date	Hour	Summary of Events and Information	Remarks and references to Appendices
MESNIL BOUCHE	17/8/16		Capt. R. D. GRAHAM, LT J. C. FRENCH and 2/LT BENNIE reported on joining the Battalion for duty at 11-30 a.m.	
			Capt Norton 2/Lt BENNIE & 100 O.R. moved at 8.30 pm to rept to 50th Bde R.A. for work	
			Lt French & 70 O.R from A.B.C Coys moved at 8.45 pm to rept to 52 Bde R.A for working party.	
MESNIL BOUCHE	18/8/16		1 Sgt - 1 Cpl & 30 men left at 8. A.M. to report to Reserve Depot Stores ~~at~~ for work near Pt SERVINS.	
			Routine:-	
			7-15 to 7.45 a.m. All Coys Extended order Drill by Sections	
			9.30 am to 10-40 am. A Coy Smoke Helmet Drill & Rapid Loading	
			Do. Do. B Coy Attack Practice	
			10-50 to 12 ~~pm~~ noon B. Coy Smoke Helmet Drill & Rapid Loading	
			Do. Do. A Coy Attack Practice.	
			10 to 12 am C Coy Route march in full marching order.	
			2-30 to 3.30 p.m. A & B Coys Do. Do.	
			2-30 to 3.30 p.m. C Coy Bayonet fighting.	
			10 to 12 noon and 2-30 to 4 p.m. Bombing instruction for Regtl Bombers.	
			2/Lieut Gemmil reported from base for duty with battalion	

Instructions regarding War Diaries and Intelligence Summaries are contained in F. S. Regs., Part II. and the Staff Manual respectively. Title Pages will be prepared in manuscript.

Page 8

Army Form C. 2118

WAR DIARY
or
INTELLIGENCE SUMMARY
(Erase heading not required.)

4th Regt Saf Infy — August 1916

Place	Date	Hour	Summary of Events and Information	Remarks and references to Appendices
MESNIL BOUCHE	18/8/16		Capt Ross in command of 250 O.R. from A.B. & C Coys moved at 7.40 pm. to report at "MAISTRE LINE" for work in trenches for 9th Signal section.	
MESNIL BOUCHE	19/8/16		Transport moved to Pt SERVINS at 1-30 p.m. Very few men left available in camp, gave them lectures on map reading, bombs &c, & practiced rapid loading. Major Hunt, 2 other officers & 8 N.C.O.s visited the trenches. A good deal of rain, muddy underfoot.	
MESNIL BOUCHE	20/8/16		Church parades:- Dull days - Muddy underfoot.	
MESNIL BOUCHE	21/8/16		Very few men in camp except specialists under instruction, & the details of Coys in camp practiced the attack & rapid loading in morning. In the evening the working parties under Capt Ross, Capt Norton & Lt French reported back from same.	

1875 Wt. W593/826 1,000,000 4/15 J.B.C. & A. A.D.S.S./Forms/C. 2118.

Instructions regarding War Diaries and Intelligence Summaries are contained in F. S. Regs., Part II. and the Staff Manual respectively. Title Pages will be prepared in manuscript.

Page 9 Army Form C. 2118

WAR DIARY
or
INTELLIGENCE SUMMARY
(Erase heading not required.)

4th Regt S Afr Infy August 1916

Place	Date	Hour	Summary of Events and Information	Remarks and references to Appendices
MESNIL BOUCHE	22/8/16		All companies bathing at GUOY SERVINS.	
MESNIL BOUCHE	23/8/16		The battalion commenced to move at 6-30 am to relieve the Black Watch in the trenches BERTHONVAL SECTOR No 1. Relief completed by 1 pm. All details went to PETIT SERVINS to 1st Line Transport.	
TRENCHES Berthonval No 1	24/8/16		Found a lot of working parties - Sent out two patrols - Intermittently shelled during Day. Wind westerly - Casualties 1 O.R. wounded	
	25/8/16		Working parties. For R.E in front line - Trench Mortar emplacements. Deepening Snargate Street. A few shells dropped into ZOUAVE VALLEY Patrol out under Lt Davies. Casualties 1 O.R Killed 4 O.R wounded	
	26/8/16		Working parties - For R.E in front line - Trench Mortar emplacements. Patrol out under Lt Gemmill. Our trench mortars shelled enemy's line	
	27/8/16		Working party - for R.E in front line - Party on battle Dug out. Intermittent shelling both sides. Patrols out at night. Proceeding with battle HQrs Dug out. Patrols out during night Casualties 1 O.R. Killed 2 O.R wounded	

1875 Wt. W593/826 1,000,000 4/15 J.B.C. & A. A.D.S.S./Forms/C. 2118.

Instructions regarding War Diaries and Intelligence Summaries are contained in F. S. Regs., Part II. and the Staff Manual respectively. Title Pages will be prepared in manuscript.

Page 10 [illegible]

Army Form C. 2118

WAR DIARY
or
INTELLIGENCE SUMMARY
(Erase heading not required.)

~~4th Regt. S. Afr. Infy~~ ~~Aug. 1916~~

4th S.A.I. August 1916

Place	Date	Hour	Summary of Events and Information	Remarks and references to Appendices
TRENCHES BERTHONVAL 1.	28/8/16		~~Very heavy rain, doing considerable damage to trenches & C.T.s.~~ Working parties repairing trenches, & 80 men under R.E. on Broad St. & Snargate St. Our artillery & T.M.s shelling during day. Proceeding with Battn Hedqrs. – Patrols out inspecting enemy's wire	Casualties 1 O.R. killed 2 O.R. wounded
	29/8/16		Working parties 80 men under R.E. on Broad St. & Snargate St. – General work. Proceeding with Battn Hdqrs dugout. Our T.M.s registering on enemy's wire. Patrols out.	
	30/8/16		Work repairing damage done by heavy rains, also 80 men under R.E. on Broad St. Proceeding with Battn Hdqrs dugout. Enemy shelling intermittently in morning & in afternoon searching west side of LOUVRE VALLEY. Patrols out, also observation posts.	
	31/8/16		Relieved by 2nd S.A.I. Relief commenced 7 A.M. completed 1 p.m. Enemy shelling slightly during relief, but no casualties. A & B Coys & Headqrs proceeded to CAMBLAIN L'ABBE, C & D Coys to MAISTRE LINE	

D. J. Hume
Major Commdg
4th S.A.I.

1/9/16

1875 Wt. W593/826 1,000,000 4/15 J.B.C. & A. A.D.S.S./Forms/C. 2118.

Instructions regarding War Diaries and Intelligence Summaries are contained in F. S. Regs., Part II. and the Staff Manual respectively. Title Pages will be prepared in manuscript.

Army Form C. 2118

4 S F Infy Vol 6

WAR DIARY
or
INTELLIGENCE SUMMARY
(Erase heading not required.)

Place	Date	Hour	Summary of Events and Information	Remarks and references to Appendices
CAMBLAIN L'ABBE	1/9/16		A & B Coys & H.Qrs. having baths at CAMBLAIN L'ABBE C & D Coys finding working parties from Meistre Line	
CAMBLAIN L'ABBE	2/9/16		Balance of A & B & H.Qrs to baths. Gas helmets inspected & foot inspection C & D Coys rejoined from MEISTRE LINE after dark.	
CAMBLAIN L'ABBE	3/9/16		A & B Coys church parade in morning C & D Coys to baths. The regt moved at 3.15 pm. to billets in ESTREE CAUCHIE billeted by 5 pm. 2/Lt G. POLSON joined for duty.	
~~CAMBLAIN~~ ~~L'ABBE~~ ESTREE CAUCHIE	4/9/16		All Coys. Route March 9 to 12 noon A & B Coys. Attack practice & close order drill 2.30 to 4 pm. C & D Coys. Inspection of Gas Helmets & Lewis gun instruction 2.30 to 4 pm	

Army Form C. 2118

Instructions regarding War Diaries and Intelligence Summaries are contained in F. S. Regs., Part II. and the Staff Manual respectively. Title Pages will be prepared in manuscript.

WAR DIARY
or
INTELLIGENCE SUMMARY
(Erase heading not required.)

Place	Date	Hour	Summary of Events and Information	Remarks and references to Appendices
ESTREE CAUCHIE	5/9/16		bayonet [illegible] morning & afternoon with Lewis gun instruction for all coys. The battalion sent 250 men [illegible] at a parade at CAMBLAIN L'ABBE where medal ribbons for Somme were presented to (amongst others) :— Capt Ross Military Cross 2/Lt Sumner Military Medal L/Cpl Hall Military Medal. Following members of regt awarded military medals were not present. Cpl Dixon Pte Prentice Pte Allen	
ESTREE CAUCHIE	6/9/16		The battalion moved at 10.45 a.m. to relieve 11th Royal Scots as support battalion in CARENCY SECTION. A & B Coy's occupied BAJULIE LINE, C & D Coys in CARENCY, and Headqrs at DALYS near HOSPITAL CORNER.	
CARENCY in Support.	7/9/16		Battalion finding 320 men for working parties & carrying parties, in front line sector.	

Army Form C. 2118

WAR DIARY
or
INTELLIGENCE SUMMARY
(Erase heading not required.)

Instructions regarding War Diaries and Intelligence Summaries are contained in F. S. Regs., Part II. and the Staff Manual respectively. Title Pages will be prepared in manuscript.

Place	Date	Hour	Summary of Events and Information	Remarks and references to Appendices
CARENCY in SUPPORT	8/9/16		Battalion finding 470 men for working parties & carrying parties in sector (front line) Carency 1.	
	9/9/16		Battalion finding 470 men for working & carrying parties in the sector. Officers visiting front line trenches.	
	10/9/16		Battalion finding 470 men for working & carrying parties in sector. Officers & men visiting front line trenches	
	11/9/16		Battalion finding 470 men for working & carrying parties in sector, front line Carency I	
	12/9/16		Battalion finding 470 men for working & carrying parties in sector, front line CARENCY I	

1875 Wt. W593/826 1,000,000 4/15 J.B.C. & A. A.D.S.S./Forms/C. 2118.

Army Form C. 2118

Instructions regarding War Diaries and Intelligence Summaries are contained in F. S. Regs., Part II. and the Staff Manual respectively. Title Pages will be prepared in manuscript.

WAR DIARY
or
INTELLIGENCE SUMMARY
(Erase heading not required.)

Place	Date	Hour	Summary of Events and Information	Remarks and references to Appendices
CARENCY in support	13/9/16		Battalion finding working parties & carrying parties in sector. Enemy shelling guns app: 200 yds west of DALY'S. Lieut FARRELL & 2/Lt VERNAL reported for duty at 4-30 pm from [illegible] England. Lt Farrell having recovered from wounds received on SOMME	
	14/9/16		Battalion finding working parties & carrying parties in sector by day & night. 1 O.R. WOUNDED	
	15/9/16		Battalion finding working parties & carrying parties by night & day in front line Carency sector I	
	16/9/16		Battalion finding working parties & carrying parties by day & night in frontline sector. Carency I	

Army Form C. 2118

Instructions regarding War Diaries and Intelligence Summaries are contained in F. S. Regs., Part II. and the Staff Manual respectively. Title Pages will be prepared in manuscript.

WAR DIARY
or
INTELLIGENCE SUMMARY
(Erase heading not required.)

Place	Date	Hour	Summary of Events and Information	Remarks and references to Appendices
VIMY RIDGE - CARENCY SECTOR Trenches Carency I & part II S.	17/9/16		Moved at 8-30 a.m. to relieve 2nd SOUTH AFRICAN Infantry by ERSATZ AVENUE. Relief completed by 1-5 p.m. A. B. and D. Coys holding front line from right to left & C Coy in reserve. Enemy quiet except for intermittent Trench mortar shelling. We put 32 men making dugouts in Lime Street.	
	18/9/16		Enemy quiet except for intermittent Trench Mortar	
	19/9/16		At 2 AM Enemy blew a small crater to south of Kennedy, which blew in two of our mining saps. Storming party of our regt took possession without serious opposition & party started to consolidate & wire until daylight leaving small post to hold crater. Enemy quiet during day. 1 O.R. died of wounds. 1 O.R. wounded	

1875 Wt. W593/826 1,000,000 4/15 J.B.C. & A. A.D.S.S./Forms/C. 2118.

Instructions regarding War Diaries and Intelligence Summaries are contained in F. S. Regs., Part II. and the Staff Manual respectively. Title Pages will be prepared in manuscript.

WAR DIARY
or
INTELLIGENCE SUMMARY
(Erase heading not required.)

Army Form C. 2118

Place	Date	Hour	Summary of Events and Information	Remarks and references to Appendices
VIMY RIDGE CARENCY SECTOR front line trenches	19/9/16		S.	
	20/9/16		General attitude of enemy quiet. At night cutting new C.T. & consolidating crater with 30 our men & R.E. At 12 midnight enemy troublesome, & worked resumed later till dawn with smaller party: our trench mortars active during day. 5 O.R. wounded (of whom 1 slightly at duty).	
	21/9/16		General attitude fairly quiet. Enemy's trench mortars active during day, ours very active retaliating. Weather fine. Again working on C.T. to new crater from 10 p.m. till dawn. Our Stokes silenced enemy maxims when they started to annoy working party. Suspect enemy relieved during night. 2 Wounded.	

Instructions regarding War Diaries and Intelligence Summaries are contained in F. S. Regs., Part II. and the Staff Manual respectively. Title Pages will be prepared in manuscript.

Army Form C. 2118

WAR DIARY
or
INTELLIGENCE SUMMARY
(Erase heading not required.)

Place	Date	Hour	Summary of Events and Information	Remarks and references to Appendices
VIMY RIDGE CARENCY SECTOR	22/9/16		Enemy a bit more aggressive. Trench Mortars quite active for awhile in evening in retaliation for 2" Mortars fired by us.	
	23/9/16		Relieved by 2/Leinsters. Relief commenced 12-30 noon & complete by 5-40 p.m. The battalion moved to CAMBLAIN L'ABBE & billeted for the night.	
CAMBLAIN L'ABBE	24/9/16.		Battalion moved at 11-15 am to VILLERS BRULIN & billeted for the night. Tunnellers from 1 & 2nd Coy, & our dugout platoon attached 64th R.E. returned	
VILLERS BRULIN	25/9/16		Battalion moved at 9-30 a.m. to HAMBRINES for training & billetted in the village.	

Instructions regarding War Diaries and Intelligence Summaries are contained in F. S. Regs., Part II. and the Staff Manual respectively. Title Pages will be prepared in manuscript.

WAR DIARY
or
INTELLIGENCE SUMMARY
(Erase heading not required.)

Army Form C. 2118

Place	Date	Hour	Summary of Events and Information	Remarks and references to Appendices
AMBRINES	26/9/16		All Coys inspecting kit, bathing & cleaning up.	
Do.	27/9/16		All Coys training - Bombing - Bayonet fighting - Rapid loading on ground S.W of AMBRINES	
Do.	28/9/16		All Coys training - Bombing - Bayonet fighting - Rapid loading & extended order work by sections	
Do.	29/9/16		All Coys training. Close order drill - Fire direction & control extended order.	
	30/9/16		All Coys training Fire control - Bayonet fighting - Bomb throwing - Extended order - Intensive digging Lt Young & 2/Lt Kirby rejoined from England	

[illegible]
Major Commanding
4th SHI

1

1875 Wt. W593/826 1,000,000 4/15 J.B.C. & A. A.D.S.S./Forms/C. 2118.

4th South African I

Army Form C. 2118

WAR DIARY
or
INTELLIGENCE SUMMARY
(Erase heading not required.)

4. S. A. I. Vol 7

Instructions regarding War Diaries and Intelligence Summaries are contained in F. S. Regs., Part II. and the Staff Manual respectively. Title Pages will be prepared in manuscript.

Place	Date	Hour	Summary of Events and Information	Remarks and references to Appendices
AMBRINES	1/10/16		Church parade	
AMBRINES	2/10/16		Training - A & B. Musketry - C & D Fire control & Extended order Raining in afternoon - Lectures & Rapid Loading in Billets	
AMBRINES	3/10/16		Training - C & D Coys Musketry - A & B Fire control. Extended order.	
AMBRINES	4/10/16		TRAINING - ATTACK Practice	
AMBRINES	5/10/16		The regt moved at 9. A.M. to BEAUVOIR via BONNIERES.	
BEAUVOIR	6/10/16		Stayed all day.	
BEAUVOIR	7/10/16		Left at 7. A.M. moved to ARBRES & waited for BUSSES - Embarked on same & went VIA AMIENS to BOHENCOURT.	

WAR DIARY
or
INTELLIGENCE SUMMARY
(Erase heading not required.)

Instructions regarding War Diaries and Intelligence Summaries are contained in F. S. Regs., Part II. and the Staff Manual respectively. Title Pages will be prepared in manuscript.

Place	Date	Hour	Summary of Events and Information	Remarks and references to Appendices
BEHENCOURT	8/10/16		Officers with the Regt.	
			Hdqrs - Major Hunt - Capt Clerk - Capt Mitchell - Lt Bayly - Lt Johnston	
			Lt Suzor - Lt Lamont.	
			A. Coy - Capt Mowat - Lt Farrell - 2/Lt Binny - 2/Lt WEBB -	
			~~2/Lt Marshall~~ 2/Lt DONALDSON. 2/Lt Aitken - 2/Lt Morrison.	
			B. Coy - Capt Ross - ~~Lt~~ 2/Lt Sumner - 2/Lt Jackson - 2/Lt McMillan	
			2/Lt Allen. - 2/Lt Halsted	
			C. Coy - Capt Graham - Capt Guest - 2/Lt Ross - 2/Lt Kirby - 2/Lt Hinton	
			2/Lt Quinton - 2/Lt Norman - 2/Lt Salaman	
			D. Coy. Capt Norton - Lt Young - 2/Lt Harris - 2/Lt Vernal -	
			2/Lt Polson - 2/Lt O.N. Hay.	
			~~Capt &~~ Lt Charlton & 2/Lt Marshall at courses.	
			The regiment moved at 11-30 (delay caused waiting for 2nd to get clear) via FRANVILLIERS thence along AMIEN-ALBERT Road to DERNANCOURT to rail at VIVIER HILL E16 B70 near MEAULTE & entrained there proceeding to X29C by train. Detrained at DUSK & proceeded by march route to X23C (57c SE map) where stayed the night in trenches. The transport proceeded under Brigade arrangements & did not join up till next day.	near MAMETZ WOOD
			The trenches we occupied are on slope of hill across to south of MAMETZ wood	

Instructions regarding War Diaries and Intelligence Summaries are contained in F. S. Regs., Part II. and the Staff Manual respectively. Title Pages will be prepared in manuscript.

Army Form C. 2118

WAR DIARY
or
INTELLIGENCE SUMMARY
(Erase heading not required.)

Place	Date	Hour	Summary of Events and Information	Remarks and references to Appendices
9/10/16. MAMETZ WOOD	9/10/16.		The regiment moved after midday meal by platoons to X Roads just north of BAZENTIN LE GRAND & halted till 6 p.m. Then moved forward via High Wood to relieve the 24th London Regt as battalion in support, the ~~1st~~ 2nd [illegible] Regt occupying the front line trenches. Hqrs & A Coy in STARFISH trench M34 due north of High Wood, D Coy in PRUE trench, and B & C Coys in FLERS Switch M28B. The transport moved to a site app S 20 C. Rations to COUGH DROP DUMP	
In front of High Wood	10/10/16		Regiment still in trenches as support battalion. At night we furnished two parties A carrying party of 80 men to carry up rations to 2nd Regt A working party of 200 men to dig communication trenches M22 Strength in trenches 21 officers 609 O.R.	
	11/11/16		Regiment still in trenches as support battalion. Trench where B & C are shelled intermittently all day. We bombarded the Germans for 20 minutes & there was very little retaliation. Our gunnery active. At night we found Carrying party of 60 men to carry rations to 2nd Regt. Working parties amounting to 310 men to dig trenches in M.22	

Instructions regarding War Diaries and Intelligence Summaries are contained in F. S. Regs., Part II. and the Staff Manual respectively. Title Pages will be prepared in manuscript.

Army Form C. 2118

WAR DIARY
or
INTELLIGENCE SUMMARY
(Erase heading not required.)

Place	Date	Hour	Summary of Events and Information	Remarks and references to Appendices
Front Line M 22-23	12/10/16		For the attack the 2nd Regt was formed up in the front line & support line trenches, the 4th Regt in the communication trench leading from behind quarry towards front line. The coys of the 4th followed one another into this communication trench from their assembly trench in FLERS SWITCH. A note dated 12/10/16 & timed 1-45 pm was received from Capt Mowat, saying his Coy "A" was in position.	
			The following reports received via phone at 2nd Batt H.Q. from the forward observer of 2nd Battalion, all pm (as taken down by Capt Mitchell at time.)	
			2.5 Barrage increasing – 2.6 Enemy shelling increasing	
			2.7 Our barrage good 2.8 Our men (2nd Regt) going over	
			2.9 Going over all along the line – 2-11 4th Regt/Scottish entering front line	
			2-12 Scottish going over & well up ridge 2.14 Barrage lifting steadily	
			2.15. Scottish going over ridge 2.18 Men continuing to advance over ridge. Scottish moving rapidly. 2.23 Wire to forward observer gone.	
			2.30 Green rockets seen – 2.35 3 groups of 3 Red lights seen then 4 then 5. 2.45 3 Single Red lights gone up & other lights reported chiefly red.	
			A report by runner from forward observing officer of 2nd as follows:– 2.30 Our men that seen in vicinity and along ridge to right of Butte, but very difficult to see on a/c of smoke. Enemy shelling heavily on our right sector.	

1875 Wt. W593/826 1,000,000 4/15 J.B.C. & A. A.D.S.S./Forms/C. 2118.

Instructions regarding War Diaries and Intelligence Summaries are contained in F. S. Regs., Part II. and the Staff Manual respectively. Title Pages will be prepared in manuscript.

WAR DIARY
or
INTELLIGENCE SUMMARY

(Erase heading not required.)

Army Form C. 2118

Place	Date	Hour	Summary of Events and Information	Remarks and references to Appendices
	12/10/16		At 3.15 p.m. Col Christian (2nd Regt) sent an order to one of his officers Lt Irwin to go forward & observe. At 4.25 p.m. an order was sent to officers holding 1st objective to bomb up trench running N W from S.W corner of 1st objective. Practically no information was received at Bn H.Q. until a runner arrived from Capt Ross to say he was to right of our original front & near the 1st objective. An order was sent to him to hold on & dig in. Capt Mowat was killed leading his company towards the 1st objective early in the afternoon, and 2/Lts Benny & Webb also of A Coy were wounded. 2/Lt Macmillan B Coy was wounded. Capt Graham (C) wounded, 2/Lt Overton (C) ~~wounded~~ killed and 2/Lt Kirby (C) wounded (for the 3rd time during this war). Capt Norton (D) wounded and 2/Lt Polson (D) killed. Thus nine officers were knocked out in the course of the afternoon. The losses amongst N.C.O.s & men were also heavy, mainly caused by enemy machine guns on our left in the 'TAIL' trench. By dusk the other men together with men of 2nd ~~[illegible]~~ were on the left of the mill holding our original front line trench under	

WAR DIARY
or
INTELLIGENCE SUMMARY
(Erase heading not required.)

Army Form C. 2118

Instructions regarding War Diaries and Intelligence Summaries are contained in F. S. Regs., Part II. and the Staff Manual respectively. Title Pages will be prepared in manuscript.

Place	Date	Hour	Summary of Events and Information	Remarks and references to Appendices
HIGH	12/10/16		The 9th Division went over the parapet at 2.5 pm to attack	
WOOD			the enemy lines. The 26th Brigade on the right & the 1st	
&			S.A.I. Bde on the left. The 44th Infy Bde holding the line	
TRENCHES			on left of 1st S.A.I. See Brigade operation order No 66 of 11/10/16	
N W of			The objective of the 1st S.A.I Brigade.	
EAUCOURT			(1) Enemy trench in M17C and	
L'ABBAYE			(2) Enemy trench from M17B27 to LE SARS - BAPAUME Road.	
			& the attack to be made by the 2nd S A I leading	
			& the 4th S A I following in waves of companies, with one platoon per coy to be employed as a carrying platoon.	
			The 4th Regt was assembled in Flers switch trench M28 13 by 11 AM in the following order from West to East. A Coy - B Coy - C Coy - D Coy & carrying platoons & D. Coy. Headqrs proceeded to Battalion H Qrs dugout at the Quarry.	
			Strength going into action as follows:	
			Headqrs 4 officers 39 O.R. Medical 1 officer & 12 Stretcher Bearers	
			A. Coy 4 officers 126 O.R. B Coy 4 officers 134 O.R.	
			C. Coy 4 officers 128 O.R. D Coy 4 officers 136 O.R.	
			TOTAL STRENGTH 4th S.A.I 20 officers 574 O.R.	
			attached 1 officer (M.O) 1 O.R. [illegible]	

1875 Wt. W593/826 1,000,000 4/15 J.B.C. & A. A.D.S.S./Forms/C. 2118.

Instructions regarding War Diaries and Intelligence Summaries are contained in F. S. Regs., Part II. and the Staff Manual respectively. Title Pages will be prepared in manuscript.

WAR DIARY
or
INTELLIGENCE SUMMARY
(Erase heading not required.)

Army Form C. 2118

Place	Date	Hour	Summary of Events and Information	Remarks and references to Appendices
	12/10/16		under 2/Lt Donaldson, to the right of the mill 2/Lt Harris was holding our original front line to strong point 77. To his right front was Capt Ross with about 100 of our own men & some men of the 2nd A Seaforths and digging in.	
			During the night these officers set about reorganising their men & evacuating their wounded through Capt Scotts advanced medical Dressing station near the mill	
			The attack ~~did not~~ was unable to obtain its objective owing to machine gun fire from left which simply mowed down our men as they advanced.	
			About 6pm a company of the 3rd regt reinforced the front line.	
Trenches West of EAUCOURT L'ABBAYE	13/10/16		About 2 AM an order from Brigade received to withdraw the regt, & orders sent out to Capt Ross & Mr Harris to withdraw. The 3rd Regt by this time having taken over the original front line. By about 4.45 practically the whole regt had rendezvoused at back of High Wood, except	

1875 Wt. W593/826 1,000,000 4/15 J.B.C. & A. A.D.S.S./Forms/C. 2118.

Instructions regarding War Diaries and Intelligence Summaries are contained in F. S. Regs., Part II. and the Staff Manual respectively. Title Pages will be prepared in manuscript.

WAR DIARY
or
INTELLIGENCE SUMMARY
(Erase heading not required.)

Army Form C. 2118

Place	Date	Hour	Summary of Events and Information	Remarks and references to Appendices
	13/10/16		stragglers, and a party of ~~14~~ 75 men under 2/Lt Donaldson which remained on in a trench to left of mill. This detachment was relieved in the evening by the 3rd Regt and rejoined us at High Wood late in the evening.	
			Our total casualties from 12 Noon on the 12th for these operations were app.	

	Killed		Wounded		Missing
Officers	3	-	6	-	0
Other Ranks	24		98		5
	27	–	104	–	5

Instructions regarding War Diaries and Intelligence Summaries are contained in F. S. Regs., Part II. and the Staff Manual respectively. Title Pages will be prepared in manuscript.

WAR DIARY
or
INTELLIGENCE SUMMARY
(Erase heading not required.)

Army Form C. 2118

Place	Date	Hour	Summary of Events and Information	Remarks and references to Appendices
High Wood S.W. edge	14/10/16		Regiment camped in trenches or shelters along S.W. border of High Wood	
			(1) 50 men away doing Stretcher Bearers at Millers Aid post	
			(2) 100 men salvaging & cleaning up from 8 to 12 noon	
			(3) 180 men on working parties deepening & improving C.T.s in front line	
High Wood	15/10/16		Still camped same place	
			(1) 50 men at Millers Aid post as Stretchers	
			(2) 150 men (in 3 parties) digging & improving trenches in front line at night	
			(3) 25 men burying dead Germans in vicinity of High Wood during day. Germans dropped about 16 5.9 shells near D Coy lines at S.W. of wood. Our artillery very active all night	
High Wood	16/10/16		Still camped same place	
			(1) 50 men employed as Stretcher Bearers at Millers Aid Post.	
			(2) 25 men employed on Dugouts at ELM TRENCH (M28d).	
			(3) 20 men burying horses during day	
			(4) Found 100 men to dig cable trench by night. A shell landed in middle of No 3 party, killing & wounding 7.	

1875 Wt. W593/826 1,000,000 4/15 J.B.C. & A. A.D.S.S./Forms/C. 2118.

Army Form C. 2118

WAR DIARY
or
INTELLIGENCE SUMMARY
(Erase heading not required.)

Instructions regarding War Diaries and Intelligence Summaries are contained in F. S. Regs., Part II. and the Staff Manual respectively. Title Pages will be prepared in manuscript.

Place	Date	Hour	Summary of Events and Information	Remarks and references to Appendices
HIGH WOOD	17/10/16		Still camped same place. (1) 50 men employed as stretcher bearers at Millers and post (2) 28 men employed on dugouts (3) 150 men in 3 parties digging trenches in front line.	
High Wood	18/10/16		The 1st regiment, with 3rd Regt in reserve & support attacked at 3.40 am. C. Coy under Capt Grant left High Wood at 11.15 a.m. to hold part of our original front line. About 3 p.m. the enemy dropped a few 5.9 s over our line of trenches & camp at High Wood landing a 100 yds from us. At 4 p.m. a draft of 147 o.r. arrived from our Transport lines & joined the regt. At 12 p.m. a 100 men under Capt Ross, with Lt Young, Lt Allen & Lt Hay left for front line or Snag Trench to make a special bombing attack on enemy trench (Tail Trench) 60 men of B and 40 men of D with Lewis Gunners & Signallers	
High Wood	19/10/16		Regt relieved by 6th K.O.S.B's by 11.30 a.m. & proceeded to Mametz Wood taking over some dugouts & shelters at S 13 d 99. Very wet day. During evening & night C. Coy returned, also small parties of Capt Ross' party	

1875 Wt. W593/826 1,000,000 4/15 J.B.C. & A. A.D.S.S./Forms/C. 2118.

Instructions regarding War Diaries and Intelligence Summaries are contained in F. S. Regs., Part II. and the Staff Manual respectively. Title Pages will be prepared in manuscript.

WAR DIARY
or
INTELLIGENCE SUMMARY

(Erase heading not required.)

Army Form C. 2118

Place	Date	Hour	Summary of Events and Information	Remarks and references to Appendices
	19/10/16		Kept coming on.	
			Of Capt Ross party Capt Ross wounded, Lt Young killed and Lt Allen wounded.	CASUALTIES K. W. M
			The bombing attack as originally planned was not carried out, as the enemy meanwhile counterattacked heavily along the Snag & against our front line trenches so that Capt Ross' party were engaged in resisting this counterattack.	Offs 1. 2. 0 O.R. 4. 34. 14 5. 36. 14
MAMETZ WOOD	20/10/16		Still camped N.E. corner of Mametz Wood. Nothing doing	
MAMETZ WOOD	21/10/16		Still camped N.E. corner of Mametz Wood. Quiet day. Mr Gemmell took over command of D Coy.	
MAMETZ WOOD	do		Officers with Regt.	
			Headqrs. Major Hunt commdg - Capt Mitchell Adjutant - 2/Lt Lamont {Lewis guns} Mr Bayley Quartermaster - Mr Johnston Tpt officer.	
	22/10/16		A Coy Lt Farrell commdg - Subaltern officers 2/Lts Marshall Donaldson, Aitken & Morrison	
			B Coy Lt Charlton commdg - Subalterns 2/Lts Sumner - Jackson Halsted & Forbes	
			C Coy Capt Guest commdg. Subalterns 2/Lts Stocks, Hinton Norman, Clune & Salaman.	

1875 Wt. W593/826 1,000,000 4/15 J.B.C. & A. A.D.S.S./Forms/C. 2118.

Instructions regarding War Diaries and Intelligence Summaries are contained in F. S. Regs., Part II. and the Staff Manual respectively. Title Pages will be prepared in manuscript.

WAR DIARY
or
INTELLIGENCE SUMMARY
(Erase heading not required.)

Army Form C. 2118

Place	Date	Hour	Summary of Events and Information	Remarks and references to Appendices
	22/10/16		D Coy 2/Lt D Gemmell commdg - Subalterns 2/Lts Vernal Hawks, Hay, Harward, Peacock & Williams Medical officer Capt Scott, Chaplain Revd Menzies Lt Maclean & 2/Lt Le Sueur with Brigade Found 300 men for road work, and 50 men for Sanitary work	
MAMETZ WOOD	23/10/16		Still camped N.E corner of Mametz Wood. Found 300 men for road work.	
MAMETZ WOOD	24/10/16		Moved at 2 p.m. to tents at X23d, to S.W of wood.	
MAMETZ WOOD	25/10/16		Still in tents. Rained most of day. Found road working parties of 4 off & 352 men	
MAMETZ WOOD	26/10/16		Still in tents. Furnished road working parties of 4 offrs & 373 O.R.	

Instructions regarding War Diaries and Intelligence Summaries are contained in F. S. Regs., Part II. and the Staff Manual respectively. Title Pages will be prepared in manuscript.

WAR DIARY
or
INTELLIGENCE SUMMARY
(Erase heading not required.)

Army Form C. 2118

Place	Date	Hour	Summary of Events and Information	Remarks and references to Appendices
MAMETZ WOOD	27/10/16		Moved from Mametz Wood by march route via CONTELMAISON & ALBERT to MILLENCOURT. Reached last named place at about 2 p.m. & occupied a camp of tents. Bde also billeted there.	
MILLENCOURT	28/10/16		Moved by march route to HERISSART by way of HENENCOURT, WARLOY & CONTAY. Left about 10-40 a.m. & got in about 2 p.m. billeting in village.	
HERISSART	29/10/16		Left at 7-30 a.m. to road junction abt one mile N.W of village where embarked on French buses & went via PUCHEVILLIERS, MARIEUX, MENDICOURT to X Roads near LOUEZ, and disembarked at 1 pm. Halted under cover of trees for an hour or two till got orders to proceed into ARRAS & entered town in by sections at 50 yds distance. Men billeted in Cavalry barracks. HdQrs in house No 69 RUE D'AMIENS, other officers billeted in the town.	
ARRAS	30/10/16		Men not allowed out during day till 6 p.m., no lights allowed to be shown. Nothing doing.	

Army Form C. 2118

Instructions regarding War Diaries and Intelligence Summaries are contained in F. S. Regs., Part II. and the Staff Manual respectively. Title Pages will be prepared in manuscript.

WAR DIARY
or
INTELLIGENCE SUMMARY
(Erase heading not required.)

Place	Date	Hour	Summary of Events and Information	Remarks and references to Appendices
ARRAS	31/10/16		Men kept in all day. Nothing done, could not get bath accomodation.	

D. M. Hunter [?] Major
Comdg S.A. Scottish

1875 Wt. W593/826 1,000,000 4/15 J.B.C. & A. A.D.S.S./Forms/C. 2118.

Instructions regarding War Diaries and Intelligence Summaries are contained in F. S. Regs., Part II. and the Staff Manual respectively. Title Pages will be prepared in manuscript.

WAR DIARY
or
INTELLIGENCE SUMMARY
(Erase heading not required.)

4th S.A.I.

Vol 8

Army Form C. 2118

Place	Date	Hour	Summary of Events and Information	Remarks and references to Appendices
ARRAS	1/11/16		The regiment furnished working parties under direction of C.R.E. 35th Division on following:	Our Transport stationed at Louez
			C Coy. Laying Tramway from Chalk farm up Monday Av via Thelus Redoubt to 7 work. Day work	
			D Coy. Reclaiming RESERVE Trench running - Fosty Street between Lille Road & Thursday Avenue. Night work one platoon by day	
			A Coy. with Dugout platoon. 5 new Dugouts. In continuous shifts	
			B Coy. Burying water pipe from Pumping Station to Thelus Redoubt. Day work	
			Strength of parties for S.A.I.: A 1 officer & 90 O.R. + 7 Dugout platoon	[illegible]
			B 1 officer & 79 O.R. + 11 do	
			C 1 officer & 65 + 11 do	
			D 2 officers & 101 O.R. + 3 do.	
ARRAS	[illegible]/11/16		Work on pipe line changed from day work to night work.	[illegible]
			[illegible] opened, sent 1 officer & 1 Warrant officer	
			Strength of working parties A 1 officer & 90 O.R. + 7 Dugout platoon	
			B 1 officer & 84 O.R. + 11 do	
			C 1 officer & 104 O.R. + 11 do	
			D 2 officers & 85 O.R. + 3 do.	
			Casualties 1 O.R. wounded.	

1875 Wt. W593/826 1,000,000 4/15 J.B.C. & A. A.D.S.S./Forms/C. 2118.

Army Form C. 2118

WAR DIARY
or
INTELLIGENCE SUMMARY
(Erase heading not required.)

Instructions regarding War Diaries and Intelligence Summaries are contained in F. S. Regs., Part II. and the Staff Manual respectively. Title Pages will be prepared in manuscript.

Place	Date	Hour	Summary of Events and Information	Remarks and references to Appendices
ARRAS	3/11/16		The regt still finding working parties as under	
			Sent 80 men to baths	
			A 1 officer + 90 OR + 4 dugout platoon	1. O.R.
			B 1 officer + 80 OR + 11 dugout platoon	Wounded
			C 1 officer + 85 OR + 11 dugout platoon	
			D 2 officers + 89 OR + 3 dugout platoon + 12 on offloading stores	
ARRAS	4/11/16		Sent 120 men to Baths	
			Regt finding working parties as under	
			A 1 officer + 90 men + 4 dugout platoon + 5 offloading stores	
			B 1 officer + 65 men + 11 dugout platoon + 5 offloading stores	
			C 1 officer + 93 men + 11 dugout platoon	
			D 2 officers + 90 men + 3 dugout platoon + 5 offloading stores	
ARR.	5/11/16		Sent balance of regt to Baths	
			Regt finding working parties as under	
			A 1 officer + 90 OR + 8 dugout platoon	
			B 1 officer + 66 OR + 13 dugout platoon + 5 offloading stores	
			C 1 officer + 86 OR + 11 dugout platoon + 5 offloading stores	
			D 2 officers + 101 OR + 2 dugout platoon + 5 offloading stores	

1875 Wt. W593/826 1,000,000 4/15 J.B.C. & A. A.D.S.S./Forms/C. 2118.

Army Form C. 2118

Instructions regarding War Diaries and Intelligence Summaries are contained in F. S. Regs., Part II. and the Staff Manual respectively. Title Pages will be prepared in manuscript.

WAR DIARY
or
INTELLIGENCE SUMMARY
(Erase heading not required.)

Place	Date	Hour	Summary of Events and Information	Remarks and references to Appendices
ARRAS	6/11/16		Battalion found working parties as under:-	
			A Coy 90 Working party + 8 dugouts	
			B 63 do + 13 do + 5 offloading	
			C 79 do + 11 do + 6 do + 2 wiring	
			D 75 do + 2 do + 5 do	
ARRAS	7/11/16		Battalion found working parties as under:-	
			A Coy 90 Working party + 8 dugouts	
			B do 49 do + 25 do + 5 offloading	
			C do 82 do + 23 do + 6 do + 4 wiring	
			D do 85 do + 7 do + 6 do.	
ARRAS	8/11/16		Battalion found working parties as under.	
			A Coy 79 working party.	
			B " 48 do + 25 dugouts + 5 offloading	
			C " 78 do + 23 do. + 6 do. + 4 wiring	
			D " 78 do + 8 do + 6 do	

1875 Wt. W593/826 1,000,000 4/15 J.B.C. & A. A.D.S.S./Forms/C. 2118.

Instructions regarding War Diaries and Intelligence Summaries are contained in F. S. Regs., Part II. and the Staff Manual respectively. Title Pages will be prepared in manuscript.

WAR DIARY
or
INTELLIGENCE SUMMARY
(Erase heading not required.)

Army Form C. 2118

Place	Date	Hour	Summary of Events and Information	Remarks and references to Appendices
ARRAS	9/11/16		Battalion found Working parties as under.	
			A Working party 90 + Dugouts 8	
			B do 39 + do 25 + offloading party 5	
			C do 74 + do 23 + do 6 + Wiring 4	
			D do 82 + do 8 + 6	
ARRAS	10/11/16		Battalion found working parties	
			A Working parties 74	
			B do 42 + Dugouts 25 + offloading party 5	
			C do 79 + do 23 + do 5 + wiring 4	
			D do 76 + do 8 + do 6	
ARRAS	11/11/16		Battalion found working parties	
			A Working party 74.	
			B do 42 + Dugout party 25 + offloading party 5	
			C do 69 + do 23 + do 5 + Wiring 4	
			D do 73 + do 8 + do. 6	

1875 Wt. W593/826 1,000,000 4/15 J.B.C. & A. A.D.S.S./Forms/C. 2118.

WAR DIARY
or
INTELLIGENCE SUMMARY
(Erase heading not required.)

Army Form C. 2118

Instructions regarding War Diaries and Intelligence Summaries are contained in F. S. Regs., Part II. and the Staff Manual respectively. Title Pages will be prepared in manuscript.

Place	Date	Hour	Summary of Events and Information	Remarks and references to Appendices
ARRAS	12/11/16.		Finding Working parties A Coy 90 Working Party + 8 Dugout men B " 46 do + 19 do + 5 offloading party C " 77 do + 16 do + 5 do + 4 wiring D " 68 do + 4 do + 5 do.	
ARRAS	13/11/16		Finding working parties A Coy 90 Working party + 7 Dugout men B " 43 do + 19 do + 5 offloading party C " 78 do + 16 do + 5 do + 4 wiring D " 81 do + 4 do + 5 do.	
ARRAS	14/11/16		Finding working parties A Coy 90 working party + 7 Dugout men B " 47 do + 19 do + 5 offloading party C " 76 do + 16 do + 5 do + 4 wiring D " 80 do + 5 do + 5 do.	

1875 Wt. W593/826 1,000,000 4/15 J.B.C. & A. A.D.S.S./Forms/C. 2118.

Army Form C. 2118

Instructions regarding War Diaries and Intelligence Summaries are contained in F. S. Regs., Part II. and the Staff Manual respectively. Title Pages will be prepared in manuscript.

WAR DIARY
or
INTELLIGENCE SUMMARY
(Erase heading not required.)

Place	Date	Hour	Summary of Events and Information	Remarks and references to Appendices
ARRAS	15/11/16		The battalion found working parties as follows:-	
			A Coy 90 working party + 6 dugout party	
			B Coy 45 do + 19 do + 5 offloading party	
			C Coy 68 do + 16 do + 5 do	+ 4 wiring
			D Coy 80 do + 5 do + 6 do	
			B. Coy having completed pipe line were put on to assist "C" Coy with tram line	
ARRAS	16/11/16		The battalion found working parties as under:-	
			A Coy 90 working party + 6 dugout men	
			B Coy 48 do. + 19 do + 5 offloading party	
			C Coy 67 do. + 16 do + 5 do	+ 4 wire
			D Coy 76 do + 5 do + 5 do	
ARRAS	17/11/16		The battalion found working parties as under:-	
			A Coy 90 working party + 6 Dug Out Men	
			B Coy 49 do + 19 do + 5 offloading party	
			C Coy 65 do + 15 do + 5 do	+ 4 wiring
			D Coy 70 do + 5 do + 5 do	

1875 Wt. W593/826 1,000,000 4/15 J.B.C. & A. A.D.S.S./Forms/C. 2118.

Instructions regarding War Diaries and Intelligence Summaries are contained in F. S. Regs., Part II. and the Staff Manual respectively. Title Pages will be prepared in manuscript.

WAR DIARY
or
INTELLIGENCE SUMMARY
(Erase heading not required.)

Army Form C. 2118

Place	Date	Hour	Summary of Events and Information	Remarks and references to Appendices
ARRAS	18/11/16		The Battalion found working parties as follows:-	
			A Coy 90 Working party + 6 Dug-out men	
			B Coy 49 do + 19 do + 5 Off loading men	
			C Coy 66 do + 15 do + 5 do + 4 Wiring	
			D Coy 70 do + 5 do + 6 do	
ARRAS	19/11/16		The Battalion found working parties as follows:-	
			A Coy 90 Working party + 6 Dug-out men	
			B " 47 " + 19 do + 5 Off-loading men	
			C " 65 " + 15 do + 5 do + 4 Wiring	
			D " 71 " + 5 do + 6 do	
ARRAS WANQUETIN	20/11/16		The Battalion moved out from Arras at 5 pm at intervals between Companies and marched through DAINVILLE, WARLUS & reached WANQUETIN at 7.45 pm. Battalion H.Qs at 3 RUE de GOUY.	
WANQUETIN	21/11/16		More billets allotted to Regiment by Town Major & men moved, which has made men more comfortable. Officers quarters very bad.	

1875 Wt. W593/826 1,000,000 4/15 J.B.C. & A. A.D.S.S./Forms/C. 2118.

Army Form C. 2118

WAR DIARY
or
INTELLIGENCE SUMMARY
(Erase heading not required.)

Instructions regarding War Diaries and Intelligence Summaries are contained in F. S. Regs., Part II. and the Staff Manual respectively. Title Pages will be prepared in manuscript.

Place	Date	Hour	Summary of Events and Information	Remarks and references to Appendices
WANGUETIN.	22/11/16		The Battalion started training as follows:- Classes started for instructing Signallers & Lewis Gunners	
			7AM – 7.30 Rapid Route march	
			9 – 9.45 Arms inspection & arms & Close order drill	
			9.45 – 10.15 Musketry & Rapid Loading	
			10-15 – 11. Company Drill	
			11.15 – 12 Bayonet Fighting	
			12.0 – 1 Small Box Respirator Drill	
			2-15 – 4 Two platoons football. Rest of Battalion route march	
WANQUETIN	23/11/16		Training continued as following programme.	
			7AM – 7.30 Physical Drill for Trench Card.	
			9 – 9.45 Arms inspection & arms & close order drill by NCOs	
			9.45 10-15 Fire Control & Target Indication.	
			10-15 11 – Company Drill	
			11-15 12 – Bayonet Fighting	
			12 – 1 Dummy Bomb Throwing	
			2.15 – 4 Route march	

Army Form C. 2118

Instructions regarding War Diaries and Intelligence Summaries are contained in F. S. Regs., Part II. and the Staff Manual respectively. Title Pages will be prepared in manuscript.

WAR DIARY
or
INTELLIGENCE SUMMARY
(Erase heading not required.)

Place	Date	Hour	Summary of Events and Information	Remarks and references to Appendices
WANQUETIN	24/11/16		Training continued as per programme:-	
			7AM – 7-30 Rapid Route March with games	
			9 – 9-45 Arms Inspection + Arms + Close Order Drill	
			9-45 – 10-15 Judging distances	
			10-15 – 11 Company Drill	
			11-15 – 12 – Small box respirator drill	
			12 – 1 Bayonet fighting	
			2-15 – 4 Route march (Two platoons football)	
			Draft of 85 men arrived today.	
WANQUETIN	25/11/16		Training continued Programme	
			7AM – 7-30 Rapid route march.	
			9 – 9-45 Arms inspection + Arms + close order Drill	
			9-45 10-15 Musketry + Rapid Loading	
			10-15 – 11 Company Drill	
			11-15 12. Bayonet fighting	
			12-0 1 – Small box respirator Drill	
			2-15 4 Route march.	

1875 Wt. W593/826 1,000,000 4/15 J.B.C. & A. A.D.S.S./Forms/C. 2118.

Instructions regarding War Diaries and Intelligence Summaries are contained in F. S. Regs., Part II. and the Staff Manual respectively. Title Pages will be prepared in manuscript.

WAR DIARY
or
INTELLIGENCE SUMMARY
(Erase heading not required.)

Army Form C. 2118

Place	Date	Hour	Summary of Events and Information	Remarks and references to Appendices
WANQUETIN	26/11/16		New form of training instituted today. Firing from hips while advancing. This took place against high bank MAP Reference K 27 c 4.8 Small box Respirators tested in room at 41 C.C.S. Gas N.C.O sent over by Brigade. All who had been fitted were tested.	
WANQUETIN	27/11/16		Training continued. Programme for day	
			7 – 7.30 a.m. Rapid Route march	
			9 – 9.45 Arms inspection & Arms Close Order Drill	
			9.45 – 10.15 Judging Distances	
			10.15 – 11 Company Drill	
			11.15 – 12 Small box respirator drill	
			12 – 1 Bayonet fighting	
			2.15 – 4 Two platoons football. Rest of Batt. Route March	
WANQUETIN	28/11/16		Church Parade in morning.	

1875 Wt. W593/826 1,000,000 4/15 J.B.C. & A. A.D.S.S./Forms/C. 2118.

Instructions regarding War Diaries and Intelligence Summaries are contained in F. S. Regs., Part II. and the Staff Manual respectively. Title Pages will be prepared in manuscript.

WAR DIARY
or
INTELLIGENCE SUMMARY
(Erase heading not required.)

Army Form C. 2118

Place	Date	Hour	Summary of Events and Information	Remarks and references to Appendices
WANQUETIN	29/11/16		A Coy to baths at Habarcq in morning	
			B " do afternoon	
			C & D Bombing with live bombs & Intensive digging	
			Route march in afternoon.	
			Bombing Ground situated Q.2.B.5.3 Intensive digging situated K.32.c.7.3	
			During the day balance of men who had not been through Gas Test were put through by Gas NCO from Brigade.	
			Brigade Rugby 1st Regt 12/16 4th Regt 0.	
	30/11/16		C Coy to baths at Habarcq in morning	
			D " do do afternoon	
			A & B bombing with live bombs & intensive digging	

[illegible signature]
Major
Commanding
4th SA Inf.

1875 Wt. W593/826 1,000,000 4/15 J.B.C. & A. A.D.S.S./Forms/C. 2118.

Instructions regarding War Diaries and Intelligence Summaries are contained in F. S. Regs., Part II. and the Staff Manual respectively. Title Pages will be prepared in manuscript.

Army Form C. 2118

WAR DIARY
or
~~INTELLIGENCE SUMMARY~~
(Erase heading not required.)

4 SA Infy Bn

Vol 9

Place	Date	Hour	Summary of Events and Information	Remarks and references to Appendices
Wanquetin	1/12/16		7-7.30 AM. Rapid Route March.	
			9-10 } A.B.C and D coys in turn } Firing from the hip	
			10-11 } Arms Inspection & Coy Drill	
			11-12 } Bayonet fighting	
			12-1 } N.C.O.'s Elementary Tactical Exercises	
			~~2.30-4~~ } Musketry	
			2.30-4 Battalion Route March.	
WANQUETIN	2/12/16		Completing Equipment & getting ready in preparation for move.	
WANQUETIN	3/12/16		Regt moved to ARRAS. Battn Hqrs at Hotel de l'Univers. A & D Coys at Convent. B Coy 3 platoons at St Nicholas & 1 platoon at Bosky Redoubt. C Coy 2 platoons at Nicholls Redoubt and 2 platoons at Forester Redoubt.	
ARRAS	4/12/16		Nothing to chronicle except Rifle & Kit inspections.	

Army Form C. 2118

Instructions regarding War Diaries and Intelligence Summaries are contained in F. S. Regs., Part II. and the Staff Manual respectively. Title Pages will be prepared in manuscript.

WAR DIARY
or
INTELLIGENCE SUMMARY
(Erase heading not required.)

Place	Date	Hour	Summary of Events and Information	Remarks and references to Appendices
ARRAS	5/12/16		B & C Coys did general repair work in their own localities.	
ARRAS.	6/12/16		B & C Coys did general repair work in their own localities. A Coy furnished 50 men to carry 2" bombs from 2 p.m. A & D Coys do 100 men at 8.30 AM till 1 p.m. to deepen trench for light railway from Candle factory & also to dig a drain along road.	
ARRAS J2 Sub Sec.	7/12/16		Battalion moved into J2 sub section Arras centre Bn HQ and took over from 2nd S.A.I. Major Hunt left on leave. Capt Mitchell assumed command. Relief completed at 6pm. A Company left flank D. Coy right flank. C support. B. Reserve. A Coy sent out 2 patrols and D Coy 2 patrols. July trench shelled 8/30pm minnenwerfer. Three men C. Coy killed. On the whole everything quiet. Minnenwerfer fell in July trench and resulted in	C Coy 2 Killed 1 wounded - since died of wounds
ARRAS	8/12/16		Moderate exchange of T.M's. Wiring parties out in front line and support trenches. Two officer patrols	

1875 Wt. W593/826 1,000,000 4/15 J.B.C. & A. A.D.S.S./Forms/C. 2118.

Instructions regarding War Diaries and Intelligence Summaries are contained in F. S. Regs., Part II. and the Staff Manual respectively. Title Pages will be prepared in manuscript.

WAR DIARY
or
INTELLIGENCE SUMMARY
(Erase heading not required.)

Army Form C. 2118

Place	Date	Hour	Summary of Events and Information	Remarks and references to Appendices
ARRAS J.2.	8/12/16 Contd.		were sent out one by D + one by A × 2/Lt. Hay in charge of the D patrol was fired on by sentry of 1st Regt. at 9.30 a.m. 9. from Sap on right of 89 bay + was wounded in leg + sent to Hospital – Inclement weather caused trenches to fall in and much revetting had to be done with A frames. No dug outs to be used in front line, all wired up.	2/Lt. Hay wounded morning 9th
ARRAS	9/12/16		Enemy dropping T.M's in supports + July avenue badly. This was repaired. Capt. Lawrence M.O. replaced Capt. Young – Wiring parties out 6 pm to 10 pm and 2 listening posts out. – Repairs to trenches caused by hostile T.M's continued and general revetting × weather bad. Care being taken to oil mens feet in trenches. Oxo + tea issued during night × D Coy patrol sniped when going out at 2 am 10th + hit through leg rather badly	1 wounded leg [illegible] D Coy
ARRAS	10/12/16		Weather continues very bad + front line trenches and condition of mens feet notwithstanding precautions gives rise to apprehension – Fatigue	

1875 Wt. W593/826 1,000,000 4/15 J.B.C. & A. A.D.S.S./Forms/C. 2118.

Instructions regarding War Diaries and Intelligence Summaries are contained in F. S. Regs., Part II. and the Staff Manual respectively. Title Pages will be prepared in manuscript.

WAR DIARY
or
INTELLIGENCE SUMMARY
(Erase heading not required.)

Army Form C. 2118

Place	Date	Hour	Summary of Events and Information	Remarks and references to Appendices
ARRAS J2	10/12/16 cont^d		Work heavy: wiring, carrying, cleaning trenches. Two posts out all night observing – our T Ms active. One man wounded behind S01 & evacuated	1 wounded A Coy
ARRAS J2	11/12/16		Decided to change front line companies B from reserve to Right flank C " supports to Left flank A " left flank to supports D " Right flank to reserve. This was essential and proved a success. The only sleeping accommodation in front line being fire steps. Wiring parties out and also listening posts One man Cooke accidentally wounded whilst correcting Lewis Gun stoppage 2/Lts Forder & Baxter arrived. 2/Lt Baxter & a draft of 150 men at Duisans. 100 men of various companies were sent to Baths at Cuptee Factory – during day.	(1 man Cooke) accidentally wounded.
ARRAS J2	12/12/16		Snow and rain making trenches very bad condition, sides falling in & parties continually engaged cleaning. Lot of duck boarding work carried out. Wiring parties and listening posts out all night.	

Instructions regarding War Diaries and Intelligence Summaries are contained in F. S. Regs., Part II. and the Staff Manual respectively. Title Pages will be prepared in manuscript.

WAR DIARY
or
INTELLIGENCE SUMMARY
(Erase heading not required.)

Army Form C. 2118

Place	Date	Hour	Summary of Events and Information	Remarks and references to Appendices
ARRAS I2	12/12/16 contd		Enemy T.Ms active and did some damage which was repaired by continued day & night effort but it interfered very appreciably with constructional work we had in hand. Two listening posts out till dawn everything reported normal. Put 100 men through Candle Factory Baths. Having good effect on men also keeping up supplies of Bea Soup & Tea during night. part of trench right flank blown in 1 man killed 1 wounded 50 men passed through baths - Fatigues very heavy & numerous -	1 man D Coy. Clearpt Trench feet. 1 Killed B 1 W B Coy
ARRAS I2	13/12/16		Trenches fully & many subsiding owing to weather resulting in heavy fatigue work. Listening posts and wire patrols out - our artillery & T.Ms active also enemy retaliation - 40 men through baths	1 Trench feet D 1 " " C 1 wounded A
ARRAS I2	14/12/16		All companies working at clearing up trench. Artillery & T.Ms fairly active - Gas alert on. working on all trenches - repairs -	1 Trench feet B

1875 Wt. W593/826 1,000,000 4/15 J.B.C. & A. A.D.S.S./Forms/C. 2118.

Army Form C. 2118

Instructions regarding War Diaries and Intelligence Summaries are contained in F. S. Regs., Part II. and the Staff Manual respectively. Title Pages will be prepared in manuscript.

WAR DIARY
or
INTELLIGENCE SUMMARY
(Erase heading not required.)

Place	Date	Hour	Summary of Events and Information	Remarks and references to Appendices
ARRAS. J2 to J3.	15/12/16		Change over from J2 (centre Bn) to J3 (Left Bn), relieving 3rd Regt. C took up Left support, B -"- -"- Right -"-, D -"- -"- Left front, A -"- -"- Right front positions. Two patrols out examining wire and fully reported upon. Gas alert on.	
J 3	16/12/16		Enemy Trench M's active. patrol inspected enemy wire from Claude crater to Trench 100. Good condition. Draft put in billets at Arras and arrangements made to employ them on daily fatigues in the line. Much progress made in revetting, duckboarding, clearing up and improvements. Our artillery & Light & Medium T.M.s did good work on enemy position.	
J 3.	17/12/16		During day the draft supplied fatigue parties up to 128 men for R.E.s and general revetting and much progress was made in repairing damage done by hostile T.M's also with constructional work.	1 man wounded [illegible] sniped D Coy
J 3.	18/12/16		Companies changed over A taking right front support, B " right front line, C " Left front, D " " support (Chance T.M. in Support line)	2 killed B Bone Telford

1875 Wt. W593/826 1,000,000 4/15 J.B.C. & A. A.D.S.S./Forms/C. 2118.

Working parties continue - patrols, wiring parties, & outposts

Instructions regarding War Diaries and Intelligence Summaries are contained in F. S. Regs., Part II. and the Staff Manual respectively. Title Pages will be prepared in manuscript.

WAR DIARY
or
INTELLIGENCE SUMMARY
(Erase heading not required.)

Army Form C. 2118

Place	Date	Hour	Summary of Events and Information	Remarks and references to Appendices
ARRAS. J III	19/12/16		Enemy T.M.s active damaging Angus Avenue – Our T.M.s were busy during morning cutting enemy wire – Full fatigue parties throughout Sub Section, wiring, revetting, shutting dugouts and generally repairing damages. Usual patrols out	
J III	20/12/16		Stokes and 2" T.M.s made good play on enemy wire. The [illegible] attack was made during day + in the evening. Enemy threw a lot of 4.5 shells over the Subsection, indiscriminately doing some damage to trenches which have been repaired working parties out all night –	
J III	21/12/16		Companies changed over. A to right front, B – " – support, C – " – left – " –, D – " – " –. Activity on both sides normal.	
J III	22/12/16		Situation generally quiet. Rain morning. Fair later. Working parties operating strenuously	
J III to J.1.	23/12/16		Relief carried out satisfactorily during day. A. B. C. left to right front companies. D. reserve. Artillery + H.T.M. shots afternoon.	2 men wounded.
J.1.	24/12/16		Wiring patrols own and enemy wire – all available men cleaning trenches. Activity normal.	2 men wounded. –

1875 Wt. W593/826 1,000,000 4/15 J.B.C. & A. A.D.S.S./Forms/C. 2118.

Instructions regarding War Diaries and Intelligence Summaries are contained in F. S. Regs., Part II. and the Staff Manual respectively. Title Pages will be prepared in manuscript.

WAR DIARY
or
INTELLIGENCE SUMMARY
(*Erase heading not required.*)

Army Form C. 2118

Place	Date	Hour	Summary of Events and Information	Remarks and references to Appendices
J1.	25/12/16		Christmas day. Fine - our artillery & T.M's active. Whole of our front closely patrolled wire reconnoitred and German wire inspected - Sentries located in German lines and sounds of merriment.	
J1.	26/12/16		Change over. - D from supports to right front C. Right front - to supports Two patrols out looking for gaps in wire and damage done by our artillery & T.M's during the day	
J1.	27/12/16		Fine - Activity in exchanges of missiles normal and even. Listening posts & patrols carried out usual duties without encountering enemy.	
J1	28/12/16		Normal activity - patrols and listening posts as usual.	
J1	29/12/16		Enemy shelled very severe rather heavily wounding three men (2 badly 1 slight). Lewis gun sent out [illegible] of "No mans land" to prevent enemy repairing the damage done by our T.M.s - dispersed several parties	3 wounded.
J1	30/12/16		Raining persistently - trenches falling in badly and extra efforts required from everyone - continually -	

1875 Wt. W593/826 1,000,000 4/15 J.B.C. & A. A.D.S.S./Forms/C. 2118.

Army Form C. 2118

WAR DIARY
or
INTELLIGENCE SUMMARY
(Erase heading not required.)

Instructions regarding War Diaries and Intelligence Summaries are contained in F. S. Regs., Part II. and the Staff Manual respectively. Title Pages will be prepared in manuscript.

Place	Date	Hour	Summary of Events and Information	Remarks and references to Appendices
J1	31/12/16		Relieved by 1st Regt & into Reserve. A {3 platoons Grand Place {1 " St Nicholas B convent C. " " D. 2 Platoons Forester, 2 platoons St Nicholas	
			Summary of casualties.	

	K.	D of W.	W.	Trench feet.
J II Sub section	3	2	5	
J III " "	2		1	
J I " "			7	7
	5	2	13	7

D. G. [illegible] Major
Comdg S. A. Scottish

9TH (SCOTTISH) DIVISION
STH AFRICAN INFY BRIGADE

4TH STH SFRICAN INFY REGT

JAN - DEC 1917

Instructions regarding War Diaries and Intelligence Summaries are contained in F. S. Regs., Part II. and the Staff Manual respectively. Title Pages will be prepared in manuscript.

WAR DIARY
or
~~INTELLIGENCE SUMMARY~~
(Erase heading not required.)

Army Form C. 2118

4th South African Infantry
January – 1917

Vol. 10

Place	Date	Hour	Summary of Events and Information	Remarks and references to Appendices
Reserve ARRAS.	1/1/17.		Cleaning up. Night working parties. Lieut Col. Christian arrived and assumed Command.	
do	2/1/17.		Baths. – working parties. Major Hunt proceeded to England.	
do	3/1/17.		Successful raid by 3rd Regt. Local Lewis Gun instruction under Sgt [illegible]. Baths. 6 per Company. Full working parties.	
do	4/1/17.		working parties. Baths. Enemy threw large number of gas shells on Arras commencing about 10pm	
do	5/1/17.		working parties. Baths. — do —	
do	6/1/17.		working parties. Baths	

Instructions regarding War Diaries and Intelligence Summaries are contained in F. S. Regs., Part II. and the Staff Manual respectively. Title Pages will be prepared in manuscript.

WAR DIARY
or
INTELLIGENCE SUMMARY
(Erase heading not required.)

Army Form C. 2118

4th South African Infantry
January – 1917.

Place	Date	Hour	Summary of Events and Information	Remarks and references to Appendices
Reserve ARRAS	7/1/17		Baths – working parties –	
J2.	8/1/17		Battalion moved into J2 Sector relieving the 2nd Regt. B. Right Company; C. Left Company; A. Support; D. Reserve. Raining. Clearing trenches.	
J2.	9/1/17.		Full wiring parties. all companies engaged in clearing trenches, revetting etc. Normal activity –	
J2	10/1/17.		Fatigue parties. patrols – wiring –	
J2	11/1/17.		Companies changed over. D. becoming Right Company; A. Left Company; B. Reserve –do–; Supports. Snow, rain. Inter relief starts 9. A.M., finishes 10-30 A.M.	
J2	12/1/17.		Working parties, two patrols, normal artillery activity	1 wounded arm Siebert

1875 Wt. W593/826 1,000,000 4/15 J.B.C. & A. A.D.S.S./Forms/C. 2118.

Army Form C. 2118

WAR DIARY
or
INTELLIGENCE SUMMARY
(Erase heading not required.)

Instructions regarding War Diaries and Intelligence Summaries are contained in F. S. Regs., Part II. and the Staff Manual respectively. Title Pages will be prepared in manuscript.

4th South African Infantry
January 1917

Place	Date	Hour	Summary of Events and Information	Remarks and references to Appendices
ARRAS J2.	13/1/17		patrol inspecting German wire. wiring & fatigue parties. weather - Snow rain	
J2	14/1/17		Companies changed over. A: to Reserve. D: Support. B: right front. C: left front. Relief started 9. A.M. " finished 11 - A.M.	
J. 2	15/1/17		Weather dull & overcast. Nothing unusual to record. Enemy activity slight	
J. 3	16/1/17		Battalion relieved in J II subsection by 2nd S.A.I, & took over J III subsection from 3rd S.A.I. Relief commenced 9-30 A.M. & completed at 12.25 p.m. A Coy Right Coy Front Line - B Coy Supports D Coy Left Coy Front Line - C Coy Reserve in Bosky & Nicoll Redoubts.	
J. III	17/1/17		Snowing most of the day. Nothing unusual to record. One O.R. Died of wounds.	

1875 Wt. W593/826 1,000,000 4/15 J.B.C. & A. A.D.S.S./Forms/C. 2118.

Instructions regarding War Diaries and Intelligence Summaries are contained in F. S. Regs., Part II. and the Staff Manual respectively. Title Pages will be prepared in manuscript.

WAR DIARY
or
INTELLIGENCE SUMMARY
(Erase heading not required.)

Army Form C. 2118

4th South African Infy.
January – 1917

Place	Date	Hour	Summary of Events and Information	Remarks and references to Appendices
J III	18/1/17		Right Front company resumed its normal posts, the order for temporary withdrawal of posts from vicinity of Clavis Crater (due to suspected enemy mining) being cancelled. Enemy trench mortars active. Killed 1 O.R. Wounded 2 O.R.	
J III	19/1/17		Enemy threw over Tear shells in morning in vicinity of BOSKY redoubt, also 12 5.9 shells in right coys section, and in evening very active with Trench mortars. No casualties.	
J III	20/1/17		Intercompany relief. B Coy Right Coy - Front Line C Coy Left Coy - Front Line A Coy Supports D Coy Reserve in BOSKY and NICOLL REDOUBTS. Enemy very active with Trench Mortars during afternoon. Casualties 2 O.R. Wounded.	
J III	21/1/17		Enemy Heavy Trench Mortars very active all day doing considerable damage to the trenches. About 6 pm. the left coy front line was being knocked about, whilst the enemy attempted a raid further north. Evening quiet & night also. Casualties Killed 1 O.R. Wounded 1 O.R.	

Instructions regarding War Diaries and Intelligence Summaries are contained in F. S. Regs., Part II. and the Staff Manual respectively. Title Pages will be prepared in manuscript.

WAR DIARY
or
INTELLIGENCE SUMMARY
(Erase heading not required.)

Army Form C. 2118

4th South African Infy.
January – 1917.

Place	Date	Hour	Summary of Events and Information	Remarks and references to Appendices
J III	22/1/17		Keen frost. Enemy fairly quiet. Busy repairing damage to trenches No casualties.	
J III	23/1/17		Hard frost, bright sunshine. Repairing & cleaning damaged trenches No casualties.	
J I Subsection	24/1/17		Relieved by 3rd Regt S.A.I. in J III subsection. Relief commenced at 9 A.M. & on relief the 4th took over J I subsection from the 1st S.A.I. Relief reported complete to Bde at 12.40 pm. A Coy took over front line from left to Sap 84 B B Coy took over Fonetrier Redoubts & 2 [illegible] in support line C Coy took over Oilworks & Laundry Post D Coy took over front line from right Hard frost all day – no casualties Major de Hartland attached to the battalion for instruction.	
J I	25/1/17		Hard frost – no casualties Usual trench mortar activity by enemy.	
J I	26/1/17		Hard frost – no casualties Nothing unusual to record.	

Instructions regarding War Diaries and Intelligence Summaries are contained in F. S. Regs., Part II. and the Staff Manual respectively. Title Pages will be prepared in manuscript.

WAR DIARY
or
INTELLIGENCE SUMMARY
(Erase heading not required.)

Army Form C. 2118

4th South African Infantry
January – 1917

Place	Date	Hour	Summary of Events and Information	Remarks and references to Appendices
J I	27/1/17		Hard frost – No casualties Nothing unusual to record.	
J I	28/1/17		Intercompany relief – Commenced 9. A.M. Complete 10·40 A.M. A Coy took over Oilworks & Laundry Post. B Coy took over front line from left to Sap 84 C Coy took over front line from right to Sap 84 D Coy took over Forrester Redoubt & 2 Dugouts in Support line Hard frost – No casualties.	
J I	29/1/17		Hard frost – Nothing unusual to report.	
J I.	30/1/17		Snow. Frost. Biting winds. Activity Normal.	
J I.	31/1/17		Snow Frost – Support line knocked about hostile fire and repaired	

[illegible]
Lt Colonel Commanding
4th South African Infantry
2–2–1917

1875 Wt. W593/826 1,000,000 4/15 J.B.C. & A. A.D.S.S./Forms/C. 2118.

Instructions regarding War Diaries and Intelligence Summaries are contained in F. S. Regs., Part II. and the Staff Manual respectively. Title Pages will be prepared in manuscript.

Army Form C. 2118

WAR DIARY
or
INTELLIGENCE SUMMARY
(Erase heading not required.)

4th S A Battn

Vol XI

Place	Date	Hour	Summary of Events and Information	Remarks and references to Appendices
ARRAS	1/2/17		Relieved in J I subsection by 1st S A I On relief Battalion moved to billets Headquarters to Hotel de l'Univers A Coy Two platoons to Forrestier Redoubt A Coy Two platoons to St Nicholas B Coy One platoon to St Nicholas B Coy Three platoons to Grand Place C & D Coys to the Convent. Hard frost. Found 45 men for 184th Tunnelling Co. Casualties - 1 O.R. Killed accidentally by support collapsing owing to frost breaking out.	
ARRAS	2/2/17		Bathed 100 men from 5.30 to 6.30 pm Found 100 men for R.E. Working parties R.E. Found 45 men for 184th Tunnelling Co. Hard frost.	

WAR DIARY
or
INTELLIGENCE SUMMARY
(Erase heading not required.)

Army Form C. 2118

Instructions regarding War Diaries and Intelligence Summaries are contained in F. S. Regs., Part II. and the Staff Manual respectively. Title Pages will be prepared in manuscript.

Place	Date	Hour	Summary of Events and Information	Remarks and references to Appendices
ARRAS	3/2/17		Hard Keen frost - Battalion found Working parties for Brigade 1 Officer - 12 N.C.Os & 275 O.R. do do for 184th Tun: Co 2 N.C.Os & 28 ~~42~~ O.R Trench Wardens [illegible] 10 O.R. allotted bathing for 150 Rank & file	
ARRAS	4/2/17		Hard, Keen frost - Battalion finding Working parties for Brigade 1 Officer - 12 N.C.O.S & 275. O.R. do do for 184th Tun: Co 2 N.C.O.S & 28 ~~42~~. O.R Trench Wardens [illegible] 10 O.R allotted bathing for 150 Rank & file	
ARRAS	5/2/17		Hard, Keen frost. Battalion finding Working parties for Brigade - 1 officer - 12 N.C.O.S & 275 O.R do do for 184th Tun: Co 3 N.C.O.S & 42 O.R Trench Wardens 10 O.R allotted bathing for 50 O.R.	

1875 Wt. W593/826 1,000,000 4/15 J.B.C. & A. A.D.S.S./Forms/C. 2118.

Army Form C. 2118.

WAR DIARY
or
INTELLIGENCE SUMMARY.
(Erase heading not required.)

Instructions regarding War Diaries and Intelligence Summaries are contained in F. S. Regs., Part II. and the Staff Manual respectively. Title pages will be prepared in manuscript.

Place	Date	Hour	Summary of Events and Information	Remarks and references to Appendices
ARRAS	6/2/17		Hard Keen frost. Battalion finding	
			Working parties for Brigade 1 officer - 12 N.C.O.s & 275 O.R.	
			Do do for 184th Tunn. Co. 3 N.C.O.s & 42 O.R.	
			Do do as Trench Wardens 10 O.R.	
			allotted bathing for 150 O.R.	
ARRAS	7/2/17		Hard Keen frost — Battalion finding	
			Working parties for Brigade - 1 officer 12 N.C.O.s & 275 O.R.	
			Do do 184th Tunnelling Co 3 N.C.O's & 42 O.R.	
			Do do Trench Wardens 10 O.R.	
ARRAS	8/2/17		Hard Keen frost. Battalion finding	
			Working parties for Brigade 1 officer - 13 N.C.O.s & 285 O.R.	
			Do do 3 N.C.O.s & 42 O.R.	
			Do Trench Wardens 10 O.R.	
J II subsection	9/2/17		Relieved the 2nd S A I in the line. Relief commenced at 8-30 a.m. & reported complete to Brigade at 11-36. A.M.	
			D. Company right Company	
			A Company left Company	
			C Company Supports	
			B Company in reserve at Brittannia Works.	
			Hard frost.	

A5834 Wt. W4973 M687 750,000 8/16 D. D. & L. Ltd. Forms/C.2118/13.

Instructions regarding War Diaries and Intelligence Summaries are contained in F. S. Regs., Part II. and the Staff Manual respectively. Title pages will be prepared in manuscript.

WAR DIARY
or
INTELLIGENCE SUMMARY.
(Erase heading not required.)

Army Form C. 2118.

Place	Date	Hour	Summary of Events and Information	Remarks and references to Appendices
Do	10/2/17		Hard frost. Water has to be carried to cookhouses. Nothing special to report.	
No. 2 Section Right Sector.	11/2/17		Our front altered as follows. Southern ~~point~~ Boundary Junction of Trench 89 & 90 & Junction of S.T. 89 & 90 to May Avenue. Northern Boundary St Pancras to "D" work inclusive to November avenue exclusive We took over from 3rd S.A.I the extra front on left flank & handed over Trench 89 to 1st S.A.I on right. 27th Brigade on our left now. Change effected at 9 A.M.	
Do	12/2/17		Nothing special to report.	
Do	13/2/17		Intercompany relief. Commenced 8.45 a.m. & completed 10.45 A.M. B Company Right Company. C Company Left Company. D Company Support Company A Company Reserve Company. Slight thaw & frost at night.	

A5834 Wt. W4973/M687 750,000 8/16 D. D. & L. Ltd. Forms/C.2118/13.

Instructions regarding War Diaries and Intelligence Summaries are contained in F. S. Regs., Part II. and the Staff Manual respectively. Title pages will be prepared in manuscript.

or

INTELLIGENCE SUMMARY.

(Erase heading not required.)

Place	Date	Hour	Summary of Events and Information	Remarks and references to Appendices
No 2 Section Right Sector	14/2/17		Successful raid by 27th Brigade on our left. Slight retaliation. 2/Lieut Hinton seriously wounded watching same. Cold not so intense. Commenced to clear out an old trench near Magazine. Still finding working party for 184th Tunnelling Coy.	
do.	15/2/17		Commenced to open up Immediate control trench in right company's sector. Situation fairly quiet.	
do.	16/2/17		Intermittent hostile shelling along front during day & night. No casualties. Thaw setting in.	
do to Reserve ARRAS.	17/2/17		Battalion relieved in No 2 section. Right sector by 2nd S.A.I commencing 8.30am. A. B. C. coys billeted in Convent. D Company Rue St Augustines Nos. 48. 50. 54. 55 billets. Officers 47 (Bis) Capt Reid arrived. Thawing & misty. No artillery work	

A5834 Wt. W4973/M687 750,000 8/16 D. D. & L. Ltd. Forms/C.2118/13.

Army Form C. 2118.

INTELLIGENCE SUMMARY.

(Erase heading not required.)

Summaries are contained in F. S. Regs., Part II. and the Staff Manual respectively. Title pages will be prepared in manuscript.

Place	Date	Hour	Summary of Events and Information	Remarks and references to Appendices
Reserve Bn – ARRAS.	18/2/17		Damp drizzle – misty – no artillery activity to speak of. Working parties A 1 Off – 45 O/Rs (daily Newcut) B – 45 O/Rs for 184th Tun: Co. Addl working parties A 1 Off. 40 men B. 35 C. 2 90 D 1 90 Baths allotted A. Coy. 25 O.R. B Coy 25 O.R.	
Reserve Bn ARRAS	19/2/17		Mild weather. Found Working parties A Coy 105 – B Coy 105 C Coy 120 – D 112 being on Spring Avenue 40. August Avenue 40. July Avenue 40 – Dump 45 Dugouts (184th) 45 and new Trench 283 Bathing Nil.	
Reserve Battn ARRAS	20/2/17		Found Working & Carrying parties New Dump 45, 184th Tunnelling 45 Aug Ave 30, S&T.M.B 30 July Ave 30, New Trench 232 Oct Ave 20, Spring Tram 40 Sundries 10 TOTAL 482 Bathing Nil.	

A5834 Wt. W4973 M687 750,000 8/16 D. D. & L. Ltd. Forms/C.2118/13.

Army Form C. 2118.

Instructions regarding War Diaries and Intelligence Summaries are contained in F. S. Regs., Part II. and the Staff Manual respectively. Title pages will be prepared in manuscript.

WAR DIARY
or
INTELLIGENCE SUMMARY.
(Erase heading not required.)

Place	Date	Hour	Summary of Events and Information	Remarks and references to Appendices
Reserve Batt. ARRAS.	21/3/17		Found Working parties. August Avenue 30, July Avenue 30, October Avenue 68, Spring Tram 61, Sundries 10, 184th Tun: Co 45, Dump Trench 45, New Trench 218, 2" T.M.S 19 } TOTAL 526. Bathing Nil.	
Reserve Battn ARRAS	22/3/17		Found Working parties. August Avenue 30, July Avenue 30, October Avenue 78, Spring Avenue 60, 184th Tunnel Co 45, Dump Trench 45, New Trench 187, Sundries 10 } TOTAL 485. Allotted Baths. A. 50. B. 50. C. 25 D 25. A & B Lewis gunners of [illegible] out on range all day.	
Reserve Battn ARRAS	23/3/17		Found Working parties. T.M.B. 40, 184th Tunnelling 108, Dump Trench 45, Spring Avenue 40, S.A.A. T.M.B. 40, October Ave 18, New Trench 209 } TOTAL 500 C & D Lewis gunners out on range all day. Casualty - 1 O.R. Wounded. Allotted Baths ~~A 50~~ 75. B 75. C 50. D 50. H.Q. 50.	

A5834 Wt. W4973/M687 750,000 8/16 D. D. & L. Ltd. Forms/C.2118/13.

Army Form C. 2118.

WAR DIARY
or
INTELLIGENCE SUMMARY.
(Erase heading not required.)

Instructions regarding War Diaries and Intelligence Summaries are contained in F. S. Regs., Part II. and the Staff Manual respectively. Title pages will be prepared in manuscript.

Place	Date	Hour	Summary of Events and Information	Remarks and references to Appendices
RESERVE BATT. ARRAS	24/2/17		Found working parties 184th Tunnelling Co 108 / S.A.L.T.M.B. 40 NEW Trench 150 / Sundries 10 } 392 x Spring Tram 42 / Fat. ? 42 Allotted Baths H.Qrs 120. A Coy 40 B Coy 10 C Coy 40 D Coy 40.	
Right Section Left Section	25/2/17		Relieved 2nd S.A.I. in line. Relief commenced 9. AM & complete by 12-10 p.m. A. Coy Left Coy D Coy Right Coy B Coy Supports C Coy Reserve. } Trenches fallen in badly & very muddy. Weather warm & bright. Casualties 1. O.R. wounded Six patrols out during night of 25/26. 2/Lt Lamont & 2 O.R. not yet returned	
do	25/2/17		Found working parties. 184th Tunnelling Coy 108 Dump Trench 45 Clearing Trenches 156 S.A.L.T.M.B. 40 } 349	2/Lt Lamont & 2 O/R still missing @ 12 midnight

A5834 Wt. W4973/M687 750,000 8/16 D. D. & L. Ltd. Forms/C.2118/13.

Army Form C. 2118.

WAR DIARY
or
INTELLIGENCE SUMMARY.
(Erase heading not required.)

Instructions regarding War Diaries and Intelligence Summaries are contained in F. S. Regs., Part II. and the Staff Manual respectively. Title pages will be prepared in manuscript.

Place	Date	Hour	Summary of Events and Information	Remarks and references to Appendices
Right Section Left Section	26/2/17		Raid by 1st Regiment. Identification established. Our Lewis guns opened fire on enemy trenches opposite during raid. Artillery active on both sides. Capt Mitchell went on short leave. 3 Patrols out to see if enemy was occupying trenches. Enemy coughing heard. Brigade wired "Special rations" but cancelled later. Patrol sent out to find 2/Lt Lamont & party. Unsuccessful. Working parties as follows:- 184th Tunnelling Co. All men turned out all day to clear trenches which are in a bad state.	
do	27/2/17.		Body seen near enemy wire. 2/Lt Lamont & Pte Leathern returned, report L/Cpl Fraser killed by bomb thrown at them from enemy sap head. 3 Officers patrols out to establish contact. Working parties as follows:- 184th Tunnelling, Brigade Dump & rest of men clearing trenches. Weather fine. Aeroplane brought down by enemy over ARRAS.	

A5834 Wt W4973 M687 750,000 8/16 D. D. & L. Ltd. Forms/C.2118/13.

Army Form C. 2118.

Instructions regarding War Diaries and Intelligence Summaries are contained in F. S. Regs., Part II. and the Staff Manual respectively. Title pages will be prepared in manuscript.

WAR DIARY
or
INTELLIGENCE SUMMARY.
(*Erase heading not required.*)

Place	Date	Hour	Summary of Events and Information	Remarks and references to Appendices
Right Section Left Section	28/7/17		Inter-company relief Situation of Coys. B right front line C Left " " A Supports D Reserve.	
			Special rations again notified but cancelled.	
			Patrols. 4 Officers patrols at various times to establish contact with enemy. Successful.	
		10-12pm	About 10-12 pm heavy barrage put on front line by enemy. Communications with RIGHT front & support broken & no news. Left Coy reported "nothing serious on the left". SOS was put through to artillery	
		10-25pm	from Battalion H.Q at 10-25 pm. Front line knocked to pieces. Working parties. 184th Tunnelling Brigade dump & the rest working all day to repair damage done by bombardment. also clearing trenches & revetting. During bombardment casualties slight.	

Irwan Christian
Lt Col
Commanding

A5834 Wt. W4973/M687 750,000 8/16 D. D. & L. Ltd. Forms/C.2118/13.

Instructions regarding War Diaries and Intelligence Summaries are contained in F. S. Regs., Part II. and the Staff Manual respectively. Title pages will be prepared in manuscript.

WAR DIARY
or
INTELLIGENCE SUMMARY.
(Erase heading not required.)

4 S A Infy Bn

Vol 12

Army Form C. 2118.

Place	Date	Hour	Summary of Events and Information	Remarks and references to Appendices
Right SECTOR. LEFT SECTION	1/3/17		Fine day. Enemy trench mortars active all day. Four officers patrols out during night.	
do	2/3/17		At 5.30 AM. Enemy heavily bombarded our front line and at 5.50 AM attempted to raid our trenches to the South of Cuthbert Crater. Owing to the heavy mist he managed to reach our wire without being seen. One German reached the parapet but was shot by an officer (Lt Wallace). The remainder of the enemy were dispersed by Lewis gun & rifle fire. Our front line badly knocked about by shell fire. Our casualties 6 killed & 7 wounded (All from shell fire). During the night our patrols were sent out to obtain identification & brought in one body, 2 identity discs, 2 box bombs (for dugouts) & several enemy hand grenades. (The enemy raiding party belonged to the 12 Pioneers). Strong wiring parties were sent out to repair damage done to our wire. Working parties also sent up to clear front line.	

A5834 Wt. W4973/M687 750,000 8/16 D. D. & L. Ltd. Forms/C.2118/13.

Army Form C. 2118.

Instructions regarding War Diaries and Intelligence Summaries are contained in F. S. Regs., Part II. and the Staff Manual respectively. Title pages will be prepared in manuscript.

or

INTELLIGENCE SUMMARY.

(Erase heading not required.)

Place	Date	Hour	Summary of Events and Information	Remarks and references to Appendices
RIGHT SECTOR LEFT SECTION	3/3/17		Everything quiet on front. Working parties cleaning trenches. Our transport moved most of spare kit in the evening. Four officers patrols out during night. Nothing special to report.	
do	4/3/17.		Regiment relieved by 10th Argyle & Sutherland Highlanders. Relief started at 10 Am & finished by 2 pm. Working parties stationed in Arras moved off at 9 Am. On relief Companies were held up at Candle Factory on instructions from Brigade. at 2 pm further instructions arrived to proceed with move. The last company reported in at Y Hutment Camp at 5.30 pm Battalion headquarters at B Block Y Hutment camp.	
Y. Hutments Near ETRUN	5/3/17		Battalion paraded for inspection by Field Marshall Sir Douglas Haig at 12.45 pm. Regiment turned out in good style. Found Working parties { 50 men at LARASSET 100 men at St Nicholas.	

A5834 Wt. W4973 M687 750,000 8/16 D. D. & L. Ltd. Forms/C.2118/13.

Army Form C. 2118.

WAR DIARY
or
INTELLIGENCE SUMMARY.
(*Erase heading not required.*)

Instructions regarding War Diaries and Intelligence Summaries are contained in F. S. Regs., Part II. and the Staff Manual respectively. Title pages will be prepared in manuscript.

Place	Date	Hour	Summary of Events and Information	Remarks and references to Appendices
Y" HUTS NEAR ETRUN	6/3/17		Battalion training from 9 A.M. to 1 pm and 2.30 pm to 4.30 pm. Two coys on rifle range. Baths allotted A. B & D Coys 100 men each from 10 A.M. to 1 pm. Found fatigue parties { Larassit Dump 50 O.R. St Nicholas 100 O.R.	
do	7/3/1917		Battalion training from 9 A.M. to 1 pm and 2.30 pm to 4.30 pm. Found fatigue parties { Larassit Dump 50 O.R. St Nicholas 100 O.R.	
do	8/3/1917		Battalion training from 9 A.M. to 1 pm and 2.30 pm to 4.30 pm. Found fatigue parties { Larassit Dump 50 O.R. St Nicholas 100 O.R.	

A5834 Wt. W4973/M687 750,000 8/16 D. D. & L. Ltd. Forms/C.2118/13.

Instructions regarding War Diaries and Intelligence Summaries are contained in F. S. Regs., Part II. and the Staff Manual respectively. Title pages will be prepared in manuscript.

WAR DIARY
or
INTELLIGENCE SUMMARY.
(Erase heading not required.)

Army Form C. 2118.

Place	Date	Hour	Summary of Events and Information	Remarks and references to Appendices
Y. Huts	9/3/17		Battalion Training from 9 AM to 1 pm and from 2 30 pm to 4 30 pm. Allotted baths. Signallers 50 Headqrs 50 D Coy 100 A Coy 50. Found Fatigues { Laurent 50 O.R St Nicholas 100 O.R.	
Y. Huts	10/3/17		Battalion training from 9 am to 1 pm and from 2 30 pm to 4.30 pm. Bathing allotted A Coy 25 men, B Coy 50 men, C Coy 50 men D Coy 100 men, Snipers 25 men, H.Q's 25 men Lewis Gunners 75 men. Fatigues found. Laurent Dump 50 O.R. Mr Farrell & 150 O.R. left at 1.30 pm for ANZIN for fatigue under Corps H.A.	

Army Form C. 2118.

Instructions regarding War Diaries and Intelligence Summaries are contained in F. S. Regs., Part II. and the Staff Manual respectively. Title pages will be prepared in manuscript.

WAR DIARY
or
INTELLIGENCE SUMMARY.
(Erase heading not required.)

Place	Date	Hour	Summary of Events and Information	Remarks and references to Appendices
[illegible]HUTS [illegible]TRUN	11/3/17		No parades for training. Found 50 men for fatigues at LARASSET. Battalion inspected in afternoon by Mr Walter Long - the Secretary of State for Colonies.	
[illegible]HUTS [illegible]TRUN	12/3/17		Found 50 men for fatigue at LARASSET. The battalion moved at 8.30 A.M. for OSTREVILLE via HERMAVILLE. Halted for midday meal just west of SAVY. All billeted by 5 p.m. Good billets. The 50 men on fatigue reported back by bus.	
[illegible]STREVILLE	13/3/17		Left billets 9. A.M. to train on ground near MONCHY BRETON. Took out field kitchens.	
[illegible]STREVILLE	14/3/17		Left billets 9 A.M. for MONCHY BRETON TRAINING AREA. Bombing - Bayonet fighting - attack formation by companies. B Coy & Snipers on range. Out all day back to billets 5 pm.	
[illegible]STREVILLE	15/3/17		Left billets 9 A.M. for MONCHY BRETON TRAINING AREA. Bombing - Bayonet fighting attack practice by companies. Out all day. Back to billets 5 p.m.	

A5834 Wt. W4973 M687 750,000 8/16 D. D. & L. Ltd. Forms/C.2118/13.

Instructions regarding War Diaries and Intelligence Summaries are contained in F. S. Regs., Part II. and the Staff Manual respectively. Title pages will be prepared in manuscript.

WAR DIARY
or
INTELLIGENCE SUMMARY.
(Erase heading not required.)

Army Form C. 2118.

Place	Date	Hour	Summary of Events and Information	Remarks and references to Appendices
OSTREVILLE	16/3/17		Left billets 1-30 p.m. for training area. Attack formation, bombing &c by companies in afternoon till 5 p.m. Then from 6.30 pm to 8 night manoeuvres. Back to billets 9 p.m. - Cold but fine	
OSTREVILLE	17/3/17		Left billets 1-30 p.m. for training area. Attack practice as a battalion in afternoon & ~~at~~ night manoeuvres after dark. Back to billets 9 p.m. Fine day.	
OSTREVILLE	18/3/17		No training - 25% of battalion allowed passes to St POL. Allotted bathing to 60 men from each company. Fine day	
OSTREVILLE	19/3/17		Training - C. Coy at range in morning. Battalion attack practice in afternoon. Cold weather.	
OSTREVILLE	20/3/17		Training - Brigade practised the attack in morning & afternoon. Bitterly cold day. Company shoulder badges put on.	

Army Form C. 2118.

WAR DIARY
or
INTELLIGENCE SUMMARY.
(*Erase heading not required.*)

Instructions regarding War Diaries and Intelligence Summaries are contained in F. S. Regs., Part II. and the Staff Manual respectively. Title pages will be prepared in manuscript.

Place	Date	Hour	Summary of Events and Information	Remarks and references to Appendices
OSTREVILLE	21/3/17		Battalion moved by companies at 200 yards interval to PENIN, leaving at 10 A.M. Battalion billeted by 1 p.m. Billets left clean & all claims for damages 32 francs 50 centimes paid.	
PENIN	22/3/17		No training. All special stores wire cutters &c issued to companies. Bathed 36 men under rifle arrangements. Snowed at night	
PENIN	23/3/17		Slight frost. Training from 9-30 to 12 noon. Inter company football matches in afternoon.	
PENIN	24/3/17		Battalion moved:- A Coy & half D Coy to Y Huts. 9 officers 259 men Headqrs - B Coy & half D Coy to HERMAVILLE - 19 officers & 451 men C Coy to TILLOY-les-Hermaville 5 officers & 181 men.	

A5834 Wt. W4973/M687 750,000 8/16 D. D. & L. Ltd. Forms/C.2118/13.

Army Form C. 2118.

WAR DIARY
or
INTELLIGENCE SUMMARY.
(Erase heading not required.)

Instructions regarding War Diaries and Intelligence Summaries are contained in F. S. Regs., Part II. and the Staff Manual respectively. Title pages will be prepared in manuscript.

Place	Date	Hour	Summary of Events and Information	Remarks and references to Appendices
	24/3/17		B Coy furnished 1 officer & 30 O.R. for duty at Bois d'Habarcq. after arrival at Hermaville, as a standing duty.	
HERMAVILLE	25/3/17		A Coy & ½ D Coy moved to ANZIN to work for Corps Heavy Arty.	
			C Coy furnished 1 officer & 50 O.R. at Savy Station for fatigue	
			D Coy do 1 officer & 50 O.R. at Haute Avesnes do	
			B Coy do 1 officer & 30 men at Bois d'Habarcq. do	
			Balance of regt training under Coy arrangements & small fatigues for Town Major	
HERMAVILLE	26/3/17		A & ½ D Coy at ANZIN working for Corps H.A.	
			C Coy furnished 1 officer & 50 O.R. at Savy for fatigue	
			B Coy do 1 officer & 50 O.R. at Haute Avesnes do	
			B Coy do 1 officer & 30 O.R. at Bois d'Habarcq.	
			Balance of regt training under Coy arrangements & small fatigues for Town Major	
			Dull & showery.	

Instructions regarding War Diaries and Intelligence Summaries are contained in F. S. Regs., Part II. and the Staff Manual respectively. Title pages will be prepared in manuscript.

WAR DIARY
or
INTELLIGENCE SUMMARY.
(Erase heading not required.)

Army Form C. 2118.

Place	Date	Hour	Summary of Events and Information	Remarks and references to Appendices
HERMAVILLE	27/3/17		A Coy and half D Coy at ANZIN on fatigue for Corps H.A.	Regtl Team
			C Coy furnished 1 Officer & 50 O.R. at Savy for fatigue	beat 6/7 R.
			D Coy furnished 1 Officer & 50 O.R at Hautes Avesnes.	S.F. 3-0
			B Coy furnished 1 Officer & 30 O.R at Bois d'Habarcq.	at Soccer
			Snow showers in morning & dull generally	
HERMAVILLE	28/3/17		A Coy & half D Coy at ANZIN on fatigue for Corps H.A.	
			C Coy furnished 1 Officer & 50 O.R. for fatigue at SAVY	
			at 3.15 pm B Coy & two platoons of D Coy left to report to 9th Div. R.A. at St Catherine's for fatigue	
			at 3.15 pm Two platoons of C Coy left for ARRAS to report to Div. Trench Mortars for fatigue	
			Hdqrs D Coy remained at HERMAVILLE	

A5834 Wt. W4973 M687 750,000 8/16 D. D. & L. Ltd. Forms/C.2118/13.

Army Form C. 2118.

Instructions regarding War Diaries and Intelligence Summaries are contained in F. S. Regs., Part II. and the Staff Manual respectively. Title pages will be prepared in manuscript.

WAR DIARY
or
INTELLIGENCE SUMMARY.
(Erase heading not required.)

Place	Date	Hour	Summary of Events and Information	Remarks and references to Appendices
HERMAVILLE	29/3/17		Moved at 10 AM to Y. Huts & occupied D Block at 5 p.m. Two platoons of C Coy & 40 men of HdQrs moved to ARRAS for fatigue with Divl Trench Mortars. Two other platoons of C still with D.T.M.O.	
			B & half D Coys still with 9th DIVN R.A.	
			A & half D Coys do — do Corps R.A	
			Practically no one left at Y Huts except officers, & batmen & Orderly Room. Staff.	
			The transport reoccupied its old lines at ETRUN with R.Q.M. Store close by.	
			Day showery & cold. Y. Hutments a mass of mud.	

A5834 Wt. W4973 M687 750,000 8/16 D. D. & L. Ltd. Forms/C.2118/13.

Army Form C. 2118.

WAR DIARY
or
INTELLIGENCE SUMMARY.

(*Erase heading not required.*)

Instructions regarding War Diaries and Intelligence Summaries are contained in F. S. Regs., Part II. and the Staff Manual respectively. Title pages will be prepared in manuscript.

Place	Date	Hour	Summary of Events and Information	Remarks and references to Appendices
~~[illegible]~~ Y. HUTS ETRUN	30/3/17		Working parties still away. Without Tpt & Q.M our strength at Y. Huts 17 officers · 66 O.R. Slight showers during day. Quiet apparently on front. 21 Carriers returned from Brigade & sent to their Coys.	
Y. Huts ETRUN	31/3/17		Working parties the same. Generally quiet. Fine morning – Hail in afternoon & rain in evening	

[signature]

In the field
1–4–1917.

Lt. Colonel Commdg
4th South African Infantry

A5834 Wt. W4973/M687 750,000 8/16 D. D. & L. Ltd. Forms/C.2118/13.

Army Form C. 2118.

WAR DIARY
or
INTELLIGENCE SUMMARY.
(Erase heading not required.)

...aries and Intelligence ...in F. S. Regs., Part II. ...espectively. Title pages ...anuscript.

4th South African Infantry – April 1917

Place	Date	Hour	Summary of Events and Information	Remarks and references to Appendices
Y. HUTS ETRUN	1/4/17		Working Parties still away as follows:	
			At ANZIN for Corps H.A. 4 officers and 262 O.R.	
			At St Catherine's for 9th Div. R.A. 7 officers and 265 O.R.	
			At ARRAS for 9th Div. T.M.O. 7 officers and 234 O.R.	
			Generally dull & cold & wet. Slight frost at night	
Y HUTS ETRUN	2/4/17		Working parties as on 1st	
Y HUTS ETRUN	3/4/17		Capt T.H. ROSS Killed by shell in trenches	
			a very great loss to the Regiment.	
			Working parties from 9th Div T.M.O. and ANZIN	
			returned to Y. HUTS. Accomodated in C Block.	

D.

Army Form C. 2118.

WAR DIARY
or
INTELLIGENCE SUMMARY.

(Erase heading not required.)

Instructions regarding War Diaries and Intelligence Summaries are contained in F. S. Regs., Part II. and the Staff Manual respectively. Title pages will be prepared in manuscript.

Place	Date	Hour	Summary of Events and Information	Remarks and references to Appendices
Y. Huts ETRUN	4/4/17		The party working for the 9th Divn R.A. returned to Y Huts. Had difficulty in getting accommodation	
Y Huts	5/4/17		Regiment all at Y Huts. Issued Bombs &c to companies. All valises stored at No 5 Billet ETRUN. A fine day	
Y Huts	6/4/17		2nd - 3rd - & 4th Regts inspected by General Smuts on ground north of E Block in morning nothing in afternoon. Very showery & heavy rain at night	

A5834 Wt. W4973 M687 750,000 8/16 D. D. & L. Ltd. Forms/C.2118/13.

Army Form C. 2118.

WAR DIARY
or
INTELLIGENCE SUMMARY.
(*Erase heading not required.*)

Instructions regarding War Diaries and Intelligence Summaries are contained in F. S. Regs., Part II. and the Staff Manual respectively. Title pages will be prepared in manuscript.

Place	Date	Hour	Summary of Events and Information	Remarks and references to Appendices
HUB ETRUN	7/4/17		Regiment moved. 2 coys & D to front line B & A & Moppers up to billets in ARRAS.	
			Officers going forward.	
			Headqrs Lt Col Christison, Capt Mitchell, 2/Lt Bonstead, 2/Lt Hunt.	
			A. Coy. Capt Grady, 2/Lt Marshall, 2/Lt Saunders 2/Lt Cumming	
			B Coy 2/Lt Morrison, 2/Lt Forbes, 2/Lt Wallace 2/Lt Bunce	
			C. Coy 2/Lt Smith, 2/Lt Lees, 2/Lt Keeling 2/Lt Roff.	
			D Coy Capt Reid, 2/Lt Williams, 2/Lt Armand 2/Lt Forder.	
			Moppers up. 2/Lt Kirby & 2/Lt Aitken.	
			Medical officer attached - Capt Lawrence	
			Chaplain attached) - Capt Menzies	

A5834 Wt. W4973 M687 750,000 8/16 D. D. & L. Ltd. Forms/C.2118/13.

Army Form C. 2118.

WAR DIARY
or
INTELLIGENCE SUMMARY.
(*Erase heading not required.*)

Instructions regarding War Diaries and Intelligence Summaries are contained in F. S. Regs., Part II. and the Staff Manual respectively. Title pages will be prepared in manuscript.

Place	Date	Hour	Summary of Events and Information	Remarks and references to Appendices
Y HUTS	7/4/17.		The battalion strength for the operations was	
			A Coy 4 officers 118 other ranks	
			B Coy 4 officers 123 other ranks	
			C Coy 4 officers 108 other ranks:	
			D Coy 4 officers 127 other ranks:	
			H qrs 4 officers 61 other ranks.	
			20 officers 537 other ranks	
			Mopping up 2 50	
			22 587	
			M.O. & PADRE 2.	
			24 587.	
			In addition the regiment furnished parties attached to	
			Div: Trench Mortars 8. O.R. A.D.M.S 15 O.R.	
			Div Bomb Store 7. O.R. 28 M.G. Coy 41 O.R. TOTAL 85 O.R.	
			Brigade 6. O.R. 197th M.G. Coy 8 O.R.	
			The 1st Line Transport & details remained at ETRUN. The details left.	

A5834 Wt. W4973/M687 750,000 8/16 D. D. & L. Ltd. Forms/C.2118/13.

Army Form C. 2118.

WAR DIARY
or
INTELLIGENCE SUMMARY.
(Erase heading not required.)

Instructions regarding War Diaries and Intelligence Summaries are contained in F. S. Regs., Part II. and the Staff Manual respectively. Title pages will be prepared in manuscript.

Place	Date	Hour	Summary of Events and Information	Remarks and references to Appendices
Y. HUTS.	7/4/17		behind included a percentage of Lewis gunners & signallers, prospective officers and C.S.M.S.	
			The move was postponed owing to enemy balloon observation, but at 7. p.m. the battalion moved from Y Huts by "7" route, by platoons at 100 yards interval. The route was via LOUEZ, south of the SCARPE to ST CATHERINES & thence via the OCTROI through St Nicholas. Headquarters reached the Candle works about 9.30 pm, followed by D Coy. Headqrs moved to Battle Headqrs Dugout 23 at junction of NEW cut with front line, A. Coy took over from 1st Regt our battalion frontage of the front line, C Coy took over Brittannia Works. A & B Coys & moppers up going to billets in houses just south of the Scarpe at G22 A 5.4. Relief reported complete 12.45 am on 8th. Whilst battalion moving in to trenches enemy was shelling about the line & NEW CUT. C T.	
J. SECTOR FRONT LINE	8/4/17		During the morning C Coy furnished a fatigue party bringing up ladders & bridges to front line, & during the afternoon & evening D Coy put them in position along battalion front. At 11-15 a.m. our artillery carried out a rehearsal barrage. At 11.20 A.M the enemy retaliated with light shells	

A5834 Wt. W4973/M687 750,000 8/16 D. D. & L. Ltd. Forms/C.2118/13.

Instructions regarding War Diaries and Intelligence Summaries are contained in F. S. Regs., Part II. and the Staff Manual respectively. Title pages will be prepared in manuscript.

WAR DIARY
or
INTELLIGENCE SUMMARY.
(Erase heading not required.)

Army Form C. 2118.

Place	Date	Hour	Summary of Events and Information	Remarks and references to Appendices
I Sect'r	8/4/17		By 3 pm the platoon boards marking the right of each platoon in its assembly position had been placed, & two guides per company sent to A & B Coys. At 6 pm an officer reported to Brigade H.Q. Battle H.Qrs to synchronise watches. At 7 pm Capt REID O.C. D Coy synchronised his watch. At 9.20 pm 2/Lt Kirby reported his moppers up in position & synchronised his watch. At 9.40 pm 2/Lt Smith O.C. "B" Coy reported his company moving into position & synchronised his watch. The night was a bright moonlight one but after dusk or night fall the Intelligence officer had his snipers out completing the cutting of paths through our own wire, whilst he himself conducted the leading waves of C & D Coys to their positions in shell holes in the centre of No Mans Land. This he succeeded in doing without apparently attracting enemy attention, though at one time the enemy opened a light barrage which died away. The shell holes had been added to by the R.E. blowing artificial craters the night before. No doubt the enemy took our leading waves for strong patrols, as he frequently swept NO MANS Land during the night with M.G. fire.	

A5834 Wt. W4973 M687 750,000 8/16 D. D. & L. Ltd. Forms/C.2118/13.

Army Form C. 2118.

WAR DIARY
or
INTELLIGENCE SUMMARY.
(Erase heading not required.)

Instructions regarding War Diaries and Intelligence Summaries are contained in F. S. Regs., Part II. and the Staff Manual respectively. Title pages will be prepared in manuscript.

Place	Date	Hour	Summary of Events and Information	Remarks and references to Appendices
[illegible] SECTOR	9/4/17		Battle Headqrs, & established itself in the trench in Sunken road west of 1st objective by 8.15 A.M. in a dugout marked LINKER FLUGEL 8/25, approx G12D99. The Medical Officer establishing his Dressing station nearby. Advancing from the 1st objective as soon as the barrage commenced to move forward A & B coys moved down the spur under fairly heavy machine gun & rifle fire, & especially as they went through a belt of low plain wire erected half way down the slope, which had not been destroyed. There were paths through it, & it was noticed that those who used the paths were generally hit. The fire came from the western edge of the cutting which overlooked this slope. A Lewis gun was left here to play on the cutting & so help our advance. Once down the slope there was protection from the steep bank, & climbing up our men waited till the barrage reached the near edge of the cutting, & by the time it reached the far side were on top of the cutting looking into it, the Germans who had lined the edge of the cutting having mostly left their rifles & got into their dugouts in the cutting itself on the approach	

A5834 Wt. W4973/M687 750,000 8/16 D. D. & L. Ltd. Forms/C.2118/13.

Army Form C. 2118.

WAR DIARY
or
INTELLIGENCE SUMMARY.

(*Erase heading not required.*)

Instructions regarding War Diaries and Intelligence Summaries are contained in F. S. Regs., Part II. and the Staff Manual respectively. Title pages will be prepared in manuscript.

Place	Date	Hour	Summary of Events and Information	Remarks and references to Appendices
J. SECTOR	9/4/17		At 12.30 am 2/Lt Morrison, O.C. "B" Coy reported his company moving in & synchronised his watch. At 1.45 am Capt Grady, O.C. A Coy reported in person his company in its assembly position, & 2/Lt Morrison O.C. B Coy returned to report in person his company in its assembly position. About 1.45 am ~~the~~ a note from O.C. "C" Coy reported that company in its assembly position (time 1.25 am). The O.C. D Coy also reported, but time not noted, that his coy was in its assembly position. At 1.45 am the Commanding Officer reported in writing to Brigade that the Battalion was in its assembly position. The message was delivered by an officer at 2.13 am, & watches compared. Beyond a few 4.2s about 2 A.M. little hostile shell fire till zero but his M Gs continually swept our front, especially [illegible] from about V.9. The battalion's disposition for the attack was as follows:– Map reference 51 B N W 3 – The battalion held the front line from Sap 89 to a pp 25 yards north of Sap 91, that is from ~~[illegible]~~ G11 D 95·16 to G.12.C 35·84, approximately 300 yards. The front was a two company one. C and D Companies leading, C on right	

A5834 Wt. W4973 M687 750,000 8/16 D. D. & L. Ltd. Forms/C.2118/13.

Instructions regarding War Diaries and Intelligence Summaries are contained in F. S. Regs., Part II. and the Staff Manual respectively. Title pages will be prepared in manuscript.

WAR DIARY
or
INTELLIGENCE SUMMARY.
(Erase heading not required.)

Army Form C. 2118.

Place	Date	Hour	Summary of Events and Information	Remarks and references to Appendices
J. Sector.	9/4/17		The assaulting companies carried one large board each marked "Black Line" or "Blue Line" to put up as the objectives were reached, & they were especially noticeable to the troops going through at the Blue Line. The moppers up carried white flagged pegs about 18" long marked "CLEARED" to put in our dugout entrances	
			Attached to the diary are the following	
			Marked "A" Copy No 27 of 2/10/2 1st S.A. Inf. Bde's Instructions regarding forthcoming operations.	
			Marked "B" Copy of Operation order 17/18 by O.C. 4th S.A.I re Operations	
			Marked C¹ C² C³ 1/5000 Scale Maps of Ground for Operations on 9th	
			Marked D. Map showing Brigade objectives on Black, Blue & Brown Lines on 9th	
J. SECTOR			ZERO was at 5-30 a.m., & contrary to the expectation that the cadence of the bombardment would not alter. At zero hour our barrage opened with a tremendous crash. At 5.31 our leading wave was reported well away closely followed by the moppers up, the second wave & supporting companies also clearing our front line & following at 5.34 in response to Golden Rain rockets sent up from their	

Army Form C. 2118.

WAR DIARY
or
INTELLIGENCE SUMMARY.
(Erase heading not required.)

Instructions regarding War Diaries and Intelligence Summaries are contained in F. S. Regs., Part II. and the Staff Manual respectively. Title pages will be prepared in manuscript.

Place	Date	Hour	Summary of Events and Information	Remarks and references to Appendices
J. Sect N.	9/4/17		D on left, with A & B Coys in support A on ~~left~~ right B on left. Each company in two waves, two platoons in each ~~wav~~ wave. C & D Coys leading waves were in shell holes in No mans land midway between our own & the German lines at 4.30 a.m. the moppers up of our battalion moved into no mans land & lined up in shell holes behind the leading wave. Our 50 moppers up extended along the Brigade front. The second wave of C and D Coys were in the front line. A & B Coys were in the immediate control trench, both waves in the same trench one behind the other. This control trench in parts did not exist, so the men lay in shell holes or depressions. The 3rd S.A.I. were on our immediate right, & the 12th Royal Scots of 27th Bde on our left. Our leading wave pushed out its Lewis guns about 50 yards ahead, also the battalion snipers were in line with these Lewis guns looking for enemy M. Gunners.	
			The battalion had two objectives, one known as the Black Line, and a further one known as the Blue Line, for the first C & D Coys led, for the 2nd A & B Coys led.	

Army Form C. 2118.

WAR DIARY
or
INTELLIGENCE SUMMARY.
(Erase heading not required.)

Instructions regarding War Diaries and Intelligence Summaries are contained in F. S. Regs., Part II. and the Staff Manual respectively. Title pages will be prepared in manuscript.

Place	Date	Hour	Summary of Events and Information	Remarks and references to Appendices
			front the German barrage dropped on our front line, missing our men who were by then clear. The leading companies moved close behind our ~~barra~~ artillery barrage, so close that some of our casualties were occasioned by men getting hit by our own barrage through their going too fast. Everyone is of opinion that our artillery barrage was good. The battalion went straight through to the 1st objective, but reached it with part of battalion a bit to the left, also the supporting companies B getting into position along the road from app. H7A0.0 to H7A10.25, & A Coy in trench from app G12D95.90 to G12B90.10. The leading companies moving forward approx 50 yards in front of the objective slightly left with part of the battalion & consolidating. The moppers up reached the trenches with the first wave close up behind our barrage before the Germans had time to get out of their dugouts & proceeded to clear them, the procedure adopted being to drop one or two "P" bombs & MILLS bombs down one entrance, the other entrance being covered by a man on top of the trench well to one side of the entrance. In most instances the Germans did not offer much resistance, & where they did especially one party of ten that had managed to get into a cross trench	

A5834 Wt. W4973/M687 750,000 8/16 D. D. & L. Ltd. Forms/C.2118/13.

Instructions regarding War Diaries and Intelligence Summaries are contained in F. S. Regs., Part II. and the Staff Manual respectively. Title pages will be prepared in manuscript.

WAR DIARY
or
INTELLIGENCE SUMMARY.
(Erase heading not required.)

Army Form C. 2118.

Place	Date	Hour	Summary of Events and Information	Remarks and references to Appendices
J. Sector.	9/4/17		were promptly dealt with by the officer in charge & a few men. The companies from the Black line were in view of the 2nd objective, & corrected their dispositions, B Coy before the second attack, & A Coy getting over to its right as it moved forward to get ready to follow the barrage. In this first phase the enemy line offered no obstacle at any place, & once our barrage dropped their machine guns in the front line ceased, there was however some machine gun fire from the Blue line, whilst at the Black Line. At 5.47 a.m. the German barrage on our own front line eased off, & the Battalion signallers under 2/Lt Hunt moved out, this officer being killed as he left the parapet. At 6.21 Batt HQ. received a message from O.C. A Coy, timed 6. A.M. stating "Have reached 2nd Line Hun system, barrage halted". At 7. A.M. Artillery Liaison officer had message from his F.O.O. to say 1st objective had been taken. Batt HQ wired Brigade that Battalion Headqrs moving forward, also advised 3rd S.A.I. H.Q on right & 12 R Scots H.Q. on left at same time. At 7.20 A.M Battalion Headqrs left	

A5834 Wt. W4973/M687 750,000 8/16 D. D. & L. Ltd. Forms/C.2118/13.

Instructions regarding War Diaries and Intelligence Summaries are contained in F. S. Regs., Part II. and the Staff Manual respectively. Title pages will be prepared in manuscript.

WAR DIARY
or
INTELLIGENCE SUMMARY.
(Erase heading not required.)

Army Form C. 2118.

Place	Date	Hour	Summary of Events and Information	Remarks and references to Appendices
	9/4/17		of the barrage, & came out to be taken prisoner. The near edge of the cutting had been cut away to form a firestep close behind a thin hedge which ran the length of the cutting. The battalion reached the cutting well on time, with good direction.	
			At Battalion Headqrs in the Black Line, our men were seen entering the cutting & at 8.30 AM wired Brigade H.Q. ~~that~~ "Have taken our second objective"	
			At 8-45 a.m. Battalion H.Q. received the following message from O.C. A Coy - "No 4" & timed 8.20 A.M. "Have reached BLUE LINE, quite a number of prisoners, few casualties ourselves, now reorganising & consolidating"	
			At 8.45 a.m. received No 1 message from 2/Lt KEELEY, commanding No 12 platoon, C Coy, timed 6.45 a.m. saying "Have reached objective Black Line in touch with 3rd Regt on right & with D Coy on left & consolidating position 50 yards in advance of Black Line.	
			X At 8.50 a.m. Bn H.Q. received the following three messages No 1 message from Mr W. R. LEES commanding No 10 platoon, C Coy, timed 6.3 a.m.	

A5834 Wt. W4973/M687 750,000 8/16 D. D. & L. Ltd. Forms/C.2118/13.

Instructions regarding War Diaries and Intelligence Summaries are contained in F. S. Regs., Part II. and the Staff Manual respectively. Title pages will be prepared in manuscript.

WAR DIARY
or
INTELLIGENCE SUMMARY.
(Erase heading not required.)

Army Form C. 2118.

Place	Date	Hour	Summary of Events and Information	Remarks and references to Appendices
J. SECTOR	9/4/17		saying "Have reached 1st objective, & in touch with 3rd regiment on right" again No 1 message from 2/Lt Smith commanding C Coy timed 6.50 a.m saying "Have reached 1st objective, in touch with 3rd Regt on right & D Coy on left. Present strength unknown." Also No 3 message from Capt Grady commanding A Coy timed 8-15 a.m. saying "Have reached trench west of railway, hostile rifle & M.G fire" At 9 A.M received message No I from Capt Reid, O.C. "D" Coy timed 7 A.M, saying "Reached as map at 6.20 A.M, in touch with C Coy on right. Cannot estimate present strength. The whole line swung too much N.E, the pace was rapid and we overran first objective. Now in shell holes waiting advance to Blue Line, am correcting direction. Estimate casualties rather severe, mostly through following barrage too closely. I have not seen Mr Foster. Mr William is wounded" At 9 A.M. & 9.15 a.m wired Brigade the gist of messages received from Capts Reid & Grady.	
			At 9.40 A.M received message from 2/Lt Morrison, commanding "B" Coy timed 8.45 a.m. Have reached 2nd objective in touch with	

A5834 Wt. W4973 M687 750,000 8/16 D. D. & L. Ltd. Forms/C.2118/13.

Army Form C. 2118.

Instructions regarding War Diaries and Intelligence Summaries are contained in F. S. Regs., Part II. and the Staff Manual respectively. Title pages will be prepared in manuscript.

WAR DIARY
or
INTELLIGENCE SUMMARY.
(Erase heading not required.)

Place	Date	Hour	Summary of Events and Information	Remarks and references to Appendices
J. Sector	9/4/17		3rd regt on right & A Coy on left. Present strength about 60 men. Forbes wounded. We have had very heavy casualties, but have sent back over 100 prisoners. All ranks are at present digging in trench EAST of cutting about 60 yards away. At 10.5 a.m. received a message from O.C. "A" Coy stating that a German plane was continuously flying low over Blue Line. The information was at once wired to Brigade Headqrs. At 11-17 a.m. a message received from O.C. A Coy saying "Consolidated position 60 yards east of railway line, advanced posts 150 yards from Railway" Message at once passed on to Brigade. At 11-45 a.m. a message received from O.C. A Coy saying "Three Hun aeroplanes flying low & attacking us. At 11-50 a.m. the message passed on to Brigade. At 12.30 p.m. wired Brigade "Am moving Battalion Headquarters to Blue Line now" Battalion Headqrs reached Blue Line & established in a dugout in cutting by 1 p.m. & advised Brigade at once. During the operations the battalion captured two machine guns numbered 7029 and 3361 respectively at the 1st objective, and again at the 2nd objective captured a machine gun numbered 3451 and a 77 mm field gun numbered 3324. At 2 p.m. 2/Lt AITKEN, who had taken some moppers up to clean up dugouts in the ravine between the Blue & Green Lines in rear of the 1st & 2nd S.A.I. as they went through, returned & reported he had collected about 60 prisoners from dugouts in trenches in vicinity. During afternoon very little hostile shell fire on cutting. All ranks engaged in deepening trench east of cutting.	

A5834 Wt. W4973 M687 750,000 8/16 D. D. & L. Ltd. Forms/C.2118/13.

Instructions regarding War Diaries and Intelligence Summaries are contained in F. S. Regs., Part II. and the Staff Manual respectively. Title pages will be prepared in manuscript.

WAR DIARY
or
INTELLIGENCE SUMMARY.
(Erase heading not required.)

Army Form C. 2118.

Place	Date	Hour	Summary of Events and Information	Remarks and references to Appendices
J. Sector	9/4/17		Battalion remained in cutting, ~~dugouts~~ dugout accomodation not sufficient at 8 p.m. posted one sentry group per company in new trench east of railway. At 11 p.m. the approximate strength of the battalion was 11 officers & 339 Other Ranks. During the attack the regtl signallers, who left at 5.47 from the British front line ran out a telephone line, but owing to wrong direction being taken, & as the Brigade signallers were coming on gave it up, as not too much wire. The regtl signallers then proceeded to our 1st objective at the Black Line, selected a station & from there ran out two lines to our 2nd objective one to each flank of the battalion, & established communication from the 2nd objective back to 1st objective within a few minutes of the 2nd objective being taken & personnel have kept open communication, until the Brigade signal section came up.	
Railway Cutting 2nd objective	10/4/17		At 2.15 a.m. the following officers reported from the 1st Line Transport for duty, Capt Clark, Capt Charlton, 2/Lt Salamon, 2/Lt Webb, 2/Lt Donaldson, 2/Lt Peacock. During morning the men rested. There was a slight snowfall. About 1 pm received message from our Brigade timed 12.40 pm saying "S.A. Brigade placed at disposal of 4th Regt AAA. Your unit must be prepared to move at a minutes notice". Coys warned accordingly. At 1 pm sent out three parties of 20 each to salvage. At 3.25 pm. received message by wire from our Brigade that our battalion would relieve a battalion of 15th Brigade in BLUE LINE by 7 A.M. This simply	

A5834 Wt. W4973 M687 750,000 8/16 D. D. & L. Ltd. Forms/C.2118/13.

Instructions regarding War Diaries and Intelligence Summaries are contained in F. S. Regs., Part II. and the Staff Manual respectively. Title pages will be prepared in manuscript.

WAR DIARY
or
INTELLIGENCE SUMMARY.
(*Erase heading not required.*)

Army Form C. 2118.

Place	Date	Hour	Summary of Events and Information	Remarks and references to Appendices
Railway Cutting 2nd Objective	10/4/17		meant we stayed where we were. During the afternoon the following details from 1st Line Transport reported for Duty:- 22 Lewis gunners, 3 Coy Sgt Majors, 4 Battalion Snipers & 6 Batmen to officers who had reported during the night. At 8 pm again posted one sentry group per company in new trench east of Railway cutting. At 8 pm. Battalion strength 18 officers 418 other Ranks.	
RAILWAY Cutting	11/4/17		About 7.45 am. the two battalions of the 10th Brigade moved from Blue Line. At 10.25 am. received following wire from our own Brigade timed 10.12 AM. "15th DIVN and troops south of river are advancing successfully past MONCHY & entering KEELING COPSE at 6.55 am. AAA. If any signs of enemy retiring press on immediately and keep touch with units in front AAA. Report immediately any forward move made by you AAA Chinese attack by field artillery will be carried out from 11.0. AM to 11.3 am. AAA acknowledge." The battalion intelligence officer was sent forward to 2nd S.A.I Battalion Headqrs to BROWN LINE to keep us informed of any move. At 12 NOON he wired to effect that O.C. 2nd S.A.I. he had been to GREEN line & found it occupied by one battalion of 12th Brigade who had no instructions to move out, & that 2nd S.A.I. occupy trenches about 800 yards west of Green Line with 1st Regt on right. At 12.20 pm. received wire from O.C. 2nd S.A.I. timed 12.20 saying "Am moving forward now into the valley beyond the brow of the hill. The Division in front are attacking now" At 1.35 pm. got orders from our Brigade timed 1.20pm saying "Brigadier orders you to occupy BROWN LINE from POINT D'JOUR to CAM TRENCH inclusive AAA (Instruct Regt (3rd S A I) occupying Brown Line from your right to river east of ATHIES."	

A5834 Wt. W4973/M687 750,000 8/16 D. D. & L. Ltd. Forms/C.2118/13.

Army Form C. 2118.

WAR DIARY
or
INTELLIGENCE SUMMARY.
(Erase heading not required.)

Instructions regarding War Diaries and Intelligence Summaries are contained in F. S. Regs., Part II. and the Staff Manual respectively. Title pages will be prepared in manuscript.

Place	Date	Hour	Summary of Events and Information	Remarks and references to Appendices
RAILWAY CUTTING	11/4/17		At 2 pm. the Battalion moved forward in artillery formation by platoons and at 3-15 pm. were in position with Battalion Headquarters at junction of CAM & LAUREL trenches, A & B Companies holding LAUREL TRENCH from CAM trench to POINT DU JOUR, A on right B on left, and C & D in LADLE TRENCH in support about 150/200 yards back. B Coy on its left in touch with 15th Royal Scots 34th Divn. We had several inches of snow during afternoon & evening. At 8pm Capt Wakefield phoned not to send patrols to H4B85. At 8.30 pm. General Dawson spoke to Co. & cancelled the patrol. At 9.30 pm. received a wire from our Brigade ordering us to send out patrols to H4B85 to get touch with Divn in front. The Co. Col Christian who had been out since 8.40 pm. seeing companies, & had also seen the acting Brigadier of Brigade on our left returned at 10 pm. & was able to give Brigade the required information. Patrol cancelled.	
BROWN LINE CAM. TRENCH	12/4/17		At 10. A.M. received wire from Brigade timed 9.40 a.m. "Commanding officers required at Bde HQ. H15C53 at 10-15 a.m. very urgent." Passed message to O.C. 2nd S.A.I. about 12.30 pm. the Co. returned & issued orders to Company Commanders as per operation order 17/24. (copy attached) MARKED "E", & explained same. At 3 pm. the Battalion moved by platoons from CAM trench in following order. HdQrs A.B.C.D. At 3 pm. received wire from Brigade timed 2.35 pm. saying "Your battalion must not proceed along ATHIES FAMPOUX road beyond a point east of H.16D35.30 AAA Beyond this the road is under enemy observation & shell fire AAA Battalion must leave road at this point and turn south." Warned companies at once & got acknowledgement. The battalion moved to ATHIES FAMPOUX ROAD striking it at H15C95 55, across it, & turned east	

Instructions regarding War Diaries and Intelligence Summaries are contained in F. S. Regs., Part II. and the Staff Manual respectively. Title pages will be prepared in manuscript.

WAR DIARY
or
INTELLIGENCE SUMMARY.
(Erase heading not required.)

Army Form C. 2118.

Place	Date	Hour	Summary of Events and Information	Remarks and references to Appendices
	12/4/17		owing to the enemy machine gun fire the attack did not succeed, the furthest any of our battalion getting being the edge of a copse at H 18 D 45.60, & our left companies about the same. On the left officers report the enemy M.G. guns appeared to be firing from X Roads I 7 A 45.30 and I 13 A 9 3, from the railway embankment at I 13 C 4 7, also from Mount Pleasant wood. On the right our officers report M.Guns at I 13 C 16, also suspected M.Guns firing from building about I 13 C 99, & trench at I 13 C 7.0. Everyone took cover in shell holes after heavy casualties, & later about 6 p.m. three German aeroplanes flew low over the ground & about 15 minutes later the enemy sent over shrapnel. After dark the brigade withdrew to the trench East of FAMPOUX originally held by the 4th DIVN & continued deepening same, keeping Lewis Gun posts out in front about 50 yards forward. The Brigade was relieved by the 26th Brigade at 1.30 a.m. on morning of 13th.	
			The battalion Headquarters was also used as such by the officers commanding 1st & 2nd S.A.I.	
			At 5.40 the O.C. 1st Regt received a message ~~for~~ to say the attack was held up by M.G. fire.	
			At 5.45 p.m. a message timed 5 p.m. came from Capt Grady O.C. A Coy 4th S.A.I. saying everything going good meeting heavy machine gun fire & hostile shell fire.	
			X At 5.45 p.m. received a message from A Coy timed 5.37 pm written by 2/Lt AITKEN saying "The attack is held up with machine	

A5834 Wt. W4973/M687 750,000 8/16 D. D. & L. Ltd. Forms/C.2118/13.

Army Form C. 2118.

WAR DIARY
or
INTELLIGENCE SUMMARY.
(Erase heading not required.)

Instructions regarding War Diaries and Intelligence Summaries are contained in F. S. Regs., Part II. and the Staff Manual respectively. Title pages will be prepared in manuscript.

Place	Date	Hour	Summary of Events and Information	Remarks and references to Appendices
BROWN LINE CAM TRENCH	12/4/17		midway between river & road, through gap in wire in front of PANSY TRENCH about H22A67 diagonally to road leading to FAMPOUX H22B-H23A. The head of the regiment commenced to enter the village outskirts at 3.45 & moved up the central street. As the head of the regiment got to about H17C83 the enemy began to shell the village. As it started three white VERY lights were observed to go up in the centre of the village. By 4.15 p.m. all four companies were in position along either side of the street from H17D47 to H17C83 A & B Coys leading, taking what shelter the walls & houses afforded. C & D Coys were close behind. After battalion in position the C.O. with Headqrs, moved to Batt Headquarters in cellar in a house on road at H17D85.75. The Headqrs mess in a cellar in house next door. Coys advised at 4.25 p.m. of Batt H.Q. From 4.15 pm onwards the enemy shelling increased in intensity. At 4.50 the battalion moved from its assembly position in the village following up the 1st & 2nd S.A.I. A & C Companies ~~debouching~~ debouching by the two roads into H18C and B & D Companies by the road into 18A. The roads ~~leaving~~ & eastern outskirts of the village were heavily barraged by the enemy as they did so, & there was considerable hostile machine gun fire, the Companies, as soon as they had cleared the enemy artillery barrage extending & passing over the trench (held by the 4th DIVN.	

A5834 Wt. W4973/M687 750,000 8/16 D. D. & L. Ltd. Forms/C.2118/13.

Instructions regarding War Diaries and Intelligence Summaries are contained in F. S. Regs., Part II. and the Staff Manual respectively. Title pages will be prepared in manuscript.

WAR DIARY
or
INTELLIGENCE SUMMARY.
(Erase heading not required.)

Army Form C. 2118.

Place	Date	Hour	Summary of Events and Information	Remarks and references to Appendices
FAMPOUX	12/4/17		gun fire from railway embankment & my flank is very weak Capt Grady Hit."	
			At 5.55 p.m. the O.C. 2nd Regt sent a pigeon message.	
			At 6.20 p.m. received a message from 2/Lt AITKEN timed 6.7 p.m. saying "In touch with "B" company on left, casualties heavy. Machine guns holding up right flank at railway embankment.	
			At 6.35 p.m. the C.O sent a message to Mr AITKEN O.C. A Coy saying "Your three messages received. Do the best you can. If you cannot get on dig yourselves in."	
			At 7.15 Capt Clark O.C. D Coy arrived, wounded, at Batt HQ He reported the attack held up on left, the trench originally held by 4th Divn fairly strongly held but casualties fairly heavy mostly caused by machine gun fire from right. There was a cross fire of M.G.s from direction of the Inn & Railway embankment, & the German barrage was good. He also said Capt Charlton wounded & 2/Lt Lees Killed.	
			At 8.10 p.m. received a message from O.C. "C" company timed 8 p.m. saying "According to your instructions to O.C. A Coy all men will retire to trench west of objective now held 4th DIVN. Have arranged for outpost for tonight. Capt Grady Killed."	
			At 8.25 p.m. Capt Charlton, O.C. B Company came in wounded & reported that our men were now retiring to trench held by the 4th DIVISION.	
			At 9.25 p.m. received message from 2/Lt Smith Commanding "C" company & timed 9 p.m. saying "The trench we now occupy is very congested owing to the 4th DIVN occupying same with the	

A5834 Wt. W4973/M687 750,000 8/16 D. D. & L. Ltd. Forms/C.2118/13.

Instructions regarding War Diaries and Intelligence Summaries are contained in F. S. Regs., Part II. and the Staff Manual respectively. Title pages will be prepared in manuscript.

or

INTELLIGENCE SUMMARY.

(Erase heading not required.)

Place	Date	Hour	Summary of Events and Information	Remarks and references to Appendices
FAMPOUX	12/4/17		remains of the 1st & 4th S.A.I., & I would suggest that the rise in front of this trench which commands all ground in front of Station, be consolidated & held."	
			At 9.30 p.m. the C.O sent the following reply to O.C. C Coy	
			" (1) Received your message timed 8 p.m. & message just now timed 9 p.m.	
			(2) You had better move down to right of trench where there is plenty of room	
			(3) It is understood that the 26th Brigade will relieve the line tonight. When that happens bring all our men out of that trench & report to Battalion Headqrs."	
			At 9.40 p.m. sent following message by runner to 2/Lt Marshall of A Coy.	
			" (1) Your message received	
			(2) It is understood that the 26th Brigade will relieve the line tonight when that happens bring all our men out of the trench & report to Battalion Headqrs."	
			At 12. M.N. The enemy commenced to shell the village intermittently.	
			During the operations east of Fampoux the regtl M.O. established his Dressing station in street about H14 D00·35, & later on as the house he was in got damaged by shell fire, moved to A.D.S of the S.A.F.A about H14 C55·50, & worked there until the battalion withdrew.	
FAMPOUX	13/4/17		About 1·30 a.m. the 26th Brigade commenced taking over the trenches east of FAMPOUX & the battalion withdrew to the Green line, occupying the southern portion of PHYSIC TRENCH from H22A65 to H22A99. At 4 A.M notified Brigade by runner that relief complete & Battalion in PHYSIC TRENCH.	
			Strength at 9. A.M. 12 officers 207 other Ranks.	

Instructions regarding War Diaries and Intelligence Summaries are contained in F. S. Regs., Part II. and the Staff Manual respectively. Title pages will be prepared in manuscript.

WAR DIARY
or
INTELLIGENCE SUMMARY.
(Erase heading not required.)

Army Form C. 2118.

Place	Date	Hour	Summary of Events and Information	Remarks and references to Appendices
PHYSIC TRENCH	13/4/17		At H22A85·45 were two captured 8" German howitzers, one of which was being used against them. Day fairly quiet with occasional shells near our trench, mostly falling near the gun emplacement & bridge just south of it. Enemy shelling FAMPOUX more or less all day with high explosive & shrapnel. Fatigue parties fetched greatcoats that were dumped on 12th at BROWN LINE. Battalion strength at 6pm. 12 officers. 220 other Ranks	
PHYSIC TRENCH	14/4/17		At 12 midnight or few minutes after the enemy opened up a gas shell bombardment, most of it going over amongst the artillery positions rearwards, but a few gas shells fell in vicinity of our trench. The bombardment lasted quite an hour. About 4 A.M. a few more gas shells. At 11·30 A.M. some 4.2's or 77 mm shells in neighbourhood of our trench. Deepened our trench in places. A very fine sunny day.	
PHYSIC TRENCH	15/4/17		Drizzling rain in morning. During day the Germans sniped our trench with 77 mm. shells especially if anyone walked on top. Their observation evidently good. At 8.30 p.m. Headqrs & A & C companies moved off by road along river at 9 p.m. the 5th Gordons relieved us with a company. B & D companies moved off at 9.30 p.m. along same road. Last of the battalion got to ARRAS at 12.30 A.M. Road taken along river south of ATHIES & then tow path on north side of river SCARPE. Men billetted in HOSPICE and officers at 36 RUE GAMBETTA. Had hot soup waiting arrival of men. The draft under Mr EARP joined battalion at HOSPICE: 1 officer & 108 O.R.	

A5834 Wt. W4973 M687 750,000 8/16 D. D. & L. Ltd. Forms/C.2118/13.

Army Form C. 2118.

WAR DIARY
or
INTELLIGENCE SUMMARY.
(Erase heading not required.)

Instructions regarding War Diaries and Intelligence Summaries are contained in F. S. Regs., Part II. and the Staff Manual respectively. Title pages will be prepared in manuscript.

Place	Date	Hour	Summary of Events and Information	Remarks and references to Appendices
ARRAS	16/4/17		Battalion moved from ARRAS at 11.45 via St Catherine & got to Hutments south of ACQ by 4 pm. All details from 1st Line Transport rejoined, also most of the men on detached duty. Fine in morning - raining in evening	
Hutments ACQ.	17/4/17		Bathed 180 men at FREVIN-CAPELLE. Regiment cleaning up. Draft under Mr Earp split up to companies. Wet day & dull - Very muddy	
Hutments ACQ	18/4/17		Bathed 240 men at ACQ baths - Wet weather. Company inspections	
Hutments ACQ			Bathed the balance of the regiment. Company inspections.	

Instructions regarding War Diaries and Intelligence Summaries are contained in F. S. Regs., Part II. and the Staff Manual respectively. Title pages will be prepared in manuscript.

WAR DIARY
or
INTELLIGENCE SUMMARY.
(Erase heading not required.)

Army Form C. 2118.

Place	Date	Hour	Summary of Events and Information	Remarks and references to Appendices
HUTMENTS ACQ.	20/4/17.		Company inspections.	
HUTMENTS ACQ.	21/4/17		Battalion moved at 11-10 a.m. to MONCHY BRETON and billetted by 4 p.m. occupying village together with 3rd S.A.I. Dull day but fine	
MONCHY BRETON	22/4/17		Church parades. A fine day.	
MONCHY BRETON	23/4/17		Company parades - Inspection & close order drill 10-10-45 a.m. Cpls & Lce Cpls under R.S.M for instruction at 11-15 to 12.15 a.m. Football in the afternoon.	

A5834 Wt. W4973 M687 750,000 8/16 D. D. & L. Ltd. Forms/C.2118/13.

Army Form C. 2118.

WAR DIARY
or
INTELLIGENCE SUMMARY.
(Erase heading not required.)

Instructions regarding War Diaries and Intelligence Summaries are contained in F. S. Regs., Part II. and the Staff Manual respectively. Title pages will be prepared in manuscript.

Place	Date	Hour	Summary of Events and Information	Remarks and references to Appendices
MONCHY BRETON	24/4/17		10-11 A.M. Battalion parade.	
			In afternoon played 3rd S.A.I. at Rugger ~~[illegible]~~. beaten 13-0	
			Lt. Col. McLeod arrived in camp.	
MONCHY BRETON	25/4/17		Lt. Colonel D. M. MacLEOD on arrival assumed command of the battalion vice Lt. Col. Ewan Christian	
			Parades under Coy arrangements - 10 to 11. A.M.	
			N.C.O.s under R.S.M. 11.30 to 12.30 am	
			In afternoon played Brigade Signallers at Soccer won 1-0	
MONCHY BRETON	26/4/17		Battalion parade 10 to 11 a.m. N.C.O. under R.S.M. 11-30 to 12.30	
			Played 107th A.S.C. at football in afternoon beaten 1-0	
			Officers had a revolver competition against 3rd Regt won 456-360.	

A5834 Wt. W4973/M687 750,000 8/16 D. D. & L. Ltd. Forms/C.2118/13.

Instructions regarding War Diaries and Intelligence Summaries are contained in F. S. Regs., Part II. and the Staff Manual respectively. Title pages will be prepared in manuscript.

WAR DIARY
or
INTELLIGENCE SUMMARY.
(Erase heading not required.)

Army Form C. 2118.

Place	Date	Hour	Summary of Events and Information	Remarks and references to Appendices
MONCHY BRETON	27/4/17.		Battalion moved to ARRAS. TRANSPORT moved at 10. A.M. Mr Saunders & 103 men left by route march at 11. A.M. The rest of the battalion moved by bus at 1.15. p.m. together with detachment of 3rd Regt. Embussed at 1 p.m. & ready to move at 1.15. Traffic on Arras St Pol road very congested, & only arrived outside ARRAS at 6 p.m. Battalion billetted by 7.30 p.m. in Rue des Augustins & close by.	
ARRAS	28/4/17		Battalion furnished 8 officers - 19. N.C.O.s & 281 O.R. for Working party under 401st R.E. at Blangy bridge. 7 hours work a day. Improving & clearing road approaches to bridge. Fine day. Men who marched previous day not taken for working party.	
ARRAS	29/4/17.		Battalion furnished 8 officers 17 N.C.O.s & 332 other Ranks. for working party with 401st Coy R.E. Fine sunny weather.	

Army Form C. 2118.

WAR DIARY
or
INTELLIGENCE SUMMARY.
(*Erase heading not required.*)

Instructions regarding War Diaries and Intelligence Summaries are contained in F. S. Regs., Part II. and the Staff Manual respectively. Title pages will be prepared in manuscript.

Place	Date	Hour	Summary of Events and Information	Remarks and references to Appendices
	30/4/17		Our casualties for the operations during the period 7th to 15th April incl.	
			Officers on 9th April, 1917.	
			Killed 2/Lt W. DORWARD - 2/Lt V. A. HUNT	
			Wounded Capt J. L. REID 2/Lt E. N. CUMMING	
			2/Lt E. J. KEELEY 2/Lt W. C. FORBES	
			2/Lt W. H. KIRBY 2/Lt G. SMITH	
			2/Lt. H. WILLIAMS 2/Lt W. WALLACE	
			2/Lt D. B. ROBB.	
			Officers on 12th APRIL, 1917	
			Killed Capt E. E. D. GRADY - 2/LT W. R. LEES	
			WOUNDED A/Major E. G. CLERK Capt W. D. CHARLTON	
			2/Lt. H. BOUSTEAD 2/Lt D. J. DONALDSON.	
			Officer casualties summarised.	

	Killed -	Wounded	TOTAL.
On 9th-4-17	2	9	11
On 12th-4-17	2	4	6
	4	13	17

A5834 Wt. W4973/M687 750,000 8/16 D. D. & L. Ltd. Forms/C.2118/13.

Instructions regarding War Diaries and Intelligence Summaries are contained in F. S. Regs., Part II. and the Staff Manual respectively. Title pages will be prepared in manuscript.

WAR DIARY
or
INTELLIGENCE SUMMARY.
(Erase heading not required.)

Army Form C. 2118.

Place	Date	Hour	Summary of Events and Information	Remarks and references to Appendices
ARRAS	30/4/17		Battalion furnished working party to 401st R.E of 8 officers 17 N.C.O.s and 327 other Ranks. Fine sunny weather	
	30/4/17		Battalion Strength 30 Officers 658 other Ranks	
			B.E.F. D.M. MacLeod Lt Colonel Commdg 30/4/17. 4th South African Infantry	

A5834 Wt. W4973/M687 750,000 8/16 D. D. & L. Ltd. Forms/C.2118/13.

Army Form C. 2118.

WAR DIARY
or
INTELLIGENCE SUMMARY.
(Erase heading not required.)

Instructions regarding War Diaries and Intelligence Summaries are contained in F. S. Regs., Part II. and the Staff Manual respectively. Title pages will be prepared in manuscript.

Place	Date	Hour	Summary of Events and Information	Remarks and references to Appendices
30/4/17			Our casualties during the operations for period 7th to 15th April were.	

OTHER RANKS.

April.	Killed	Died of Wounds	Wounded	Missing	TOTAL.
8th	-	-	5		5
9th	59	3	171	1	234
10th	0	-	-		-
11th	3	-	4		7
12th	19	1	163	6	189
13th	1		3		4
14th	-		2		2
15th	2		3		5
	84	4	351*	7	446

* Includes 17 remained at duty

A5834 Wt. W4973 M687 750,000 8/16 D. D. & L. Ltd. Forms/C.2118/13.

Map Reference
Trench Map 1/20,000

A

SECRET.

Z.10/2.

Copy No. 27....

1st SOUTH AFRICAN INFANTRY BRIGADE.

INSTRUCTIONS REGARDING FORTHCOMING OPERATIONS: THIS ISSUE CANCELS ALL PREVIOUS INSTRUCTIONS.

1. INTENTION.

The primary object of the operation is to establish a line along the GERMAN 3rd. line system, which runs from the SCARPE near FEUCHY through Le POINT du JOUR - MAISON de la COTE - COMMANDANTS HOUSE and when this line has been established to make a further advance later.

2. DISTRIBUTION.

The 9th.Division will be the RIGHT Division of XVII Corps and will have a frontage of 1800 yards from RIVER SCARPE to St. PANCRAS TRENCH (inclusive).

It will have three Brigades in line :-

26th. Infantry Brigade on the RIGHT.
S.A. Infantry Brigade in the CENTRE.
27th Infantry Brigade on the LEFT.

The following troops will be attached to the Brigade and will be accommodated in the Brigade Area :-

1 SECTION 90th FIELD COY., R.E.- to assist in the consolidation of the BROWN LINE.

½ COY. 9th SEAFORTHS (PIONEERS).-to join up communication trenches across " NO MAN'S LAND".

3. OBJECTIVE.

There will be three separate main objectives involving :-

(i) The capture of the front system (BLACK LINE ON MAP.)

(ii) The capture of the second line (BLUE LINE ON MAP).

(iii) The capture of the third line (BROWN LINE ON MAP).

4. The boundaries of the 1st South African Infantry Brigade are :-

RIGHT BOUNDARY ESAR GABEL (exclusive), Road junction G.18.b.5.8. (inclusive), Trench Junction H.13.a.0.8. (inclusive), Railway Bridge H.8.c.05.05. (inclusive), Trench Junction H.15.b.3.3.

LEFT BOUNDARY - A line from G.12.c.7.8. eastwards to the bend in INN TRENCH at G.12.d.5.8 thence to trench junction G.12.d.95.90 (exclusive), Railway Crossing H.7.d.7.8 (inclusive) and thence due EAST.

(5).

5. COMMUNICATION TRENCHES.

"IN" JULY AVENUE from St NICHOLAS - QUATRE VENTS ROAD about G.16.a.7.4 by old trench into AUGUST AVENUE (North of CANDLE FACTORY) up AUGUST to BRITANNIA WORKS and across to JULY up to NEW CUT Junction thence by NEW CUT.

"OUT" MAY AVENUE - By MAY to BRITANNIA WORKS thence along BRITANNIA WORKS to JULY, along JULY through CANDLE FACTORY to G.16.b.5.3 and by old trench to about G.16.a.5.8.

6. PREPARATION OF THE ATTACK.

The wire along the enemy's front trenches will be systematically cut from now onwards and special artillery bombardments of selected strong points will be carried out periodically.

A continuous bombardment will be carried out for 96 hours preceding the attack.

Special attention will be paid to effective night firing to hamper movement in rear of the enemy's front trenches.

Infantry, Machine guns and Trench Mortars will co-operate in this task and in keeping the wire cut.

Patrols will be sent out daily under cover of darkness or smoke where necessary, to ascertain the damage done by our artillery fire.

It will be the business of the Infantry to find out what wire has or has not been cut in their front and to report thereon to the artillery.

7. PLAN OF ATTACK.

(a) The 3rd and 4th Regiments will be the assaulting Battalions of the Brigade.

ASSEMBLY TRENCHES.

The front wave, namely four platoons from each of the 3rd and 4th S.A. Infantry will be assembled in shell-holes in front of our line, not more than 200 yards from the enemy's wire.

The second wave, consisting of four platoons of the same two Battalions will be drawn up together with the MOPPERS UP in our Front line.

The two remaining companies of each of the 3rd and 4th S.A. Infantry will be assembled in the immediate Support trenches.

One Stokes gun will be attached to each Battalion and will assemble with the rear company.

Two companies of each 1st and 2nd S.A. Infantry in SUPPORT TRENCH

One company of 2nd. S.A. Infantry in ARTILLERY Trench EAST of junction with NEW CUT.

Two companies of 1st S.A. Infantry in ARTILLERY trench WEST of Junction with NEW CUT.

One company 2nd. S.A. Infantry in BRITANNIA WORKS.

C OP Y.

4th. S.A.I.,

12.4.1917.

OPERATION ORDER 17/24.

Time Synch. at 1.5 p.m.

1. INFORMATION.

The enemy are holding the line Mount Pleasant Wood Railway Station at I 13 central and fom there to H.12.B.0.6.

2. INTENTION.

G.O.C's. intention is to take the line Roeux - Railway Station I 13 Central, thence along road to INN at I.7.A.25.80. The 4th. Division will protect the left flank of the Division.

3. OBJECTIVE.

1st. Objective.

S.A.Brigade on right will take the line Station I.13. Central to I.7.C.7.3. 27th. Brigade on left will take the line from this latter point to the Inn.

2nd. Objective.

When the first objective has been attained the 26th. Brigade will attack from the Railway line and take the line Roeux - Railway Station.

4. ZERO HOUR. 5 p.m.

5. FORMATION.

S.A.Brigade will attack, 1st. and 2nd. Regiments in front line, 1st. on right, 2nd, on left. 4th. Regiment in Support, 3rd. Regiment in Reserve.

6. FORMING UP.

The 4th. Regiment will be formed in the area marked on the map in FAMPOUX by 4.30 p.m.

7. ATTACK.

The Regiment will support the attack 250 yards behind 1st. and 2nd. Regiments, and will cover the whole frontage of the Brigade. "A" and "B" Companies in front line. "A" on right "B" on left.
"C" and "D" Companies in Support. "C" on right "D" on left.

They will move the head of "A" and "B" Companies out of FAMPOUX at 4.50 p.m. by the roads shown on the map.

7a. SPECIAL POINTS.

The right Companies will pay special attention to the Railway and the small trenches just to North of the Railway.

The left Companies will pay special attention to a strong point at H.18.D.5.7.

8. Battalion Headquarters will be vicinity of a house at H.18.C.35.65.

9. DRESS.

Fighting order. Greatcoats to be dumped under cover in our present lines.

10. MARCH TO THE ATTACK.

The Battalion will advance to the ATTACK down the valley to ATHIES - FAMPOUX Road, and thence along road to FAMPOUX. Order of March "A", "B", "C", "D".

Starting point 50 yards to East of Battalion Headquarters. Time 3 p.m.

Sgd. F.McE. Mitchell.

Captain and Adjutant.

7. PLAN OF ATTACK - ASSEMBLY TRENCHES CONTD.

The two companies of each Battalion in the SUPPORT LINE to go forward immediately in rear of the attacking battalions. The remaining companies (all in ARTILLERY TRENCH) to wait there until the time for advance from BLACK to BLUE LINE when they will move forward to trenches in the vicinity of the Sunken Road WEST of BLACK LINE.

1 SECTION R.E., with 25 Infantry } in trenches at N.E.end of JULY AVENUE.
½ COMPANY (PIONEERS) }

MACHINE GUN COMPANY - 1 Section at G.17.a.

1 Section in ARTILLERY TRENCH N.E.end.

2 Sections in BRITANNIA WORKS.

T.M.BATTERY. after preliminary bombardment four guns in dug-outs.

METHOD OF ADVANCE.

In each phase, except the third, the two front waves will go right through to the objective and those in rear, if not required to re-inforce will occupy convenient trenches when the front waves reach their objective.

FORMATION.

Each assaulting battalion on a two-company front, the two front companies being in two waves of two lines each.

MOPPERS UP will be between the first and second waves. Waves to be about 100 yards distant. The two rear companies to be in columns of sections in file.

Two sections of each company of every battalion will be Carriers. They will advance with their companies. The rear Battalion will advance in lines of columns of sections.

FRONTAGE.

Each battalion 300 yards, equals 150 yards a Company and 75 yards a platoon.

FIRST ADVANCE - "BLACK LINE".

(a) At Zero the assaulting Battalions will move out of the trenches and advance as close as possible under the Field Artillery barrage, which will open 50 yards in front of the GERMAN front line trench where "NO MAN'S LAND" is [illegible] 200 yards or more in width or on the front line trench where No Man's Land is less than 200yds.
The barrage will lift on to the front trench, where not already on it, at Zero plus 1 minute, and at Zero plus 4 minutes will commence to move forward till it reaches a line 300 yards beyond the BLACK LINE. It will be followed by the Infantry through the successive lines of the enemy's front trench system, clearing parties occupying each line in succession.

(b) The pace at which the barrage will advance is shown in para.8.

(c) The first two waves will proceed straight to the BLACK LINE, clear and consolidate it. The two rear companies, if not required to re-inforce, will occupy the Sunken Road to the WEST of the BLACK LINE. They will leave the clearing of dug-outs to the MOPPERS UP.

The two front companies of each of the 1st and 2nd S.A.Infantry will advance at Zero immediately in rear of the 3rd and 4th S.A.Inf. and will occupy the two lines of trenches immediately to the EAST of the GERMAN front line.

7. PLAN OF ATTACK (contd).

(d) The Pioneers at Zero will proceed to the Sap South of Sap 91 and will dig a Communication trench to (GERMAN) Sap V.10.

(e) The BLACK LINE should be reached about Zero plus 34 minutes. The consolidation of the line will be commenced and the troops will move into position in rear of the Field Artillery barrage, preparatory to the commencement of the advance on the BLUE LINE.

SECOND ADVANCE - BLUE LINE.

(f) At Zero plus 1 hour 48 minutes the two rear companies of the 3rd and 4th S.A.Infantry will advance from the Sunken Road WEST of the BLACK LINE and will form up and lie down until the time to attack the BLUE LINE, when they will advance supported by the two Companies which had attacked the BLACK LINE. This advance and the subsequent one will be made in section columns as long as it is possible to retain that formation. The two front waves will occupy the Railway cutting, and the two rear ones the trench to the WEST of it, if not required to re-inforce.

The two front companies of the 1st and 2nd S.A.Infantry will now advance to the BLACK LINE and the two rear companies to the Sunken Road WEST of the BLACK LINE.

(g) At Zero plus 2 hours the advance on the BLUE LINE will commence and the Field Artillery creeping barrage will move forward as shown in para.8, followed by the assaulting battalions, till it reaches a line 300 yards beyond the BLUE LINE.

It is estimated that the BLUE LINE should be reached at ZERO plus 2 hours 43 minutes.

(h) The BLUE LINE having been gained, an outpost line will be pushed out as far as the artillery barrage will allow, and the consolidation of the BLUE LINE will commence.

The artillery will then carry out a concentrated bombardment of the enemy's third line and the two battalions of each Brigade which are to carry out the attack on the BROWN LINE will be brought up and passed through the two leading battalions, and form up close in rear of the artillery barrage, preparatory to the commencement of the advance on the BROWN LINE.

It is also proposed to move forward 3 Brigades of Field Artillery to fully prepared positions in G.17.a.and G.11.d during this period. Routes for this move have been reconnoitred and will be marked out.

THIRD ADVANCE - BROWN LINE.

(i) At Zero plus 6 hours 46 minutes the creeping barrage will move forward as shown in para.8, to a line 300 yards beyond the enemy's third system, followed by the Infantry, who should reach the front line of the system by Zero plus 7 hours 32 minutes.

(j) The rear battalions will remain in the BLACK LINE till Zero plus 6 hours 15 minutes when they will advance to the valleys to the WEST of the BLUE LINE, halting there until Zero plus 6 hours 41 minutes, when they will pass through the battalions holding the BLUE LINE and at Zero plus 6 hours 46 minutes proceed to their objective. The two rear waves, if not required to re-inforce, will halt at the first trench (i.e. most Westerly) of the Point du Jour Line, the second wave at the CENTRE trench and the first wave at the most Easterly trench.

(k) The consolidation of the BROWN LINE will be commenced as soon as it is captured and will be continued until the Division is relieved by troops of the 4th Division other than those who pass through to attack the GREEN LINE.

(l) During the advance every endeavour will be made by troops who have reached their objective to assist those on their flanks, who may have been held up, by attacking the flanks and rear of any

8. ARTILLERY BARRAGE.

Details of the Artillery barrage will be issued separately. The following table gives a summary of the times at which certain lines will be reached :-

1st ADVANCE. ZERO plus 4 MINUTES LIFT OFF FRONT LINE.

Zero plus 4 to Zero plus 10.	Advance at rate of 50 yards every 1½ minutes.
Zero plus 10 to Zero plus 14.	Advance 50 yards every 2 minutes.
Zero plus 14 to Zero plus 34.	Advance 100 yards " 4 "

Zero plus 34. Lift off BLACK LINE.

Zero plus 34 to Zero plus 46.	Advance 100 yards " 4 " till 300 yards E.of BLACK LINE.
Zero plus 46 to Zero plus 2 hrs. 6 mins.	Barrage stationary 300 yards E.of BLACK LINE.

2nd.ADVANCE.

Zero plus 2 hours 6 mins. to Zero plus 2 hours 12 mins.	Advance 100 yards every 3 mins.
Zero plus 2 hours 12 mins. to Zero plus 2 hours 43 mins.	Advance 100 yards " 4 "

Zero plus 2 hours 43 minutes LIFT OFFBLUE LINE.

Zero plus 2 hours 43 mins.to Zero plus 2 hours 55 mins.	Advance 100 yards every 4 " " till 300 yards E.of BLUE LINE.
Zero plus 2 hours 55 mins.to Zero plus 6 hours 46 mins.	Barrage stationary 300 yards E. of BLUE LINE.

3rd ADVANCE.

Zero plus 6 hours 46 mins.to Zero plus 6 hours 52 mins.	Advance 100 yards every 3 mins.
Zero plus 6 hours 52 mins.to Zero plus 7 hours 32 mins.	Advance 100 yards " 4 "

Zero plus 7 hours 32 mins. Lift off FRONT LINE of ATHIES - POINT DU JOUR SYSTEM.

Zero plus 7 hours 32 mins.	Advance 100 yards every 3 mins. for 200 yards, then 100 yards every 4 minutes till 300 yards beyond the BROWN LINE.

9. RESERVE DIVISION.

(a) The 4th.Division will be held in Reserve.

(b) From the BLUE LINE the attacking Brigades of the 4th. DIVISION will follow up the 9th.DIVISION so as to reach the GERMAN third system of trenches at Zero plus 8 hours 40 minutes.

(c) They will pass through the 9th.Division on the BROWN LINE at Zero plus 9 hours 40 minutes and proceed to the attack of the GERMAN 4th.system.

(9).

(d) The consolidation of the BROWN LINE by the troops of the 9th.DIVISION will be continued until they are relieved by troops of the 4th Division other than those who pass through them to the attack of the GREEN LINE.

(e) Units of the 1st South African Infantry Brigade will not leave the BROWN LINE until properly relieved by troops of the 4th DIVISION.

10. POINTS REQUIRING SPECIAL ATTENTION.

1. The village of St.LAURENT BLANGY has been strongly fortified apparently with a view to flanking any advance by us to the North of it.

(a) Two Tanks will be employed to assist in its capture.

(b) If it holds out the troops to the North must push past it, and endeavour to isolate it.

11. CONSOLIDATION OF OBJECTIVES.

(a) The lines to be consolidated will be :-

(i) The BLACK LINE.
(ii) The BLUE LINE.
(iii) The BROWN LINE.

(b) The work of consolidation will be carried out by the Infantry, and must commence immediately each line is captured, and be undertaken by the troops who are detailed to halt on that line.

(c) The consolidation will be carried out on the principles laid down in " Instructions for the Training of Divisions for Offensive action."

On reaching the objective an outpost line will immediately be established 100 to 200 yards in front of the line, and as close as possible to the final barrage, the Commander of each assaulting Company being responsible for thus protecting his own front.

(d) The outpost line will consist of a line of small posts 150 to 200 yards apart, each held by a N.C.O., about six riflemen and a Lewis Gun.

(e) Communication trenches running through the line towards the enemy must be DOUBLE blocked, and Bombers, both hand and rifle, posted at the block together with a Trench Mortar as soon as it can be got up.

(f) At the same time selected localities in the captured line will be put in a state of defence by converting the captured trench into a fire trench facing the enemy.

The exact siting of these localities must depend on the result of reconnaissances of local Commanders, and on the number of men available for work, but they must be so designed as to afford each other mutual support.

12. CONSTRUCTION OF COMMUNICATION TRENCHES ACROSS "NO MAN'S LAND."

The following Communication trenches will be made across "NO MAN'S LAND." :-

(a) CENTRE BRIGADE.

Old Sap from Trench 90 (G.12.C.20.45) to be joined up with MANGFALL trench (G.12.C.55.35). This will be continued by MANGFALL trench and MINDEL trench to H.8.C.0.0. and will be the main communication trench for the CENTRE BRIGADE.

It will be called DAWSON AVENUE.

COMMUNICATIONS (Cont'd.).

(e) LIGHT SIGNALS (Cont'd.).

The increase increment will be 100 yards
These signals can be given by Company Commanders.

14. MARKING OF CAPTURED LINES.

As soon as objectives are captured Boards will be put up marked "BLACK LINE", BLUE LINE", for the use of following troops.

15. PRISONERS OF WAR.

Prisoners of War will be handed over to "MOPPERS UP". Walking wounded should be utilised as far as possible for escorts.

16. "MOPPERS UP".

The first line of "MOPPERS UP" will proceed straight to the sunken road West of the Black Line and clear it.
The second line will clear the"PETER GRABEN" and all trenches between that and the sunken road.
The third line will clear all trenches West of PETER GRABEN.
"MOPPERS UP" will not be employed between the BLACK and BLUE LINES.

17. MEDICAL.

(a) AID POSTS. South African Infantry Brigade at G.11.d.8.7. (July Avenue).
(b) ADVANCE DRESSING STATION. St. NICHOLAS at G.16.c.4.9.

18. DUMPS.

Battalion Dump will be in dug-out 22 a, near Trench 90, this will also be a forward Brigade Dump.

BRIGADE DUMPS. R.E. Material head of SUMMER TRAMWAY.

S.A.A., Grenades head of SUMMER TRAMWAY and CANDLE FACTORY.

On gaining and making good the blue line the Brigade Dump will be moved to approximately H.7.d.70.30. and, on securing the BROWN LINE, it will be moved to approximately H.8.c.80.30. All carriers are to know the position of the Dumps.

19. ARMS" CLOTHING, and EQUIPMENT.

Officers will be armed and equipped the same as the men.
The following clothing and equipment will be worn :-

Leather jerkins, web equipment without valise but with haversack on back, waterproof sheet, box respirator and P.H. Helmet.

Every man, with the exception of signallers, Lewis Gunners, and runners, will carry either a pick or shovel in addition to his entrenching tool, in the proportion of 1 pick to 2 shovels.

Every man will carry 170 rounds of ammunition, with the exception of signallers, Lewis Gunners, Runners and Carriers, who will carry 50 rounds each.

Every man/

13. EMPLOYMENT OF MACHINE GUNS.

(i) Four Machine guns are at the disposal of the Division during operations.

(ii) During the attack a proportion of the guns will be used :-

(a) To afford covering fire to the Infantry during the advance. The barrage will be 500 yards in front of the attacking Battalions.

(b) To form a protective barrage covering the BLACK, BLUE and BROWN LINES respectively, when captured.

(iii) The Guns of the 28th.Coy.M.G.Corps to be employed for covering fire during the advance will be :-

(1) First Advance 4 Guns.
(2) Second Advance 4 Guns.
(3) Third Advance 4 Guns (mentioned in/1).

(iv) The remaining 8 Guns of 28th.M.G.Coy will be employed as follows :-

IN RESERVE	2 Guns.
IN STRONG POINT at approx. H.7.d.15.65.	2 Guns.
IN STRONG POINT at approx.H.8.d.90.50.	2 Guns.
At approximately H.8.c.60.60	2 Guns.

(v) There will be a supply of S.A.A.for Machine Guns at the BRIGADE DUMP.

14. TRENCH MORTARS.

(a) The LIGHT Trench Mortar Batteries will be utilised in the preliminary bombardment and in subsequent operations under the orders of the Brigade Commanders.

(b) O.C., S.A.L.T.M.Battery will arrange before-hand with the O.C.,3rd. and 4th. Regiments as to the disposal of the one gun to accompany the Battalion and will also send one gun to 1st. and 2nd. Regiments. These guns will proceed to Units of S.A.Infantry Brigade immediately on conclusion of preliminary bombardment.

(c) After the preliminary bombardment the remaining four guns and teams will occupy dug-outs near by their emplacements and await orders.

15. REMOVAL OF OUR WIRE AND PROVISION OF TRENCH BRIDGES.

In order to facilitate the movement of troops through the front system of trenches, the wire in front of the various trenches will be gradually thinned out and removed. The work will be so arranged that only one belt of wire remains standing in front of the firing line on the day preceding the assault and that will be removed during that night.

Trench Bridges will be provided, one to every 30 yards and will be placed in position by Units 15 minutes before ZERO.

The number of Trench Bridges and ladders required will be :-

	Trench Bridges.	6'foot Ladders.
S.A.INFANTRY BRIGADE.	200.	300.

(16).

16. BATTLE HEADQUARTERS.

These will be located as follows :-

9th.DIVISION ETRUN L.3.d.1.2.

S.A.I.BRIGADE,New Dug-outs G.17.a.23.48.

Front RIGHT Battalion G.17.b.8.9.)No.6.Dug-out(

" LEFT " G.11.d.85.15.(Nos 23.24 and 25 dug-outs.)

Rear RIGHT " G.17.a.25.70 (No.32 Dug-out).

" LEFT " G.17.a.10.70 (No.35 Dug-out).

As soon as the BLACK LINE is reached, the H.Qrs. of the 3rd. and 4th. Regiments will make arrangements to move to suitable dug-outs which may be in the Sunken Road. Should there not be suitable dug-outs there, it is suggested that the left front battalion occupy the dug-out slightly to the North of the Junction of TRIM and TROT trenches, and the right front Battalion, the dug-out at the junction of WYE and WIND trenches. These dug-outs are shown on the map (Scale 1/5,000) issued to Units on 20th.instant and giving the English names of German Trenches.

When the Headquarters of the assaulting Battalions have moved forward the Headquarters of the two rear Battalions will then move up and occupy the dug-outs vacated by the front Battalions.

When the BLUE LINE is reached the H.Qrs.of the two rear Battalions will select Dug-outs near that line and will occupy them until their Units have reached the BROWN LINE. They need not necessarily move forward until their Battalions advance from the BLUE LINE.

It is suggested that the right rear Battalion occupy the dug-out EASTERN END OF KISS TRENCH and the left rear Battalion the dug-out shown as just South of the first 'K' in "KNUCKLE."

When the BROWN LINE is reached these two Battalions will select Headquarters in the POINT DU JOUR - L'ABBAYETTE LINE and it is suggested that the RIGHT Battalion occupies the dug-out at the SOUTHERN part of KICK trench and the LEFT Battalion in the NORTHERN part of KICK Trench.

BRIGADE HEADQUARTERS.

When the BROWN LINE has been gained an advanced BRIGADE H.Q. will be established in a dug-out near the EASTERN end of KNAVE trench. Battalions will be notified when this has been done.

17. SIGNALLING COMMUNICATIONS.

(a) VISUAL SIGNALLING.

1. Two main receiving stations will be established at :-

(a) G.23.c.35.20.
(b) G.10.c.9.4.

At the commencement of the Offensive, each BRIGADE H.Q. will be in visual communication with one or other of these two receiving stations.

As the advance proceeds, it will be possible to maintain signalling communication with these points.

17. SIGNALLING COMMUNICATIONS - VISUAL SIGNALLING CONTD.

(ii) The above mentioned receiving stations will be manned day and night and a constant look out kept.

They will be pointed out to all signallers concerned previous to the advance to enable them to be picked up readily.

(iii) Brigade and Battalion Signallers will be detailed to form Signal stations for the H.Q.of their respective Units.

(iv) Daylight lamps will be used throughout.

Two daylight lamps (LUCAS or FRENCH) will be available for the use of the two attacking Regiments, and they will be handed over by the 3rd and 4th Regiments to the 1st and 2nd Regts. after the second objective has been gained.

(v) To maintain secrecy and to reduce the length of messages the B A B Trench Code will be used whenever possible.

(vi) The following forward Brigade Stations will be established in the forthcoming operations :-

G.12.d.07.35.

G.12.d.7.3
or G.12.d.85.60.
or H.13.a.05.85. } Whichever is left vacant by the Regiments.

H.7.d.05.25.
*H.7.d.95.25.
H.8.c.95.40.

H.8.d.95.70.
or H.8.d.90.40.
or H.8.d.90.25. } Whichever is left vacant by the Regiments.

*This post will be "FORWARD BRIGADE SIGNAL STATION" until Brigade Headquarters moves forward or the 1st and 2nd Regiment Headquarters moves to the vicinity of the BROWN LINE.

VISUAL. The main Divisional Visual Receiving Station will be at G.23.c.~~35.30~~ 35.20 - All the Brigade Front (with the exception of the NORTHERN part of the BROWN LINE is visible from this Station.

(b) POWER BUZZERS & WIRELESS.

Power Buzzers will be allotted as follows :-

2 Power Buzzers to S.A.I.BRIGADE. One to go forward with a leading Battalion and one to be with a rear Battalion of each Brigade.

Only one Power Buzzer is to go forward with the attacking Infantry. It will be sent with the 4th.Regiment S.A.Infantry in the first place,and be handed over by them to the 2nd.Regiment S.A.I.,after the second objective has been gained. The receiving amplifier for it will be with the 27th.Brigade Headquarters at G.12.c.00.95.and the Earth base must be set out N.N.E. to S.S.W. The receiving Station's call will be AB. The sending station will have no call letters. The signalling from this Power Buzzer will be done only between the five minutes 6 to 10, 16 - 20, 26 - 30, 36 - 40, 46 - 50 and 56 - 60 of each hour. It is important that these times be adhered to, otherwise the signals will clash with those of another power buzzer which will be working to the same receiving station during the alternate five minutes.

(c) PIGEONS.

Pigeon Lofts have been established near DIVISIONAL H.Qrs.from which birds will be issued to each Battalion.

Messages intended for Brigades will be communicated from Divisional H.Qrs.by any means available at the time.

17. PIGEONS CONTD.

Only six pigeons will be available for issue to the Brigade. One will accompany each Regiment, and two kept in Reserve at BRIGADE HEADQUARTERS for issue as required. If those carried by the 3rd and 4th Regiments are still on hand when the second objective has been gained, and the telephone line completed to that point, they will be handed over to the 1st and 2nd.Regiments.

(d) RUNNERS.

Brigades and Battalions will detail and train runners who will wear the distinguishing badge of a RED band as laid down in S.S.135 para. XXXII.

(e) CONTACT AEROPLANES.

In addition to the above means of communication,contact aeroplanes will be employed to receive signals from Brigade and Battalion Headquarters by means of :-

(i) Ground signal Panels.
(ii) Lamps,

and from attacking Infantry by means of Flares.

Information thus obtained will be dropped at the Corps Dropping Station at F.29.a.3.3 whence it will be transmitted to the Unit concerned.

N OR E.7.B.2.1.

The Infantry will be prepared to light their Flares and will be on the look out for the contact planes at :-

(a) Zero plus 1 hour, i,e,after BLACK LINE is expected to be captured.

(b) Zero plus 3 hours 10 mins. i,e,after BLUE LINE is expected to be captured.

(c) Zero plus 8 hrs.10 mins. i,e,after BROWN LINE is expected to be captured.

The Flares will be lit when the aeroplane actually calls for them.

(f) LIGHT SIGNALS.

Light Signals will be used for communication from the Front line to Batteries through any intermediate station which it may be found necessary to establish.

Light signals will be used according to the following Code :-

Succession of GREEN LIGHTS	OPEN FIRE.
Succession of WHITE LIGHTS	LENGTHEN RANGE.

The signal for "OPEN FIRE" and to "LENGTHEN RANGE" can be given by a Company Commander.

Signals will be continued until the required response is made by the ARTILLERY.

The increment by which the Range will be increased will be 100 yards.

The above Light Signals are to be used for calling for Artillery Support, they will not be used during the actual progress of an attack to recall the barrage or accelerate its lift.

There will be no Signal to " CEASE FIRE " or "SHORTEN RANGE".

/The Very Light.

17. LIGHT SIGNALS CONTD. (11).

The VERY LIGHT SIGNAL for "OPEN FIRE" will be equivalent to the S.O.S. and will be used by day as well as by night.

In making the S.O.S. and LENGTHEN RANGE Signals, they should be fired along the front of the area in which Artillery Support is required and care should be taken that lights are sent up on both flanks of the line so that it may be clearly marked.

(g) Each Battalion will take into battle not more than 24 Signallers. This does not include men specially detailed for Power Buzzer Sets. The remainder of the Signallers, except two, will stay with the Battalion Transport. The two will be attached to Brigade Headquarters under the orders of the Brigade Signal Officer. They will be used for forming the Brigade Visual Receiving Station and to assist the Brigade Linesmen or Operators if necessary.

18. REPORTS.

Situation Reports by platoon, Company and Battalion Commanders will be rendered frequently, by the latter at least once every two hours. It is to be impressed on all ranks that negative reports are frequently as valuable to the higher commands as those that contain a lot of information.

If no reports are received from the front Companies, this fact should be so stated in the reports sent to Brigade Headquarters by Battalion Commanders.

19. NOTICE BOARDS TO ~~MAKE~~ MARK ENEMY'S TRENCH SYSTEM.

In order that the troops who follow up the leading Battalions in the attack may recognize what portion of the Battlefield they have reached, Brigades will arrange to send forward with their assaulting battalions a number of Notice Boards or canvas screens marked "BLACK LINE", "BLUE LINE" and "BROWN LINE" which will be erected on the various objectives as they are reached.

MARKING OF CAPTURED LINES.

As soon as a line is captured and consolidated, Units will be responsible for the erection of the boards marking the positions i.e., BLACK LINE, BLUE LINE, BROWN LINE.

Boards showing the German and English names of the trenches will be put up by the MOPPERS UP.

20. PRISONERS OF WAR.

Prisoners taken by the fighting troops will be handed over to the MOPPERS UP who will send them under as small a escort as possible to St NICHOLAS where they will be taken over by special escorts under the A.P.M. Walking wounded should be utilised for escorts as far as possible.

Strict orders will be issued that no documents of any kind whatever are to be removed from a Prisoner until he reaches the Divisional Collecting Station unless the Prisoner shows an inclination to destroy those he possesses, in which case they will be removed and sent to the Divisional Collecting Station with the escort.

21. MOPPERS UP. See also page 13

Moppers Up will not be employed between the BLACK and BLUE LINES. Those in the Sunken Road will however join the 1st and 2nd. Regiments and be used for clearing the Ravine about 400 yards EAST of the BLUE LINE. The remainder will be collected and will occupy and proceed with the consolidation of the BLACK LINE.

22. MEDICAL.

The sites of AID POSTS, COLLECTING POSTS and DRESSING STATIONS are as follows :-

(a) AID POSTS.

1st S.A.I.BRIGADE. G.11.d.8.7.(JULY AVENUE)

(b) ADVANCED DRESSING STATION.

St NICHOLAS (G.16.c. 4.9.)

23. DUMPS.

(a) R.E.

Main Divisional Dump	ANZIN (G.7.b.50.60.)
Advd. =do=	G. 16. d. 3. 7.
S.A.I.BRIGADE.	Head of Summer Tramway. and New cut

(b) S.A.A.&.GRENADES.

Main Divisional Dump	ETRUN.
Advd. =do=	BRASSERIE, ST NICHOLAS.
S.A.I.BRIGADE.	~~CANDLE FACTORY~~ and HEAD OF SUMMER TRAMWAY. Dug Outs 4 and 22a

On gaining and making good the BLUE LINE the Brigade Dump will be moved up to approximately H.18.b.5.9.and on securing the BROWN LINE it will be moved to approximately H.7.d.7.3.

Reserves of S.A.A. and GRENADES are also kept at :-

FORRESTIER REDOUBT	14,000	Rounds	S.A.A.	375	GRENADES	
NICHOLAS REDOUBT	12,000	"	"	375	"	
OIL WORKS	14,000	"	"	375	"	
LAUNDRY	12,000	"	"	60	"	

(c) RESERVE SUPPLIES.

Dumps of Reserve Supplies will be placed at the CANDLE FACTORY consisting of 8,000 rations for 3 days.

RESERVE SUPPLIES are also kept at :-

FORRESTIER REDOUBT	400	Rations	400	galls.	Water.
NICHOLAS REDOUBT	400	"	400	"	"
OIL WORKS	400	"	400	"	"
LAUNDRY	60	"	60	"	"

24. GAS MORTARS.

(a) 8, 4" Trench Mortars have been allotted to the Division.

These will be employed under the command of Lieutenant BERRY, L.Section, No.3, Special Company R.E., in the 27th Brigade Area to fire Gas shells into " CHANTECLER TRENCH 6 hours before ZERO."

(b) 500 LIVENS GAS PROJECTORS have been allotted to the Division and will be employed against St LAURENT BLANGY.

(c) The following precautions will be taken for the protection of our troops :-

(i) "GAS ALERT" precautions will be maintained while the GAS BOMBS are in the trenches.

(ii) BOMBS will not be discharged over the heads of our troops.

25/(13).

25. CARRYING PARTIES.

Officers and N.C.O's in charge of Carrying parties will always march in rear of their parties.

26. STRAGGLERS POSTS.

These will be established at the JULY and MAY ends of BRITANNIA WORKS and will consist of one N.C.O. and three men each, whose duty it will be to collect all unwounded men and send them back to their Units. Names of the N.C.O's and men so collected will be taken by the N.C.O. in charge of the post.

27. GENERAL.

BOX RESPIRATORS are to be carried.

Its is suggested that all private belongings should be packed up in bags by platoons and these bags then put together in a Company sack. If this is done it is not a matter of importance that men get their own packs back. Only Government kit should be put in the packs.

(Sgd.) Pepper.

Captain,
Brigade Major.
Ist S.A. Infantry Brigade.

ADD.

21. MOPPERS UP.

Para. A. Moppers Up will be furnished as follows :-

2 Platoons 1st Regiment S.A.I.
2 Platoons 2nd Regiment S.A.I.
50 other ranks 4th Regiment S.A.I.,

the whole under the command of 2nd/Lieut KIRBY, 4th. Regiment South African Infantry.

They will be drawn up in three lines, the first of which will proceed straight to the Sunken Road WEST of the BLACK LINE and will clear the Dug-outs there.

The Second line will clear the PETER GRABEN and all the trenches between that trench and the Sunken Road, and the THIRD line will clear all trenches WEST of PETER GRABEN.

SECRET.

B

4th. SOUTH AFRICAN INFANTRY.

Ref. Map.
Trench Map
1/10,000.

3rd. April, 1917.

OPERATION ORDER NO. 17/18.

1. INTENTION.

The primary object of the operation is to establish a line along th GERMAN 3rd. line system, which runs from the SCARPE near FEUCHY through Le POINT du JOUR - MAISON de la COTE,- COMMANDANTS HOUSE and when this line has been established to make a further advance later.

2. DISTRIBUTION.

The South African Infantry Brigade will be the centre Brigade of the 9th. Division. It will have two Battalions in the front line.:-

3rd. S.A. Infantry on the RIGHT, and
4th. S.A. Infantry on the LEFT,

and two Battalions in Support,

1st. S.A. Infantry on the RIGHT, and
2nd. S.A. Infantry on the LEFT.

One Stokes gun will be attached to each Battalion.

3. OBJECTIVE.

There will be two separate main objectives for the Battalion :-

(a) The capture of the front system (BLACK LINE ON MAP).

(b) The capture of the second line (BLUE LINE ON MAP).

The third line (BROWN LINE ON MAP) will be captured by the Supporting Battalion.

4. BOUNDARIES.

The boundaries of the Battalion are :-

Right Boundary. The line from G.12.c.59.18 to H.7.c.00.23. and thence to H.7.d.90.40.

Left Boundary. A line from G.12.c.7.8. Eastwards to the bend in INN TRENCH at G.12.d.5.8. thence to trench junction G.12.d.95.90 (exclusive) Railway Crossing H.7.d.7.8.(inclusive).

5. COMMUNICATION TRENCHES.

"IN" JULY AVENUE from St. NICHOLAS - QUATRE VENTS ROAD about G16.a.7.4. by old trench into AUGUST AVENUE (North of CANDLE FACTORY) up AUGUST to BRITANNIA WORKS and across to JULY up to NEW CUT junction thence by NEW CUT.

"OUT" MAY AVENUE - By MAY to BRITANNIA WORKS thence along BRITANNIA WORKS to JULY, along JULY through CANDLE FACTORY to G.16.b.5.3. and by old trench to about G.16.c.5.8.

6. PREPARATION FOR THE ATTACK.

A continuous bombardment will be carried out for 96 hours preceding the attack.

7. PLAN OF ATTACK.

FORMATION.

The Battalion will attack on a two Company front.

"C" and "D" Companies will be in FRONT LINE, "C" on the RIGHT and "D" on the LEFT.

"A" and "B" Companies will be in support, "A" on the RIGHT and "B" on the LEFT.

The two front Companies will be in two waves of two lines each. "MOPPERS UP" will be between the first and second waves. Waves to be about 100 yards distant. The two rear Companies to be in column of sections in file.

One N.C.O. and ten men from each Company will be CARRIERS. They will advance with their Companies. N.C.O's. in charge of carrying sections will always be in rear of their parties.

ASSEMBLY TRENCHES.

The front wave, namely two platoons each from "C" and "D" Companies, will be assembled in shell holes in front of our lines, not more than 200 yards from the enemy wire.

The second wave, consisting of two platoons each of the same two Companies, will be drawn up, together with the "MOPPERS UP" in our front line.

"A" and "B" Companies will be assembled in the IMMEDIATE SUPPORT trenches.

The right of each platoon will be marked with a board with the number of the platoon on it.

METHOD OF ADVANCE.

In each phase the two front waves will go right through to the objective and, those in rear, if not required to reinforce, will occupy convenient trenches when the front waves reach their objective.

FRONT.

Battalion.	300 yards.
Each Company.	150 yards.
Each Platoon.	75 yards.

ZERO HOUR.

The date and time of ZERO will be notified later.

ADVANCE TO BLACK LINE.

(a) At ZERO the Battalion will move out and advance as close as possible under the Artillery Barrage, which will open 50 yards in front of the GERMAN front line trench.

The barrage will lift on to the front trench at ZERO plus 1 minute and at ZERO plus 4 minutes will commence to move forward until it reaches a line 300 yards beyond the BLACK LINE. It will be closely followed through the successive lines of the enemy's front system, "MOPPING UP" parties occupying each line in succession.

(b) The pace at which the barrage will advance is shown in para 8.

(c)

ADVANCE TO BLACK LINE (Cont'd.).

(c) "C" and "D" Companies will proceed direct to the BLACK LINE and, having gained it, will push out an outpost line in front as far as the Artillery Barrage will allow, and then clear the BLACK LINE and consolidate it.

"A" and "B" Companies, if not required to reinforce, will occupy the sunken road to the West of the BLACK LINE. They will leave the clearing of dug-outs to "MOPPERS UP".

SECOND ADVANCE TO THE BLUE LINE.

(d) At ZERO plus 1 hour and 45 minutes "A" and "B" Companies will advance from the sunken road West of the BLACK LINE and will form up and lie down as close to the barrage as possible until the time to attack the BLUE LINE when they will advance supported by "C" and "D" Companies. This advance will be made in section columns as long as it is possible to retain that formation.

(e) At ZERO plus 2 hours and 6 minutes the advance on the BLUE LINE will commence and the barrage will move forward till it reaches a line 300 yards beyond the BLUE LINE.

(f) The BLUE LINE having been gained an outpost line will be pushed out as far as the Artillery barrage will allow and the consolidating of the BLUE LINE will commence.

"A" and "B" Companies will clear the Railway ~~line~~ cutting and consolidate that position.

"C" and "D" Companies will clear the trench to the West of the Railway Cutting and, if required, will help in the consolidating of the position.

(g) At ZERO plus 6 hours and 41 minutes the 2nd. South African Infantry will pass through the Regiment and attack the BROWN LINE.

During the advance every endeavour will be made by troops who have reached their objective to assist those on their flanks who may have been held up, by attacking the flanks and rear of any hostile troops opposing them.

STOKES MORTAR GUN.

The Stokes Mortar gun will advance in rear of the two Supporting Companies in each advance.

SMOKE BARRAGE.

During the operations a smoke barrage will be put on the BLUE LINE if the wind is blowing from the West, or on the BROWN LINE if blowing from the EAST.

8. ARTILLERY BARRAGE.

A percentage of smoke shells will be fired in the artillery barrage to show where the barrage is falling.

The following table gives a summary of the times at which certain lines will be reached :-

1st. ADVANCE.

ZERO plus 4 minutes lift off FRONT LINE.

Zero plus 4 to Zero plus 10.	Advance at rate of 50 yards every 1½ minutes.
Zero plus 10 to Zero plus 14.	Advance 50 yards every 2 minutes.
Zero plus 14 to Zero plus 34.	Advance 100 yards every 4 minutes.

ARTILLERY BARRAGE (Cont'd.).

Zero plus 34. Lift off BLACK LINE.

Zero plus 34 to Zero plus 46.	Advance 100 yards every 4 minutes till 300 yards E. of BLACK LINE.
Zero plus 46 to Zero plus 2 hrs. 6 minutes.	Barrage stationery 300 yards E. of BLACK LINE.

2nd. ADVANCE.

Zero plus 2 hrs. 6 mins. to Zero plus 2 hrs. 12 mins.	Advance 100 yards every 3 minutes.
Zero plus 2 hrs. 12 mins. to Zero plus 2 hrs. 43 mins.	Advance 100 yards every 4 minutes.

Zero plus 2 hrs. 43 mins lift off BLUE LINE.

Zero plus 2 hrs. 43 mins. to Zero plus 2 hrs. 55 mins.	Advance 100 yards every 4 minutes till 300 yards E. of Blue Line

9. POINTS REQUIRING SPECIAL ATTENTION.

It is suspected that there is a strong point near the cross road about G.12.b.90.00. and suspected M.G. emplacements at G.12.c.80.65., G.12.c.65.15., H.7.c.05.14., H.7.b.65.00., H.8.d.85.50., H.8.d.82.08., and H.8.d.65.10.

10. CONSOLIDATION OF .OBJECTIVES.

(a) The lines to be consolidated will be :-
(1) The Black Line.
(2) The Blue Line.

(b) The work of consolidation will be carried out by the Infantry and must commence immediately each line is captured, and be undertaken by the troops who are detailed to halt on that line.

(c) The consolidation will be carried out on the principles laid down in "Instructions for the Training of Divisions for Offensive Action."

On reaching the objective an outpost line will immediately be established 100 to 200 yards in front of the line, and as close as possible to the final barrage, the Commander of each assaulting Company being responsible for thus protecting his own front.

(d) The outpost line will consist of a line of small posts 100 to 150 yards apart, each held by a N.C.O., about 6 riflemen and a Lewis Gun.

(e) Communication trenches running through the line towards the enemy must be double blocked, and bombers, both hand and rifle, posted at the block, together with a trench mortar as soon as it can be got up.

(f) At the same time selected localities in the captured line will be put in a state of defence by converting the captured trench into a fire trench facing the enemy.

(The exact siting of these localities must depend on the result of reconnaissances of Local Commanders, and on the number of men available for work, but they must be so designed as to afford each other mutual support.

11. PROVISION OF TRENCH BRIDGES AND LADDERS.

Trench bridges will be provided, one to every 30 yards. and will be placed in position fifteen minutes before zero. 6'0" trench ladders will also be provided to lead out of the front and immediate/

PROVISION OF TRENCH BRIDGES AND LADDERS (Cont'd.).

immediate support trenches.

12. BATTLE HEADQUARTERS.

Battalion Battle Headquarters will be at G.11.d.85.15. (Dug-outs Nos. 23, 24, and 25).

As soon as the BLACK LINE is reached the Battalion Headquarters will be moved forward to the sunken road, probably to a dug-out at G.12.d.85.60.

Companies will be notified directly Battalion Headquarters are being moved.

13. COMMUNICATIONS.

(a) REPORTS. Situation Reports by Platoon and Company Commanders will be rendered frequently and at least once every hour, It is to be impressed on all ranks that negative reports are just as valuable as those which contain a lot of information.

(b) VISUAL SIGNALLERS.

A Divisional Signal Station will be established in ARRAS at G.23.c.35.30.

When the BLACK LINE has been captured a Battalion Signal Station will be established at G.12.d.90.60.

To maintain secrecy and reduce length of messages the "B.A.B." Trench Code will be used whenever possible.

(c) CONTACT AEROPLANES.

Front line Companies will be prepared to light their flares and will be on the look out for Contact Aeroplanes, at (1) Zero plus 1 hour, that is, when the BLACK LINE is expected to be captured, and (2) Zero plus 3 hours and 10 minutes, that is, when the BLUE LINE is expected to be captured. The flares will be lit when the aeroplane actually calls for them by sounding a succession of "A's. on Klaxton Horn or dropping a white light.

(d) RUNNERS.

Runners will wear the distinctive badge of a red band worn round the left forearm.

(e) LIGHT SIGNALS.

Light signals will be used for communicating from the front line to Batteries. They will be according to the following Code :-

Succession of Green Lights.	Open Fire.
Succession of White Lights.	Lengthen Range.

The above light signals are to be used for calling for Artillery support, they will not be used during the actual progress of an attack to recall the barrage or accelerate its lift.

There will be no signal to "CEASE FIRE" or "SHORTEN RANGE".

The VERY LIGHT signal for "OPEN FIRE" will be equivalent to the S.O.S. and will be used by day as well as by night.

In making the S.O.S. and LENGTHEN RANGE signals, they should be fired along the front of the area in which artillery support is required and care should be taken that lights are sent up on both flanks of the line so that it may be clearly marked.

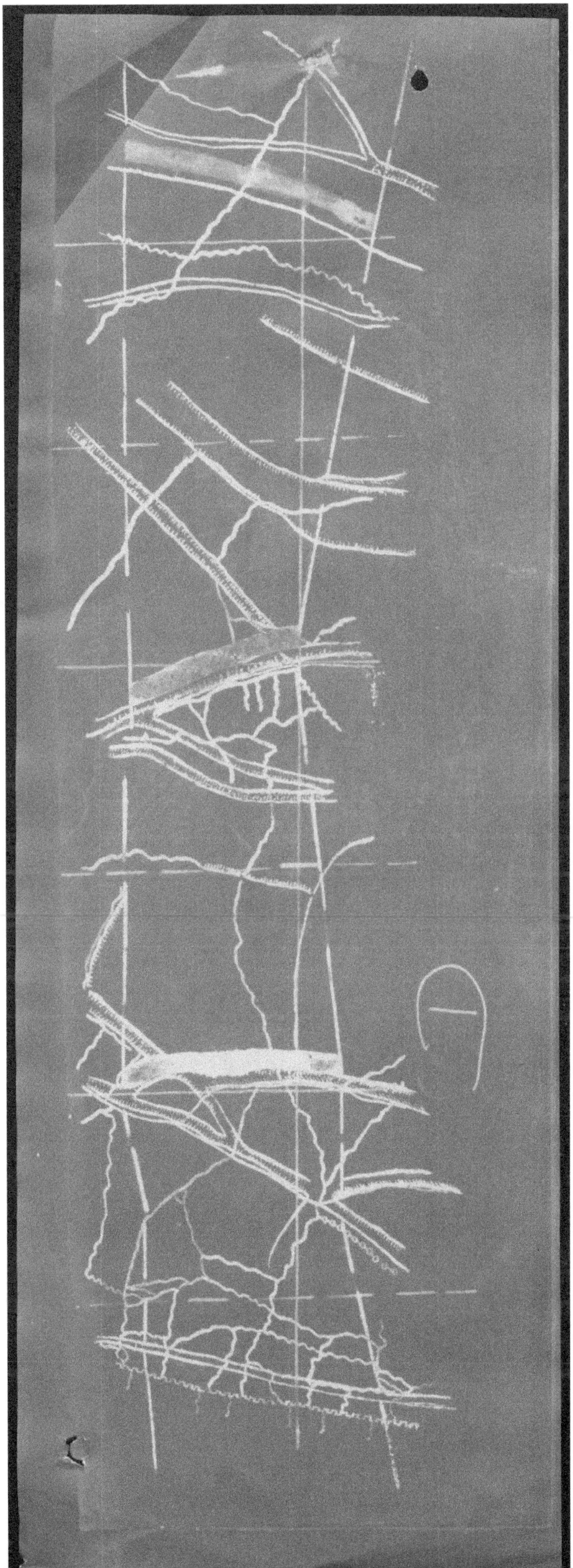

Army Form C. 2118.

WAR DIARY
or
INTELLIGENCE SUMMARY.
(Erase heading not required.)

Instructions regarding War Diaries and Intelligence Summaries are contained in F. S. Regs., Part II. and the Staff Manual respectively. Title pages will be prepared in manuscript.

4th SOUTH AFRICAN INFANTRY Bn Sht 14

Place	Date	Hour	Summary of Events and Information	Remarks and references to Appendices
ARRAS	1/5/17		Battalion furnished working party to 401st R.E 8 officers 17 N.C.O.s 314 other Ranks. Fine sunny weather. A small ammunition dump near Rue St Augustin set on fire by long range shell.	
ARRAS	2/5/17		Battalion found working party to 401st R.E. 8 officers 17 N.C.O.s and 273 other Ranks. O.C. R.E said could reduce strength of party. Fine sunny weather	
ARRAS	3/5/17		Battalion found working party for 401st R.E 4 officers 17 NCOs & 260 O.R. Enemy shelled the town during the day & evening	
ARRAS	4/5/17		Battalion found working party for 401st R.E. 4 officers 17 N.C.O.s & 255 O.R. In evening about 8 pm an ammunition dump went on fire near gasometers. Everybody kept under cover, or box respirators worn "alert" in case of gas shells exploding. Quite a lot of stuff flying about from it, & kept on till 11 pm. when it died down, & then intermittent explosions during night.	

A5834 Wt. W4973 M687 750,000 8/16 D. D. & L. Ltd. Forms/C.2118/11.

Instructions regarding War Diaries and Intelligence Summaries are contained in F. S. Regs., Part II. and the Staff Manual respectively. Title pages will be prepared in manuscript.

WAR DIARY
or
INTELLIGENCE SUMMARY.
(Erase heading not required.)

Place	Date	Hour	Summary of Events and Information	Remarks and references to Appendices
ARRAS	5/5/17		Got orders about 6 A.M. to cease work for R.E. & prepare to go into line. Drew from DADOS Lewis guns &c to complete also drew Very lights &c. At 6pm the Battalion moved via Blangy bridge to Black Line and by 7-30 pm. established in TRAY, TRASH and TREE TRENCHES. Strength 22 officers (including M.O.) and 373 other ranks. Battalion under the orders of G.O.C 26th BDE.	
BLACK LINE	6/5/17		In morning C.O. visited Green Line to arrange relief with O.C 10th A & S.H. Battalion moved from Black Line at 8 pm. being met by A & S H guides at Bde H.Q. in RWY cutting at H 7 D 95.25. thence by Infantry track straight across to Adv Bde H.Q. at H 10 D 4 5 app & thence north along Green Line Trench system. Relief completed by 1 AM. 7/5/17. Position held by regt CUBA trench 2 platoons - CLASP TRENCH 3 platoons - CLOVER trench 1 platoon - CADIZ 2 platoons. HUDSON - HAZARD & HONEY TRENCHES 8 platoons. Rations had been issued at Black Line before going in.	

A5834 Wt. W4973/M687 750,000 8/16 D. D. & L. Ltd. Forms/C.2118/13.

Instructions regarding War Diaries and Intelligence Summaries are contained in F. S. Regs., Part II. and the Staff Manual respectively. Title pages will be prepared in manuscript.

WAR DIARY
or
INTELLIGENCE SUMMARY.
(Erase heading not required.)

Army Form C. 2118.

Place	Date	Hour	Summary of Events and Information	Remarks and references to Appendices
GREEN-LINE	7/5/17		At 4.15 A.M. enemy sent up Golden Rain Rockets & maxim fire opposite sector on our right. Intermittent shelling of our trenches all day. Between 4 & 7 pm we shelled the enemy trenches. At 8.30 pm guides from 7th Seaforths reported at our Battn H.Q. to guide our two back companies to front line to take over CUBA trench to Brickfields at H7A69 & to CHILI TRENCH. Relief complete by 11-45 p.m. At 11-30 pm enemy actively shelled neighbourhood of Hudson trench. GAVRELLE & POINT DE JOUR Road to GAVRELLE heavily shelled by enemy heavies all day. Our battalion now holding 26th Brigade front line & support line CUBA TRENCH from H7D15.35 to H7A60.90.	
GREEN LINE	8/5/17		From 3 AM to 6 AM enemy shelling fairly active on our sector & again at 10.30 a.m. fairly quiet otherwise until 3 p.m. At 7 p.m. we had a practice barrage on	

A5834 Wt. W4973/M687 750,000 8/16 D. D. & L. Ltd. Forms/C.2118/13.

Instructions regarding War Diaries and Intelligence Summaries are contained in F. S. Regs., Part II. and the Staff Manual respectively. Title pages will be prepared in manuscript.

Army Form C. 2118.

WAR DIARY
or
INTELLIGENCE SUMMARY.
(Erase heading not required.)

Place	Date	Hour	Summary of Events and Information	Remarks and references to Appendices
GREEN LINE	8/5/17		enemy trenches opposite our Divl front. At 7.2½ the enemy sent up double green rockets & golden rain rockets, & at 7.3 his barrage opened on CUBA & CLASP especially the latter trench. His retaliation lasted 20 minutes about.	
GREEN LINE	9/5/17		Intermittent enemy shelling. At 12 and 12.30 noon & again at 4 & 4.30 pm we opened up practice barrages on enemy front line opposite our sector, but little retaliation. At night withdrew all our men from CLASP. Disposition now CUBA TRENCH 10 platoons & 12 Lewis guns, CLOVER TRENCH 1 platoon & 1 Lewis Gun, CADIZ trench 3 platoons, CHILI TRENCH 2 platoons & 2 Lewis guns, CLYDE TRENCH 1 Lewis gun (between CLOVER & CADIZ). At 6 pm one of our aeroplanes came down near CADIZ.	
	10/5/17		Enemy shelling our trenches at intervals. In afternoon our heavies shelling opposite GAVRELLE to break up reported enemy concentration, & enemy retaliation there	

A5834 Wt. W4973 M687 750,000 8/16 D. D. & L. Ltd. Forms/C.2118/13.

Instructions regarding War Diaries and Intelligence Summaries are contained in F. S. Regs., Part II. and the Staff Manual respectively. Title pages will be prepared in manuscript.

WAR DIARY
or
INTELLIGENCE SUMMARY.
(Erase heading not required.)

Army Form C. 2118.

Place	Date	Hour	Summary of Events and Information	Remarks and references to Appendices
Green Line	10/5/17		commenced at ~~8.45~~ 7.20 p.m. app. & all sorts of signals sent up	
			Fairly heavy till about 8 p.m. when practically done.	
			About 8.6 p.m. a mutual bombardment [illegible] our right	
			enemy sent up double green rockets all along his	
			line & opened a heavy barrage all along our	
			line shelling front & back trenches. Finished	
			by 9 p.m. Our relief postponed. At 9.30 p.m. sent	
			our guides to A&V Bde H.Q. At 9.50 p.m. 2 platoons	
			platoons of C Coy passed out at 10.20 3 platoons	
			of D Coy. ~~At [illegible] A Coy passed at 2.40 a.m.~~	
Green Line	11/5/17		At 1 AM A Coy passed, at 2.40 a.m. the 2	
			platoons of C Coy from CUBA, at 2.50 a.m. 1 platoon of D	
			from Blow trench, at 3 AM B Coy passed.	
			At 3.5 a.m. received 2[illegible] Bde relief complete	
			& C.O. left. The battalion was relieved by 2 Coys	

A5834 Wt. W4973/M687 750,000 8/16 D. D. & L. Ltd. Forms/C.2118/13.

Army Form C. 2118.

WAR DIARY
or
INTELLIGENCE SUMMARY.
(Erase heading not required.)

Instructions regarding War Diaries and Intelligence Summaries are contained in F. S. Regs., Part II. and the Staff Manual respectively. Title pages will be prepared in manuscript.

Place	Date	Hour	Summary of Events and Information	Remarks and references to Appendices
Y Huts.	11/5/17		of 7th East Yorks & 1 coy of 9th Duke of Wellingtons.	
			The 7th E Yorks took over our Batt. H.Q. The battalion on relief went back to ARRAS, embussed at the octroi & billeted at Y HUTS for by 7 AM.	
			Our total casualties from 6th to 11th inclusive were:-	
			Other ranks Killed Wounded Missing	
			During our tour of duty it was noticed that the enemy artillery had greatly increased since the regt was last in the line, & largely using his 4.2s & 5.9s, & very little of the 7.7 c.m. gun. He was very jumpy, & his S.O.S was the double green rocket.	
			The battalion rested at Y Huts the rest of the 11th	

A5834 Wt. W4973 M687 750,000 8/16 D. D. & L. Ltd. Forms/C.2118/13.

Instructions regarding War Diaries and Intelligence Summaries are contained in F. S. Regs., Part II. and the Staff Manual respectively. Title pages will be prepared in manuscript.

WAR DIARY
or
INTELLIGENCE SUMMARY.
(Erase heading not required.)

Army Form C. 2118.

Place	Date	Hour	Summary of Events and Information	Remarks and references to Appendices
Y HUTS ETRUN	12/5/17		The regiment moved by march route from Y Huts leaving at 7.15 am. to Monchy Breton, billetted by 12.30 noon. Moved in shirtsleeves & fighting order	
MONCHY BRETON	13/5/17		At 11 A.M. Brigade inspected by Third Army Commander. Capt Browne reported for duty from England. Draft arrived at 8 p.m.	
MONCHY BRETON	14/5/17		Physical Drill 7-15 to 7.45 A.M. Training under company arrangements 9 A.M. to 12 NOON. Rain in afternoon. Bathing for 240 men in afternoon at ROCOURT. 18 men per company detailed for Lewis gun course.	
MONCHY BRETON	15/5/17		Physical Training 7-15 to 7.45 A.M ~~for Lewis g~~ All Coys 1 Hours Company Drill - 2 hours Musketry. Sergeants 1 hours instruction under R.S.M. Subalterns 1 hours map reading.	

A5834 Wt. W4973 M687 750,000 8/16 D. D. & L. Ltd. Forms/C.2118/13.

Army Form C. 2118.

WAR DIARY
or
INTELLIGENCE SUMMARY.
(*Erase heading not required.*)

Instructions regarding War Diaries and Intelligence Summaries are contained in F. S. Regs., Part II. and the Staff Manual respectively. Title pages will be prepared in manuscript.

Place	Date	Hour	Summary of Events and Information	Remarks and references to Appendices
MONCHY BRETON	16/5/17		All Companies Physical Training 7.15 to 7.45 A.M. All Companies – Extended order drill – Lewis gun instruction Rifle Grenade firing – Bayonet fighting & company drill – 40 minutes each from 9 – 12 noon.	
MONCHY BRETON	17/5/17.		All Companies Physical Training 6-45 a.m. to 7.15 a.m. As a wet days Companies trained in billets from 9 A.M. to 12 noon under company arrangements. Corporals & L/Corporals in horns instruction in Guard mounting.	
MONCHY BRETON	18/5/17		All Companies Physical Training 6-45 to 7.15 a.m. All Companies – Judging distance – Fire Control – Rapid Loading – Lewis Gun instruction – Artillery formations from 9 A.M. to 12 NOON. Subalterns arms drill & firing positions from 3 to 4 p.m.	

Instructions regarding War Diaries and Intelligence Summaries are contained in F. S. Regs., Part II. and the Staff Manual respectively. Title pages will be prepared in manuscript.

WAR DIARY
or
INTELLIGENCE SUMMARY.
(Erase heading not required.)

Army Form C. 2118.

Place	Date	Hour	Summary of Events and Information	Remarks and references to Appendices
MONCHY BRETON	19/5/17		Intensive digging competition - Time allowed 1¼ hours. Won by D Coy. in the morning. Then in the afternoon held a snapshooting competition at a disappearing target - 70 men per company. Won by B Coy. The regt scored 40% of hits.	
MONCHY BRETON	20/5/17		Church parades - Had a field Kitchen competition won by A Coy. absolutely perfect weather.	
MONCHY BRETON	21/5/17		Divisional 1st Line Transport Show - Regt got a 3rd prize for pack pony. Artillery formations 9-10-30 am. Rest of training for day cancelled on a/c of wet weather	

Instructions regarding War Diaries and Intelligence Summaries are contained in F. S. Regs., Part II. and the Staff Manual respectively. Title pages will be prepared in manuscript.

WAR DIARY
or
INTELLIGENCE SUMMARY.
(Erase heading not required.)

Army Form C. 2118.

Place	Date	Hour	Summary of Events and Information	Remarks and references to Appendices
MONCHY BRETON	22/5/17		Training in billets 9-12 A.M owing to wet weather. Practised Rapid Loading Blindfold, with respirators &c. 1 officer & 46 O.R. on duty to Corps school.	
MONCHY BRETON	23/5/17		Regimental sports all day - Lovely weather. D. company the best company at sports. At 10 p.m practised assembly for attack from trenches. Draft of 48 O.R. arrived	
MONCHY BRETON	24/5/17		Training from 9 A M to 12.30 Noon - Carried on with Bayonet fighting - Rapid Loading - Demonstration of Indication of Targets - Use of German Bomb & Bomb Throwing (Dummies) - Extended order Drill. Coy Signallers & Lewis gunners separately instructed.	

A5834 Wt. W4973/M687 750,000 8/16 D. D. & L. Ltd. Forms/C.2118/13.

Instructions regarding War Diaries and Intelligence Summaries are contained in F. S. Regs., Part II. and the Staff Manual respectively. Title pages will be prepared in manuscript.

WAR DIARY
or
INTELLIGENCE SUMMARY.
(Erase heading not required.)

Army Form C. 2118.

Place	Date	Hour	Summary of Events and Information	Remarks and references to Appendices
MONCHY-BRETON	25/5/17		Divisional Bayonet Fighting Instructor (CSM Law) took the Battalion in Bayonet Fighting from 11 to 12.30. Companies instructed in billets in Lewis Gun from 10 – 11 am. NIGHT:- Attack Practice from 10 pm to 11.45 pm carried out on Training Ground. Weather – Clear but hot	
do	26/5/17		BRIGADE SPORTS. Commenced at 10.30 am on Training Ground. The Battalion secured 2nd place in Brigade Championship with 28 points losing to the 1st Regiment with 32 points. Battalion won 100 yards, 440 yards, N.C.Os Race, Half mile, 5 aside Football, but lost to 1st Regt in Tug of War. Weather – Excellent	
do	27/5/17		Fine bright Day. Inter-Company Shooting Competition at Fixed Target. Grouping & Rapid Firing. Result 1st A Coy, B Coy, C Coy, D Coy. Shooting on the whole Good. Voluntary Church Service in the Evening.	

Army Form C. 2118.

Instructions regarding War Diaries and Intelligence Summaries are contained in F. S. Regs., Part II and the Staff Manual respectively. Title pages will be prepared in manuscript.

WAR DIARY
or
INTELLIGENCE SUMMARY.
(Erase heading not required.)

Place	Date	Hour	Summary of Events and Information	Remarks and references to Appendices
MONCHY BRETON	28/5/17		Weather continues perfect. Training from 9 a.m. to 12 noon. Battalion practice Artillery Formation. Concert by 7th [illegible] Concert Party - Excellent.	
do	29/5/17		Change in weather - overcast with rain. Battalion marched out at 5.30 [illegible] practice attacks from "Artillery formation to Assault" - [illegible] [illegible] [illegible] formation [illegible] by Colonel [illegible] [illegible] [illegible] - abandoned and training [illegible] [illegible] [illegible] [illegible] Pack [illegible] 7th [illegible] [illegible] Cour [illegible] [illegible] [illegible] for ARRAS at [illegible] a.m.	
do	30/5/17		Weather Good. [illegible] Ceremonial Parade at 10.30 a.m. for Presentation of Decorations by the Corps Commander. [illegible] [illegible] [illegible] Capt. R. E. Marrion M.C. No. 4150 L/Sgt. M. McKendrick. No. 6896 [illegible] [illegible] C.J. No. 7435 [illegible] Barker C. No. 3304 L/Cpl. MacGuire J.R. No. 1302 L/Cpl. MacLachlan [illegible] - Military Medal. [illegible] [illegible] Court [illegible] [illegible] 3rd [illegible] - [illegible] [illegible] [illegible] [illegible] [illegible] [illegible] [illegible] [illegible] 3 S.A.I. - [illegible] [illegible] [illegible]	

A5834 Wt. W4973/M687 750,000 8/16 D. D. & L. Ltd. Forms/C.2118/13.

6

Instructions regarding War Diaries and Intelligence Summaries are contained in F. S. Regs., Part II. and the Staff Manual respectively. Title pages will be prepared in manuscript.

WAR DIARY
or
INTELLIGENCE SUMMARY.
(Erase heading not required.)

Army Form C. 2118.

Place	Date	Hour	Summary of Events and Information	Remarks and references to Appendices
Monchy Breton	3/5/17		Weather – Bright & hot. Training on training area from 9 am to 1 pm. Each Company one hour Bayonet Fighting under CSM LAW – Divisional Bayonet Fighting Instructor. Also – Indication & Recognition, Rapid loading, V.T. and T.D. Explanation of Map Reading. Practice in Mutual Support. Billeting Party 1 Officer & 15 NCOs left for ARRAS by rail from LIGNY. Operation Order No 17/33 issued – Re move to ARRAS.	

D W MacLeod Lt Col
4th S A Infy.

A5834 Wt. W4973/M687 750,000 8/16 D. D. & L. Ltd. Forms/C.2118/13.

Instructions regarding War Diaries and Intelligence Summaries are contained in F. S. Regs., Part II. and the Staff Manual respectively. Title pages will be prepared in manuscript.

INTELLIGENCE SUMMARY.

(Erase heading not required.)

4th South African Infantry

Place	Date	Hour	Summary of Events and Information	Remarks and references to Appendices
MONCHY BRETON	1/6/17		Battalion left by route march for Ligny St Flochel Station at 7.30 AM Entrained & left about 10.30 A.M. & detrained at ARRAS station about 1-30 p.m. Regiment billetted in oil Works - Place St Croix. Billets the district were taken over.	
ARRAS	2/6/17		Working Party of 46 O.R. from Corps school reported. Battalion bathed in swimming pool during morning. Cleaning up billets. Town bombed at 11-30 p.m.	
ARRAS	3/6/17		Church parade - Inspection - Cleaning billets	
ARRAS	4/6/17.		Training in billets 9-30 to 12. C. Coy bathed in morning. Very fine day & quiet. Furnished Working party of 100 O.R. as a water party for 64th R.E. Hostile bombing in vicinity of town.	

Army. Wt W... ... D. D. & L. Ltd. Forms/C.2118/...

Instructions regarding War Diaries and Intelligence Summaries are contained in F. S. Regs., Part II. and the Staff Manual respectively. Title pages will be prepared in manuscript.

WAR DIARY
or
INTELLIGENCE SUMMARY.
(Erase heading not required.)

Army Form C. 2118.

4th South African Infantry

Place	Date	Hour	Summary of Events and Information	Remarks and references to Appendices
ARRAS	5/6/17		Battalion moved out to G 13 A & B for training. Did Bayonet fighting - Instruction in Flares - Indication of Targets. & Extended order Drill. Returned by 12 NOON. At 6.30 pm the Battalion (less A Coy working party) moved out 13 officers & 264 O.R. to Balmoral Camp G18 A 25 25. to act as reserve to 26th & 27th Bde operations. A party of 2nd Regt attached 4 officers and 136 O.R.	
ARRAS	6/6/17		Stayed at Balmoral camp all day. At 7 pm. Battalion moved back to billets in ARRAS.	
ARRAS	7/6/17		Battalion in billets all day. Rifle inspection - cleaning billets & Lewis gun instruction.	

A5834 Wt W4973/M687 750,000 8/16 D. D. & L. Ltd. Forms/C2118/13

Army Form C. 2118.

WAR DIARY
or
INTELLIGENCE SUMMARY.
(Erase heading not required.)

Instructions regarding War Diaries and Intelligence Summaries are contained in F. S. Regs., Part II. and the Staff Manual respectively. Title pages will be prepared in manuscript.

4th South African Infantry

Place	Date	Hour	Summary of Events and Information	Remarks and references to Appendices
ARRAS	8/6/17		At 7.30 am moved out to G13B for training - Practised Bayonet fighting - Rapid Loading with & without respirators. Laying out trenches. Indication of Targets. Returned to billets 11.30 am	
ARRAS	9/6/17		Furnished working party of 3 Officers & 100 OR to cut wire in H.16. During the night.	
ARRAS	10/6/17		Sunday - Brigade HQrs moved to "Y" Huts near ETRUN. Battalion plus 100 Rifles of 2nd Regt (less A Coy wkg party) moved to Stirling camp H13d89 as reserve battalion under orders G.O.C 26th Bde. Moved from ARRAS 6.45 pm. on arrival found not required & moved back to ARRAS Billets at once. All back by 10 pm. Rained heavily during night. Parties of 1st - 2nd & 3rd Regts attached to us whilst left in ARRAS area. All working parties	

Instructions regarding War Diaries and Intelligence Summaries are contained in F. S. Regs., Part II. and the Staff Manual respectively. Title pages will be prepared in manuscript.

Army Form C. 2118.

WAR DIARY
or
INTELLIGENCE SUMMARY.
(Erase heading not required.)

4th South African Infantry

Place	Date	Hour	Summary of Events and Information	Remarks and references to Appendices
ARRAS	11/6/17		Rifle Inspection in morning:- Furnished working party 200 O.R. under Capt Gemmell to cut wire in H 16 west of German trenches. Party left 8.30 p.m. Draft of 55 O.R. and 9 O.R. (ex Divisional Area) reported from SAVY. Mostly old hands.	
ARRAS	12/6/17		Arras shelled with 11" shells from app: 7-30 a.m. to 9 a.m. one fell within 50 yards of Regtl mess. Very hot day:-	
ARRAS	13/6/17		Battalion found 10 officers & 310 O.R. plus 2 officers & 80 O.R. of 1st Regt attached as working party under Chief Engineer XVII Corps making up repairing road from G24 B88 to H19 B46. Work from 8 AM to 5 p.m. Fine weather.	

Instructions regarding War Diaries and Intelligence Summaries are contained in F. S. Regs., Part II. and the Staff Manual respectively. Title pages will be prepared in manuscript.

Army Form C. 2118.

WAR DIARY
or
INTELLIGENCE SUMMARY.
(Erase heading not required.)

4th South African Infantry

Place	Date	Hour	Summary of Events and Information	Remarks and references to Appendices
ARRAS	14/6/17		Battalion found 10 officers & 318 O.R. plus 2 officers and 75 O.R. of 1st S.A.I. for working party as yesterday. Very fine weather.	
ARRAS	15/6/17		Battalion found 10 officers and 313 O.R. plus 2 officers and 75 O.R. of 1st S.A.I. for working party as yesterday. Draft of 90 reinforcements & 2 from hospital joined the Battalion, & isolated as being measles contacts	
ARRAS	16/6/17		Battalion found 7 officers & 210 O.R. plus 1 officer & 50 O.R. of 1st S.A.I. for working party as yesterday	
ARRAS	17/6/17		Town shelled with either 11" or 15" shells in morning. At 5 p.m. Battalion with all details of 1st, 2nd & 3rd Regts attached moved to Y Huts near ETRUN approx L.1.D.6.8 Map 51 C N.E. 2nd Regt details rejoined their regt on arrival	

Instructions regarding War Diaries and Intelligence Summaries are contained in F. S. Regs., Part II. and the Staff Manual respectively. Title pages will be prepared in manuscript.

Army Form C. 2118.

WAR DIARY
or
INTELLIGENCE SUMMARY.
(Erase heading not required.)

4th South African Infantry

Place	Date	Hour	Summary of Events and Information	Remarks and references to Appendices
Y. HUTS	18/6/17		Kit inspection in morning. In afternoon details of 1st & 3rd Regts reformed their battalions.	
Y. HUTS	19/6/17		Parade 6 to 7 A.M. Saluting drill & arms drill. Heavy Rain interfered with training from then on till 1 p.m.	
Y. HUTS	20/6/17		Rain 6. A M to 8. A.M. stopped parades. From 9 A M to 1 P.M. carried on judging distance. Extended order drill. Bayonet fighting & rapid loading. In afternoon the whole regiment cleaned their equipment. Had a regimental Guest night	

A5834 Wt. W4973 M687 750,000 8/16 D. D. & L. Ltd. Forms/C.2118/13

Army Form C. 2118.

WAR DIARY
or
INTELLIGENCE SUMMARY.
(Erase heading not required.)

Instructions regarding War Diaries and Intelligence Summaries are contained in F. S. Regs., Part II. and the Staff Manual respectively. Title pages will be prepared in manuscript.

4th South African Infantry

Place	Date	Hour	Summary of Events and Information	Remarks and references to Appendices
Y. HUTS ETRUN	21/6/17		6 A.M. to 8 A.M. Marching and Bayonet fighting. 9 A.M. to 1 NOON. Route March & artillery formations by platoons, companies, & as a battalion, also extending for attack from same. Signallers - Bombers & L. G. classes as usual. Draft of 48 arrived about 4.30 pm. all but 6 were B.E.F. men. Officers instructed in map reading	
Y Huts ETRUN	22/6/17		Each company had two hours on the rifle range. 5 Rounds application & 15 Rounds Rapid. The last two Lewis Gun classes did two hours practice. Weather showery all day. Classes & Coys in addition did two hours training	
Y Huts	23/6/17		Training 6 to 8 & 9 to 1. Use of Smoke Bombs & flares - Firing rifle grenades & Rapid Loading - Demonstration of rapid wiring - attack practice - Passing orders	

Wt. W. ... D. D. & L. Ltd. Forms/C. 2118/13.

Instructions regarding War Diaries and Intelligence Summaries are contained in F. S. Regs., Part II. and the Staff Manual respectively. Title pages will be prepared in manuscript.

WAR DIARY
or
INTELLIGENCE SUMMARY.
(*Erase heading not required.*)

Army Form C. 2118.

4th South African Infantry

Place	Date	Hour	Summary of Events and Information	Remarks and references to Appendices
	23/6/17		Battalion drilled by C.O. Instructional classes for Signallers, Lewis Gunners & Bombers.	
	24/6/17		Church parades - Lovely weather. Inter platoon football.	
	25/6/17		Training 6-8 & 9-1. Saluting & Marching - Grenadiers firing rifle Grenades; N.C.O.s under Bayonet Instructor, Rest of Coy on Lewis Guns - Pamphlet SS 163 read & explained to men - Rapid Wiring - Platoon attacks - attack formation & changing direction in Artillery formation - Had specimen ~~[illegible]~~ shown to all ranks of correct Dress for Marching Order & Fighting Order. Signallers - Bombers - Lewis Gun instructional classes.	

Instructions regarding War Diaries and Intelligence Summaries are contained in F. S. Regs., Part II. and the Staff Manual respectively. Title pages will be prepared in manuscript.

WAR DIARY
or
INTELLIGENCE SUMMARY.
(Erase heading not required.)

Army Form C. 2118.

4th South African Infantry

Place	Date	Hour	Summary of Events and Information	Remarks and references to Appendices
Y Huts	26/6/17		Training 6–8 & 9–1 noon – Physical Drill & Bayonet fighting –	
			Company Drill – Throwing Dummy Bombs & wearing box respirators –	
			Platoon attack – Grenadiers firing rifle grenades and Lewis Guns	
			Instruction in Guard Mounting –	
			Instructional classes in Signalling – Bombing – Lewis Guns	
Y Huts	27/6/17		Training 9 A.M. to 12 noon and 9 p.m. to 12 midnight	
			In morning Physical Drill & Bayonet fighting – Antigas	
			instruction & Drill. Battalion Drill.	
			In evening Outposts & Patrols	
			Instructional classes in Signalling – Lewis guns & Bombers	
			Subaltern Officers under instruction	

Instructions regarding War Diaries and Intelligence Summaries are contained in F. S. Regs., Part II. and the Staff Manual respectively. Title pages will be prepared in manuscript.

Army Form C. 2118.

WAR DIARY
or
INTELLIGENCE SUMMARY.
(Erase heading not required.)

4th South African Infantry

Place	Date	Hour	Summary of Events and Information	Remarks and references to Appendices
Y. Huts	28/6/17		9 am to 1 noon. Bathing – antigas instructions – 7th Co's under Gym Instructor. Rain interfered with proposed night training.	
Y. Huts	29/6/17		9 A.M. to 2 pm Training in platoon attack Instructional classes for Signallers – Lewis gunners & bombers. Fine day.	
Y Huts	30/6/17		6 A.M. to 3 pm. A. B & C. Coys on range & Bombing ground. Each man firing Lewis gun & throwing live bombs. Weather rainy & D Coy still to go through as too wet for good training after 3 pm.	

D M MacLeod
Lt Col Commdg
4th S A I

B E F.
30/6/17

Forms/C. 2118/[illegible]

Instructions regarding War Diaries and Intelligence Summaries are contained in F. S. Regs., Part II. and the Staff Manual respectively. Title pages will be prepared in manuscript.

WAR DIARY
or
INTELLIGENCE SUMMARY.
(Erase heading not required.)

Army Form C. 2118.

4th South African Infantry – July-17

Vol 16

Place	Date	Hour	Summary of Events and Information	Remarks and references to Appendices
Y. Huts ETRUN	1/7/1917		Church parades. Fine weather.	
Y. Huts	2/7/1917		6 am to 8 A.M. Training. Saluting Drill – Marching – Instruction in use of extended order signals – Bayonet fighting. 9-15 to 9.45 March to training ground. 9.45 to 1. pm. Platoon attack, Instruction in use of German machine gun – Instruction in use of tank signals. Platoon attack. Extended order drill. Specialists – Signalling, Lewis Gun, Grenadiers and Scout classes. Draft of 130 O.R. joined of whom 29. B.E.F. & 101 new. Divisional Gas Cpl inspected all P.H. helmets	
Y. Huts	3/7/17		8-10 am D. Coy Lewis gun practice & musketry. 10-4 pm. All Coys 5 Rounds application and 15 Rounds rapid. 4-6 Lewis Gunners practising with ball cartridge. Divisional Gas Cpl inspected all Box Respirators.	

Instructions regarding War Diaries and Intelligence Summaries are contained in F. S. Regs., Part II. and the Staff Manual respectively. Title pages will be prepared in manuscript.

WAR DIARY
or
INTELLIGENCE SUMMARY.
(Erase heading not required.)

Army Form C. 2118.

4th South African Infantry - July - 1917

Place	Date	Hour	Summary of Events and Information	Remarks and references to Appendices
Y. HUTS	4/7/17		Wet morning. After breakfast practised a battalion attack.	
Y HUTS	5/7/17		Carried out a battalion attack for some officers from Salonika.	
Y. HUTS ETRUN	6/7/17		Moved to Berneville at 2-30 p.m. Spent morning cleaning up. Camp Commandant very satisfied with way the block of hutments handed over. On arrival in Berneville battalion billetted partly in huts partly in barns. Draft of 14 joined in evening.	
BERNEVILLE	7/7/17		A day off. Men cleaning up equipment and new quarters: Inoculated ~~all~~ men who had not been done for 12 months.	

Army Form C. 2118.

WAR DIARY
or
INTELLIGENCE SUMMARY.

(Erase heading not required.)

Instructions regarding War Diaries and Intelligence Summaries are contained in F. S. Regs., Part II. and the Staff Manual respectively. Title pages will be prepared in manuscript.

4th South African Infantry – July – 1917

Place	Date	Hour	Summary of Events and Information	Remarks and references to Appendices
Bernsville	8/7/17		Church parades	
Bernsville	9/7/17		Training 6 AM to 8 AM. Saluting Drill – Physical Drill – Bayonet Fighting – Marching. Battalion Bathing all day, & so many men off through inoculation that parades after 9 A.M. cancelled.	
Bernsville	10/7/17		8.30 AM Battalion moved to Training ground R.16.B. Dinners on ground. 10 – 12.30 Platoon attacks. After dinner company attack practice & marched home. Back about 4 p.m. Draft of 34 O.R. joined	
Bernsville	11/7/17		Range at Simencourt. All coys 5 Rounds at Head & Shoulders & 15 Rounds Rapid. All Lewis gunners firing with Lewis guns. All companies also did two hours attack practice. Sent D Coy & part A Coy – 6 officers & 191 O.R. to AUXI. [10 3rd Army School]	
Bernsville	12/7/17		6.15 Battalion moved to Training Ground. Breakfast on ground. Did Platoon & Company attack practice. Dismissed about 2 p.m.	

Instructions regarding War Diaries and Intelligence Summaries are contained in F. S. Regs., Part II. and the Staff Manual respectively. Title pages will be prepared in manuscript.

WAR DIARY or INTELLIGENCE SUMMARY.

(Erase heading not required.)

Army Form C. 2118.

4th S.A.I. July - 1917.

Place	Date	Hour	Summary of Events and Information	Remarks and references to Appendices
Bernaville	13/7/17		At 6-15 A.M. Battalion moved off to Training ground south of River Brinchon. Practised in company & in Battalion attack on trenches. Home & dismissed about 2 p.m.	
Bernaville	14/7/17		Carried out a battalion scheme as per O.O. I 3. in morning. Brigade Aquatic sports in afternoon.	
Bernaville	15/7/17		Church parades.	
Bernaville	16/7/17		Range at Simencourt. 5 Rounds Rapid, 2 lots of 10 Rounds Rapid - 4 Rounds at Disappearing Targets. In afternoon competitions. 15 O.R. Draft arrived.	
Bernaville	17/7/17		Battalion moved out at 8 A.M. to R23a29, & practised a Battalion attack on trenches each platoon, leapfrog fashion, taking a trench. Marched home at 12.30 p.m. The grenadiers in afternoon put through live grenade practice.	

Instructions regarding War Diaries and Intelligence Summaries are contained in F. S. Regs., Part II. and the Staff Manual respectively. Title pages will be prepared in manuscript.

WAR DIARY
or
INTELLIGENCE SUMMARY.
(Erase heading not required.)

Army Form C. 2118.

4th S. A. I. July - 1917.

Place.	Date	Hour	Summary of Events and Information	Remarks and references to Appendices
BERNEVILLE	22/7/17		Church parades in morning Tug of war against 5th Camerons in afternoon & lost to them.	
Berneville	23/7/17		8 A.M. to 2 p.m. Marched to & from training ground at R 17 D. Practised outposts & advancing in open order from 10 p.m. to 1 p.m. Played 5th Camerons at Soccer.	
BERNEVILLE	24/7/17		Musketry in morning. Each company did two hours. Ordinary men doing 5 Rounds application and 15 Rounds. All bad shots specially coached & fired 15 rounds each under supervision. In evening paraded at 9 p.m. & did patrols & general trench work in the dark.	
BERNEVILLE	25/7/17		Each company did a three hours route march from 7 to 10 A.M. in full marching order.	

A5834 Wt. W4973 M687 750,000 8/16 D. D. & L. Ltd. Forms/C.2118/11.

Instructions regarding War Diaries and Intelligence Summaries are contained in F. S. Regs., Part II. and the Staff Manual respectively. Title pages will be prepared in manuscript.

WAR DIARY
or
INTELLIGENCE SUMMARY.

(Erase heading not required.)

Army Form C. 2118.

4th S. A. I. July 1917

Place	Date	Hour	Summary of Events and Information	Remarks and references to Appendices
BERNEVILLE	18/7/17		Battalion took part in a Brigade Tactical Scheme attacking a front line system of trenches. Moved from billets at 7.45 a.m. back about 2 p.m.	
Berneville	19/7/17		Battalion moved at 8 AM to R17, & carried out an outpost scheme – Back in billets 1 p.m. Draft of 3 O.R. arrived	
Berneville	20/7/17		Battalion training at R.1.C from 8-30 to 12-30 p.m. Physical Drill & Bayonet fighting – Throwing Dummy bombs – Squad Drill & Saluting – Rapid Loading	
Berneville	21/7/17		Battalion training at R 1 C. 8 30 to 12 30 p.m. Rapid Loading with & without Box respirators – Antigas Drill & lecture – Physical Drill & Bayonet fighting – Handling arms Saluting & marching. Bathing allotted for whole day.	

Instructions regarding War Diaries and Intelligence Summaries are contained in F. S. Regs., Part II. and the Staff Manual respectively. Title pages will be prepared in manuscript.

Army Form C. 2118.

WAR DIARY
or
INTELLIGENCE SUMMARY.
(Erase heading not required.)

4th S.A.I. July 1917.

Place	Date	Hour	Summary of Events and Information	Remarks and references to Appendices
BERNEVILLE	26/7/17		No parades. Cleaning up quarters & generally squaring up. Part of our transport left by road at 8 AM, rest at 8 pm to entrain at SAULTY	
BERNEVILLE	27/7/17		~~Mat~~ Battalion moved at 2-20 p.m. Reached BEAUMETZ les LOGES at 3-10 p.m. and entrained. Left at 4.40 p.m. via ARRAS & ACHIECOURT LE GRAND to BAPAUME where detrained at 7-30 p.m. At 9.30 p.m H.Q. A & B Coys left by light railway & got to south end of YTRES about 2.30 AM & marched to BERTINCOURT with part of A & B not following later. C Coy left BAPAUME at 2 AM & reached YTRES siding No 27 about 5 AM & bivouacked. Left our billets at BERNEVILLE very clean.	
BERTINCOURT	28/7/17		Moved at 9-20 AM to YTRES & relieved 6th London Regt of 174th Bde at YTRES as 9th DIVISIONAL reserve. 6th London one of the cleanest regiments we have taken our billets from. At 2 p.m. found a working party of 100 O.R. for O.C. Depot Battalion at BUS. Had only 5 men at sick parade.	

A5834 Wt. W4973/M687 750,000 8/16 D. D. & L. Ltd. Forms/C.2118/13.

Army Form C. 2118.

WAR DIARY
or
INTELLIGENCE SUMMARY.
(Erase heading not required.)

[..]ructions regarding War Diaries and Intelligence Summaries are contained in F. S. Regs., Part II. and the Staff Manual respectively. Title pages will be prepared in manuscript.

4th S.A.I. JULY 1917

Place	Date	Hour	Summary of Events and Information	Remarks and references to Appendices
YTRES	29/7/17		Heavy rain all morning – Cleaning up camp.	
YTRES	30/7/17		Found a working party of 100 O.R. for Depot Battalion. Drilled under company arrangements from 9 to 12 noon. Company commanders visited the line. 2/Lt Bell reported	
YTRES	31/7/17		Drilled from 9 to 10.30 and cleaned up for tomorrow's inspection. Heavy rain afternoon & evening. 2/Lt Allen Reported.	
			In the field 1–8–17. D. M. MacLeod Lt Col. Commdg 4th South African Infantry	

A5834 Wt. W4973/M687 750,000 8/16 D. D. & L. Ltd. Forms/C.2118/13.

Army Form C. 2118.

Instructions regarding War Diaries and Intelligence Summaries are contained in F. S. Regs., Part II. and the Staff Manual respectively. Title pages will be prepared in manuscript.

WAR DIARY
or
INTELLIGENCE SUMMARY.
(Erase heading not required.)

4th South African Infantry. August - 1917.

Place	Date	Hour	Summary of Events and Information	Remarks and references to Appendices
YTRES	1/8/17		A.B.T.C. boys inspected by 4th Corps Commander at YTRES at 10 A.M. Drizzling rain nearly all day. D Coy returned from Auxi le Chateau in afternoon. D Company reported back from AUXI LE CHATEAU.	
YTRES	2/8/17		Wet weather. Companies lectured, & specialists under instruction.	
YTRES	3/8/17		Drizzly rain all day. - Supplied Divisional Guard. Battalion moved into line & relieved 2nd Regt in TRESCAULT left Sub Sector with Battalion Headquarters at Q 10 A 44 Map 57CSE. The Battalion has in line 3 platoons per Coy. The other platoons & underage men moved to NEUVILLE BOURJONVAL at 1-30 p.m, the Transport & Q M Stores to lines at V 6 A. The battalion going into line entrained at CANTEEN SIDING, YTRES on DECAUVILLE railway at 8 p.m. in 4 trains of 7	

A5834 Wt. W4973/M687 750,000 8/16 D. D. & L. Ltd. Forms/C.2118/13.

Instructions regarding War Diaries and Intelligence Summaries are contained in F. S. Regs., Part II. and the Staff Manual respectively. Title pages will be prepared in manuscript.

WAR DIARY
or
INTELLIGENCE SUMMARY.
(Erase heading not required.)

Army Form C. 2118.

4th S.A.I. August-1917.

Place	Date	Hour	Summary of Events and Information	Remarks and references to Appendices
YTRES	3/8/17		trucks each, leaving at 10 minutes interval, detrained clear of wood in Q 9 D, each platoon met by a guide. Relief went smoothly & relief reported complete to Brigade at 11-45 pm. No patrols out.	
TRESCAULT LEFT SUB.SECTOR	4/8/17		Drizzling day. Companies working improving trenches. Support company finds fatigues for R.E on dugout construction. Cosy Copse shelled at intervals otherwise quiet on our sector. Two patrols out. Explosions heard in HAVRINCOURT Village. ONE O/R WDD at Duty	
TRESCAULT LEFT SUB-SECTION	5/8/17		Companies in Line deepening & improving trenches. Support Coy on fatigue for R.E on dugout construction. Artillery quiet. Enemy dropped a few shells near Regents Crater & Cosy Copse. Explosions heard in HAVRINCOURT VILLAGE	
TRESCAULT LEFT SUB SECTION	6/8/17		Companies in front line. Deepening & improving trenches also put in 35 coils of wire in front of Sapheads. Support company finding same fatigue for R.E.	

A5834 Wt.W4973/M687 750,000 8/16 D. D. & L. Ltd. Forms/C.2118/13.

Instructions regarding War Diaries and Intelligence Summaries are contained in F. S. Regs., Part II. and the Staff Manual respectively. Title pages will be prepared in manuscript.

WAR DIARY or INTELLIGENCE SUMMARY.

(Erase heading not required.)

Army Form C. 2118.

4th S.A.I. August 1917

Place	Date	Hour	Summary of Events and Information	Remarks and references to Appendices
TRESCAULT LEFT Sub Section	6/8/17		Our artillery more active – Enemy shelled neighbourhood of COSY COPSE at intervals. Fine weather. Enemy & our aeroplanes active. No patrols sent out.	
TRESCAULT LEFT Sub Section	7/8/17		Companies in front line deepening & improving trenches & firebays & berms, also put up 34 coils of wire in front of sapheads chiefly. Misty weather. Very quiet. One patrol out. R.E. fatigue party as usual on dugouts.	
TRESCAULT LEFT SUB SECTION	8/8/17		Companies in front line deepening & improving trenches, firebays & berms; also pumping out water, especially improving trench which connects A & B saps app at Q4B66 to Q4B46. Also put up 30 coils of wire along & in front of saps. Support Coy furnished fatigues for R.E. on dugout construction. Heavy rainstorm for about 1½ hours in evening. Our artillery shelling intermittently. Enemy artillery occasionally. Fairly quiet. Two patrols out – enemy wire good	

A5834 Wt W4973/M687 750,000 8/16 D. D. & L. Ltd. Forms/C.2118/13.

Army Form C. 2118.

WAR DIARY
or
INTELLIGENCE SUMMARY.
(Erase heading not required.)

Instructions regarding War Diaries and Intelligence Summaries are contained in F. S. Regs., Part II. and the Staff Manual respectively. Title pages will be prepared in manuscript.

Place	Date	Hour	Summary of Events and Information	Remarks and references to Appendices
TRESCAULT LEFT SUB SECTION	9/8/17		Companies working as usual. Relieved in evening by 2nd S.A.I. 2nd S.A.I. commenced to pass Batt H.Q. at 9.20 p.m. Relief complete in trenches at 12.46 a.m. On relief Battalion moved to METZ as Battalion in Brigade Reserve.	
METZ EN COUTURES	10/8/17		Battalion found two working parties of 50 each. Divisional Baths allotted from 2.30 to 4 p.m.	
METZ EN COUTURES	11/8/17		Battalion found the following working parties:- 5 Officers and 200 O.R. for Divisional Signal Coy. 3 Officers and 150 O.R. for 65th Field Coy R.E. and 3 Officers and 91 O.R. for left Battalion (2nd S.A.I.). 2nd Lieut. C.C.W. LE SUEUR appointed Acting Adjt. during Capt & Adjt. F.McE. Mitchell's absence on leave	
METZ EN COUTURES	12/8/17		Battalion found Divisional Signal Coy party and R.E. party also 2 officers and 65 O.R. for left Battn. Capt. J.E.N. Marshall and 31 O.R. Reinforcing draft:- draft inspected by Divisional Commander on arrival	
METZ EN COUTURES	13/8/17		Occasional heavy showers. Battalion working as usual and finding 10 Officers and 425 O.R. in all.	

A5834 Wt. W4973 M687 750,000 8/16 D. D. & L. Ltd. Forms/C.2118/13

Instructions regarding War Diaries and Intelligence Summaries are contained in F. S. Regs., Part II. and the Staff Manual respectively. Title pages will be prepared in manuscript.

WAR DIARY
or
INTELLIGENCE SUMMARY.
(Erase heading not required.)

Army Form C. 2118.

Place	Date	Hour	Summary of Events and Information	Remarks and references to Appendices
METZ EN COUTURES	14/8/17		Lieut R.D. Grierson reported for duty from U.K. One casualty on working party last night (seriously wounded). Battn working as usual. Draft of 8 O.R. B.E.F. men.	
METZ EN COUTURES	15/8/17		Capt Marshall to command "B" Coy. a/Capt R.E. Morrison M.C. assumes his former rank of 2nd Lt on ceasing to command a Company. Capt T. Farrell returned from Course and assumes command of "A" Coy. Promotion of to "Additional Acting Captain" of Lieut J. McCubbin and Lieut a/Capt D. Gemmell as from 20/7/17. Work as usual. Lieut R.D. Grierson temporarily attached to D Coy.	
METZ EN COUTURES	16/8/17		Heavy showers. Work as usual.	
METZ EN COUTURES	17/8/17		Weather fine. Battalion moved into line and relieved 2nd Regt in TRESCAULT left Sub-Section. The Battalion	

A5834 Wt. W4973 M687 750,000 8/16 D. D. & L. Ltd. Forms/C.2118/

Army Form C. 2118.

WAR DIARY
or
INTELLIGENCE SUMMARY.

(*Erase heading not required.*)

Instructions regarding War Diaries and Intelligence Summaries are contained in F. S. Regs., Part II. and the Staff Manual respectively. Title pages will be prepared in manuscript.

Place	Date	Hour	Summary of Events and Information	Remarks and references to Appendices
METZ EN COUTURES	17/8/17		~~will~~ hold the line with 3 Companies - one Platoon per Company with details to EQUANCOURT. The Battalion left METZ EN COUTURES at 8-30 p.m. moving by Platoons with an interval of 100 yards - The relief went very smoothly and was complete at 11-45 p.m. No Patrols out.	
TRESCAULT SUB-SECTION	18/8/17		Weather fine: Quiet all day. A minor operation took place on our left at 10.50 p.m. Our Artillery put down a heavy barrage lasting until 11-30 p.m. Enemy retaliation weak - quite a number of heavy T.Ms were put over our sub-section without much damage. The operation appeared to have been very successful	

Army Form C. 2118.

WAR DIARY
or
INTELLIGENCE SUMMARY.
(Erase heading not required.)

Instructions regarding War Diaries and Intelligence Summaries are contained in F. S. Regs., Part II. and the Staff Manual respectively. Title pages will be prepared in manuscript.

Place	Date	Hour	Summary of Events and Information	Remarks and references to Appendices
TRESCAULT SUB-SECTION	19/8/17		Companies working hard. Sub-section fairly quiet until 3.30pm when heavy minnenwerfer began firing into "D" Sap causing two casualties & some damage. Casualties were 2nd LIEUT. T. M. MACMILLAN and SERGT R.S. KINGWELL both Killed. The bodies were taken over by 2nd SAI who very kindly arranged all details of burial at METZ for tomorrow. 2nd LIEUT H.W. BACKEBERG sent to hospital suffering from poisoned right arm. 2nd LIEUTS BENNINGFIELD and PATTERSON wired for from Detail Camp to replace. Weather Fine.	
TRESCAULT SUB-SECTION	20/8/17		Weather fine. Companies working as usual. New trench connecting Bass Lane with "A" Sap begun, under supervision of R.E. - 2 Platoons "A" Coy and 60 OR of 2nd SAI on work. Minnenwerfer which is doing great damage to "D" Sap & also killed 2nd Macmillan and Sgt Kingwell located at K 34. C. 15. 90. - Artillery have	

A5834 Wt. W4973/M687 750,000 8/16 D. D. & L. Ltd. Forms/C.2118/

Army Form C. 2118.

Instructions regarding War Diaries and Intelligence Summaries are contained in F. S. Regs., Part II. and the Staff Manual respectively. Title pages will be prepared in manuscript.

WAR DIARY
or
INTELLIGENCE SUMMARY.

(Erase heading not required.)

Place	Date	Hour	Summary of Events and Information	Remarks and references to Appendices
Trescault Sub Section			it marked and retaliate at given signal from us – Minenwerfer ceases fire immediately guns get on. The burial of 2nd Lt. MACMILLAN and Sgt. KINGWELL was carried out with military honours at 11.15 AM. at METZ EN COUTURE military cemetery. (Q.27.A.2.5) The firing party of 1 Officer and 20 O.R. was supplied by the 2nd S.A.I. The burial service was conducted jointly by the Revds MENZIES and WILSON. MAJOR HUNT & 5 of our officers attended.	
Trescault Sub Section	21/8/17		Weather continues fine. Companies working well. New Trench developing rapidly. Acting Brigadier accompanied by the Divisional Commander visits this sub section. Our signallers pick up a message from German observation balloon who is signalling to somebody on ground. – message forwarded to B.H.Qrs. Aircraft active otherwise day very quiet.	
Trescault Sub-Section	22/8/17		Weather still fine. Companies working hard. Day very quiet. 2 O.R. put out in Femy Bank last night were out all day and	

Army Form C. 2118.

WAR DIARY
or
INTELLIGENCE SUMMARY.
(Erase heading not required.)

Instructions regarding War Diaries and Intelligence Summaries are contained in F. S. Regs., Part II. and the Staff Manual respectively. Title pages will be prepared in manuscript.

Place	Date	Hour	Summary of Events and Information	Remarks and references to Appendices
TRESCAULT SUB-SECTION	22/8/17		returned at 9.30 pm with useful information. One O.R. casualty - Gunshot wound ~~right~~ left arm. New trench completed but for five days.	
TRESCAULT. SUB-SECTION	23/8/17		Fairly quiet day - some small shells towards BILHEM FARM and near "C" Coy Headquarters. Two casualties: O.R. 1 wounded at duty and one self inflicted revolver wound, right hand, not serious. 2nd Lieuts C.A.A. MacLean and F.A. Webb and 36 O.R. reported at Detail Camp today. 2/Lt. C.A.A. MacLean readmitted to S.A.F.A. suffering from old wound. 2nd Lt. S.D.M. SALAMAN returned from hospital. Capt. F. McE. Mitchell returned from leave.	
TRESCAULT SUB-SECTION	24/8/17		Very fine weather. Fairly quiet. Enemy aircraft active.	

A5834 Wt. W4973 M687 750,000 8/16 D. D. & L. Ltd. Forms/C.2118/13.

Army Form C. 2118.

WAR DIARY
or
INTELLIGENCE SUMMARY.

(Erase heading not required.)

Instructions regarding War Diaries and Intelligence Summaries are contained in F. S. Regs., Part II. and the Staff Manual respectively. Title pages will be prepared in manuscript.

Place	Date	Hour	Summary of Events and Information	Remarks and references to Appendices
RESCAULT R.E. SECTION	25/8/17		25 Officers and some O.R. of 36th Division inspected the sub section. Weather fine. Fairly quiet all day. A few shells fell near Cosy Copse without damage. Heavy Minnenwerfer still troublesome in D Sap and caused 4 casualties early on morning of 24th 3 wounded & one very badly shaken. 2nd Lt Backeberg reported back from Hospital. Capt. F McE Mitchell assumes duty as Adjutant.	
RESCAULT R.E. SECTION	26/8/17		Cloudy day. Enemy shelling back areas very heavily and vicinity of Cosy Copse shelled. Colonel Dalrymple accompanied by the Acting Brigadier visited the Regiment and was taken round the trenches and personally fired a Lewis Gun etc at the enemy's lines. Lt Col Macleod D.S.O. proceeds on leave to U.K. Major C.M. Browne M.C. takes command of Battalion and Capt F McE Mitchell second in Command. 2 Casualties (G.S.W.) 1 wounded at duty and one to CCS not serious	

A3834 Wt. W4973 M687 750,000 8/16 D. D. & L. Ltd. Forms/C.2118/13

Instructions regarding War Diaries and Intelligence Summaries are contained in F. S. Regs., Part II. and the Staff Manual respectively. Title pages will be prepared in manuscript.

WAR DIARY
or
INTELLIGENCE SUMMARY.
(Erase heading not required.)

Army Form C. 2118.

Place	Date	Hour	Summary of Events and Information	Remarks and references to Appendices
TRESCAULT SUB-SECTION	27/8/17	27/8/17	Raining hard all day. Very Quiet but for a about 40 small shells on Cory Copse. Officers and NCOs of 36th Division inspected the trenches.	
TRESCAULT SUB-SECTION	28/8/17		Cloudy and a high wind blowing. Very Quiet. 1 casualty bullet wound left arm - not serious. The Battalion was relieved by the 10th Royal Irish Rifles. The 10th R.I.R. came up by light Railway and arrived at 8.35 pm. Relief was complete at 10.35 pm - everything went very smoothly. The Battalion proceeded by light Railway to the outskirts of BUS and marched into Camp for the night at BARASTRE - 4 trains were used - the last trainload arriving in Camp at 1 AM. Details under Major Hunt had moved into camp during the day and had everything prepared.	

A5834 Wt. W4973/M687 750,000 8/16 D. D. & L. Ltd. Forms/C.2118/13.

Instructions regarding War Diaries and Intelligence Summaries are contained in F. S. Regs., Part II. and the Staff Manual respectively. Title pages will be prepared in manuscript.

WAR DIARY
or
INTELLIGENCE SUMMARY.

(Erase heading not required.)

Army Form C. 2118.

Place	Date	Hour	Summary of Events and Information	Remarks and references to Appendices
BARASTRE to ACHIET LE PETIT.	29/8/17		The Battalion minus "C" Coy, with the remainder of the Brigade embussed at BARASTRE at 9AM for ACHIET LE PETIT arriving about 11.30AM – owing to lack of accommodation in BEDFORD Camp "D" Coy is billeted in the village. 12 buses returned to BARASTRE for "C" Company which arrived at BEDFORD CAMP at 3.30 PM. Raining steadily. Major D.R. HUNT assumes command and MAJOR C.M. Browne M.C. 2nd in Command.	
ACHIET LE PETIT.	30/8/17		Intermittent showers of rain all day. The day was devoted to cleaning up and making Camp more comfortable.	
ACHIET LE PETIT.	31/8/17		8.30 AM to 9AM Battalion inspection by C/O. 9AM to 11.20 Bayonet fighting and Physical Exercises. Anti Gas instruction, arms drill etc with Gas appliances fixed. 10.40am to 12.10 pm Musketry – Rapid Loading with Ball ammunition. Saluting 12.10 pm to 12.30 pm. Battalion drill under C/O. Bathing allotted for whole afternoon.	

B.E.F.
3/9/17

D.R. Hunt Major
Temp. Commdg 4th R. S. Fusiliers

A5834 Wt. W4973/M687 750,000 8/16 D. D. & L. Ltd. Forms/C.2118/13.

Instructions regarding War Diaries and Intelligence Summaries are contained in F. S. Regs., Part II. and the Staff Manual respectively. Title pages will be prepared in manuscript.

WAR DIARY
or
INTELLIGENCE SUMMARY.
(Erase heading not required.)

4 S A Infy Bn 1/9

Vol 18

Army Form C. 2118.

Place	Date	Hour	Summary of Events and Information	Remarks and references to Appendices
ACHIET LE PETIT.	1/9/17		Weather cloudy. Strong wind blowing. Training 8.30 AM to 12.30 p.m. Battalion drill, Saluting, Musketry: firing 15 rounds rapid on Range, Squad drill, bayonet fighting. In the afternoon ~~[illegible]~~ the Battalion played the 2nd S.A.I. at Soccer, good clean, fast game: result 5 goals to Nil in our favour.	
ACHIET LE PETIT.	2/9/17		Church parades. Lovely weather. Inter Platoon football (Soccer). The Battalion team played the S.A.M.C. at Rugby. Very good clean football. Result: 13 points to 3 in favour of S.A.M.C.	
ACHIET LE PETIT.	3/9/17		Training: 8.30 AM to 12.30 pm. Musketry, lecture to Section Leaders on [illegible] in attack. Extended order and covering fire with [illegible] fixed. Platoon and Company drill. Bayonet fighting & physical drill. 2-4 pm Attack scheme "A" & "B" Coys attacking & "C" & "D" defending & counter attacking [illegible]. Draft of 1 WO & 12 OR of whom 11 are old B.E.F. men.	

A5834 Wt. W4973/M687 750,000 8/16 D. D. & L. Ltd. Forms/C.2118/13.

Army Form C. 2118.

WAR DIARY
or
INTELLIGENCE SUMMARY.
(Erase heading not required.)

Instructions regarding War Diaries and Intelligence Summaries are contained in F. S. Regs., Part II. and the Staff Manual respectively. Title pages will be prepared in manuscript.

Place	Date	Hour	Summary of Events and Information	Remarks and references to Appendices
ACHIET LE PETIT.	4/9/17		Lovely weather. Training 8.30 to 11 Am Battalion drill by C/O. Bayonet fighting and Physical exercise Close order drill as a Company. Dinner at 11-30 Am 12-15 to 6 p.m. Tactical exercise of Platoon in Attacks with ball ammunition on field firing Range. Companies formed into 3 strong Platoons for this exercise. 6 p.m. we played Soccer against Brigade H.Q. signals. good football. Result: 2 goals to nil in our favour.	
ACHIET LE PETIT	5/9/17		Training 8.30 to 12.30. Battalion inspection after which Battalion marched to Training Ground. Demonstration of Company in attacks as carried out by "D" Company at AUXI LE CHATEAU - NO ball ammunition used. From 1 pm onwards Battalion Sports: "D" Company won most events. Lovely weather.	
ACHIET LE PETIT.	6/9/17		Training 8.30 to 9.15. Battalion inspection and march to training ground	

A5834 Wt. W4973/M687 750,000 8/16 D. D. & L. Ltd. Forms/C.2118/

Army Form C. 2118.

WAR DIARY
or
INTELLIGENCE SUMMARY.
(Erase heading not required.)

Instructions regarding War Diaries and Intelligence Summaries are contained in F. S. Regs., Part II. and the Staff Manual respectively. Title pages will be prepared in manuscript.

Place	Date	Hour	Summary of Events and Information	Remarks and references to Appendices
ACHIET LE PETIT	6/9/17		9.15 - to 12.30 p.m. Trench to trench attack by Companies on two Platoon frontage as per S.S. 135. and the same attack repeated under command of Section leaders only. 2 pm. to 3.30 pm Companies practice advancing over the open and making use of shell holes 3.30 - 4 pm. marching back to camp. The Battalion team played a team of the 5th Camerons at Soccer. ground very wet and slippery. result 2 goals to NIL in our favour.	
ACHIET LE PETIT	7/9/17		7.15 A.M. The Battalion proceeded by Route March to the BUTTE dE WARLENCOURT and went over the ground where the Regiment was engaged during the second operations on the SOMME in October last year. Field Kitchens were taken. 1.15 pm. return march by same Route. Weather cloudy in morning, bright in the afternoon.	
ACHIET LE PETIT.	8/9/17		Training: 8.30. to 12.30. Battalion inspection, proceeded to training ground close	

Army Form C. 2118.

WAR DIARY
or
INTELLIGENCE SUMMARY.
(Erase heading not required.)

Instructions regarding War Diaries and Intelligence Summaries are contained in F. S. Regs., Part II. and the Staff Manual respectively. Title pages will be prepared in manuscript.

Place	Date	Hour	Summary of Events and Information	Remarks and references to Appendices
ACHIET LE PETIT.	8/9/17		Practiced the new assembly formation on a 3 Company front. also attack practice on a 3 Company front. In afternoon 2 hours were allotted for bathing. Played Soccer against 8th Black Watch team. interesting hard fought game we won by 3 goals to 1. Boxing match between DRUMME CLARK 8th Black Watch and PRIVATE THOMPSON. & 6 three minute rounds. Latter lost on points. hard, clean fight. Lovely weather.	
CHIET LE PETIT.	9/9/17		Weather misty. Church Parades. Brigade Sports from 11 A.M. Did not do well. Sports very successful. Div Commander attended and distributed prizes.	
CHIET LE PETIT.	10/9/17		Training on the ground taped off and representing the ground over which the operations up North will be carried out. Morning and afternoon attack carried out as a Battalion. Played the Seaforths team at Soccer, good game, result: draw 1 goal each.	

Army Form C. 2118.

WAR DIARY
or
INTELLIGENCE SUMMARY.
(Erase heading not required.)

Instructions regarding War Diaries and Intelligence Summaries are contained in F. S. Regs., Part II. and the Staff Manual respectively. Title pages will be prepared in manuscript.

Place	Date	Hour	Summary of Events and Information	Remarks and references to Appendices
ACHIET LE PETIT	11/9/17		Training. Morning Attack practice as a Brigade over the same ground as yesterday. Div Commander present. He also presented a parchment to Pte WOOLMORE for gallantry in the field. Rugby against the 3rd S.A.I. result 12 points to 3 in our favour. Bathing all afternoon	
ACHIET LE PETIT	12/9/17		Morning spent preparing for move from the 6th Corps Area. Leave Camp at 8.30 pm. to entrain at BAPAUME WEST for POPERINGHE AREA. Battalion moved at 8 p.m. via GREVILLERS to BAPAUME WEST. Camp handed over very clean. Reached station at 10-15 p.m. & had tea for men. Entrained at 11-30 p.m. less D Coy. Left VI th Corps.	
WATOU AREA 2 L	13/9/17		Train left 12-30 am via St POL & HAZEBROUCK & detrained at GODEWAERSVELDE at 1 p.m. app. & marched to SHRINE CAMP at L14B94. Billeted by 3.30 p.m. D Coy leaving BAPAUME WEST about 3.30 AM	

Army Form C. 2118.

WAR DIARY
or
INTELLIGENCE SUMMARY.
(Erase heading not required.)

Instructions regarding War Diaries and Intelligence Summaries are contained in F. S. Regs., Part II. and the Staff Manual respectively. Title pages will be prepared in manuscript.

Place	Date	Hour	Summary of Events and Information	Remarks and references to Appendices
	13/9/17		reached camp at about 7.30 p.m.	
SHRINE Camp WATOU AREA	14/9/17		Rested all morning. Moved at 2.20 by SWITCH ROAD north of Poperinghe to THISTLE CAMP BRANDHOEK near approx G11 B central. Billeted by 4.15 p.m. Quiet night.	
BRANDHOEK	15/9/17		Men resting. Weather fair. Commanding Officer & 2nd Lt Morrison went up to the trenches & will spend the night there returning tomorrow.	
BRANDHOEK	16/9/17		NCOs proceeded to POPERINGHE in morning to see clay model of ground over which forthcoming operations will take place – a fair percentage of officers went in the afternoon. Lecture by Div Gas Officer to Battalion on use of Gas bombs at 4.30 pm. Adjutant & Signal Officer visited the line early this morning returning at 10 AM. Weather clear.	

A5834 Wt. W4973/M687 750,000 8/16 D. D. & L. Ltd. Forms/C.2118/13.

Instructions regarding War Diaries and Intelligence Summaries are contained in F. S. Regs., Part II. and the Staff Manual respectively. Title pages will be prepared in manuscript.

Army Form C. 2118.

WAR DIARY
or
INTELLIGENCE SUMMARY.
(Erase heading not required.)

Place	Date	Hour	Summary of Events and Information	Remarks and references to Appendices
BRANDHOEK	17/9/17		Weather misty & cloudy. Battalion viewing by half companies the new clay model at Brigade HQ of ground over which attack will take place. Commanding Officer attended conference at BHQ at 10 Am At 2pm Company Commanders summoned by CO for final instructions. At 5pm the Battalion marched to Railway siding in platoons at 200 yards interval and at 6pm entrained. On account of the the line being shelled the Regiment detrained 2 Kilos ~~this s~~ West of Ypres & marched in platoons at intervals along main road to Ypres & to the Menin Gate. Two guides per platoon waiting at Menin Gate & regiment moved into trenches without a casualty. Disposition in the trenches as follows:- Nos 1.2.3 platoons of A Coy & No 9 platoon of C Coy held the front line. No 10 platoon & No 13 to 16 platoons held a trench slightly in rear on left flank. The latter trench was camouflaged during day.	

Army Form C. 2118.

WAR DIARY
or
INTELLIGENCE SUMMARY.
(Erase heading not required.)

Instructions regarding War Diaries and Intelligence Summaries are contained in F. S. Regs., Part II. and the Staff Manual respectively. Title pages will be prepared in manuscript.

Place	Date	Hour	Summary of Events and Information	Remarks and references to Appendices
Trenches	17/18/9/17	9pm	Platoons No 4, 11, 12, 16 in Cameron Drive & B Coy in Old German Front Line	
			The following officers took part in the attack	
			Head Quarters Lt Col McLeod DSO Capt & Adjt Mitchell 2/Lt Morrison MC 2/Lt Neilla	
			A Coy Capt Tassell 2/Lt Webb, 2/Lt Arthur 2/Lt Trethewy	
			B Coy Capt McCubbin 2/Lt Saphir 2/Lt Oates 2/Lt Douglas	
			C Coy Major Browne MC 2/Lt Allen 2/Lt Salaman 2/Lt Backenberg	
			D Coy Capt Gemmill 2/Lt Forder 2/Lt Benningfield 2/Lt Mason	
			Medical Officer Capt Lawrence Chaplain Capt Menzies	

A5834 Wt. W4973 M687 750,000 8/16 D. D. & L. Ltd. Forms/C.2118

Army Form C. 2118.

WAR DIARY
or
INTELLIGENCE SUMMARY.
(*Erase heading not required.*)

Instructions regarding War Diaries and Intelligence Summaries are contained in F. S. Regs., Part II. and the Staff Manual respectively. Title pages will be prepared in manuscript.

Place	Date	Hour	Summary of Events and Information	Remarks and references to Appendices
Square Farm	17/18th 9/17		The Battalion Strength as follows	
			A Coy 4 off 143 OR	
			B " 4 " 128 OR	
			C " 4 " 132 OR	
			D " 4 " 140 O/R	
			HQ 5 " 29 O/R.	
	18th		At 6am we put down a barrage. Enemy retaliates on Frezenberg Ridge & around Square Farm. Fairly quiet the rest of the day. Rations arrived at 7.45 pm & 36 tins of Water.	
	19th		At 3AM & 5 Am our artillery very active. Enemy retaliated with very strong barrage. Our Casualties up to night of 19th 26 OR + 4 OR. At 8pm 2/Lt Morrison laid down tapes for assembly positions & at 12-30 Am on 20th report all Coys in position for attack. Raining very hard but men very cheerful & eager.	

A5834 Wt. W4973/M687 750,000 8/16 D. D. & L. Ltd. Forms/C.2118/13.

Instructions regarding War Diaries and Intelligence Summaries are contained in F. S. Regs., Part II. and the Staff Manual respectively. Title pages will be prepared in manuscript.

WAR DIARY
or
INTELLIGENCE SUMMARY.
(Erase heading not required.)

Army Form C. 2118.

Place	Date	Hour	Summary of Events and Information	Remarks and references to Appendices
	19th		At 9-30pm. HQ moved from Square Farm to Low Farm	
Low Farm	20th	4 Am	Stopped raining & at 5.40 ZERO hour our Barrage of Smoke shells & then proper barrage. As barrage lifted our men up & away. Enemy put up Golden Rain & Double Green lights and at 5.45 am his barrage came down but our men had all got clear of assembly positions.	
		6-10 Am	At 6-10 Am Intelligence Officer who had been at Borry Farm came back & reported Borry Farm captured & our men 150 yards past. At 7-10 Am C Coy reported objective taken At 7-30 Am Morrison wired from Borry Farm that Mitchells Farm had been taken. No definite news from Left Coy At 7.35 Left Coy reported that Beck House & M G position North of Beck House captured. Vickers Guns in position at Beck & Borry. At 7.45 Am Head Quarters moved to Borry Farm	

A5834 Wt. W4973 M687 750,000 8/16 D. D. & L. Ltd. Forms/C.2118/13.

Army Form C. 2118.

WAR DIARY
or
INTELLIGENCE SUMMARY.
(Erase heading not required.)

Instructions regarding War Diaries and Intelligence Summaries are contained in F. S. Regs., Part II. and the Staff Manual respectively. Title pages will be prepared in manuscript.

Place	Date	Hour	Summary of Events and Information	Remarks and references to Appendices
[Borr]y Farm	20th		About 3 pm the enemy opened exceptionally strong barrage & searched the whole front line and as far back as Beck House. Our officer casualties up to this time were. Killed 2/Lt Aitken 2/Lt Trethewy Wounded:- Capt Farrell 2/Lt. Backenbury 2/Lt Benningfield 2/Lt Mason and also Capt Mitchell who was wounded while rescuing a wounded man under heavy barrage. This barrage lasted until 6 pm when things quietened down. Rations arrived at Borry Farm but no water. During the night intermittent shell fire on both sides & night spent in consolidating further our positions.	

Army Form C. 2118.

WAR DIARY
or
INTELLIGENCE SUMMARY.

(*Erase heading not required.*)

Instructions regarding War Diaries and Intelligence Summaries are contained in F. S. Regs., Part II. and the Staff Manual respectively. Title pages will be prepared in manuscript.

Place	Date	Hour	Summary of Events and Information	Remarks and references to Appendices
Dolly Farm	20th		During the attack Mr Saphir who was on the left of the Regiment discovered that the 55th Brigade had not reached their first objective and that he was under fire from Kay North. He immediately swung his platoon round & captured the Position time 7-15 Am at about 7-25 Am 7th Kings Regiment turned up & helped consolidate.	
			Estimated our casualties about 40 %.	
			At 9-45 Am received wire from Brigade stating that enemy massing for counter-attack in valley on left front. Warned left Companies & sent 2/Lt Oates & 35 men to re-inforce 2nd Regiment left front line. Counter attack beaten off by Artillery & Rifle fire	

A5834 Wt. W4973/M687 750,000 8/16 D. D. & L. Ltd. Forms/C.2118/13.

Instructions regarding War Diaries and Intelligence Summaries are contained in F. S. Regs., Part II. and the Staff Manual respectively. Title pages will be prepared in manuscript.

WAR DIARY
or
INTELLIGENCE SUMMARY.

(Erase heading not required.)

Army Form C. 2118.

Place	Date	Hour	Summary of Events and Information	Remarks and references to Appendices
Bolly Farm	21st 9/17		At dawn rations were issued & later on water.	
			At about 10 Am Enemy aeroplanes over & dropped two bombs at Beck House & two near Bolly Farm. 2/Lt Folder wounded at Beck House.	
			At 5 pm received orders from Brigade to evacuate half the regiment but owing to 3rd Regiment showing a tremendous amount of movement, enemy immediately started very heavy artillery barrage & this kept up to 8.5 pm. This stopped all movement until 8-15 pm, guides were then sent down to Square Farm to guide up relieving platoons. During this strafe Capt Gemmell was killed.	
			The Regiment was finally relieved at about 6 Am on 22nd inst	

A3834 Wt. W4973 M687 750,000 8/16 D. D. & L. Ltd. Forms/C.2118/13.

Army Form C. 2118.

Instructions regarding War Diaries and Intelligence Summaries are contained in F. S. Regs., Part II. and the Staff Manual respectively. Title pages will be prepared in manuscript.

WAR DIARY
or
INTELLIGENCE SUMMARY.
(Erase heading not required.)

Place	Date	Hour	Summary of Events and Information	Remarks and references to Appendices
O.G. Line	22/9/17		The Battalion slept in O.G. line until 8 Am when we moved	
+ Track			to ground 200 yards W. of Mill Cott & had breakfast.	
			Battalion moved off in platoons at 200 yards interval at	
			9 Am & marched to X roads at H.7.C.4.5. (Sheet 28 NE)	
			Details joined the Regiment at 12-30 pm & the battalion	
			embussed at 2 pm for Winnezeele.	
			The Battalion arrived at Winnezeele at 5. pm	
			& took over Arras No. 1 & Arras No. 2 camps at J.11.a & J.5.c.	
WINNEZEELE	23/9/17		At 9.30 am the Commanding Officer addressed the Officers,	
			N.C.O's & men of the Battalion & thanked them for the work	
			done in the operations of the 20th inst: & following days.	
			The rest of the day was devoted to cleaning	

A5834 Wt. W4973/M687 750,000 8/16 D. D. & L. Ltd. Forms/C.2118

Army Form C. 2118.

WAR DIARY
or
INTELLIGENCE SUMMARY.
(Erase heading not required.)

Instructions regarding War Diaries and Intelligence Summaries are contained in F. S. Regs., Part II. and the Staff Manual respectively. Title pages will be prepared in manuscript.

Place	Date	Hour	Summary of Events and Information	Remarks and references to Appendices
INNEZEELE	23/9/17		clothing equipment & to bathing.	
VINNEZEELE	24/9/17		Training from 9 a.m. to 12 noon – Physical drill & Bayonet fighting, Lecture & demonstration in the use of the German machine gun, Arms drill & Lewis Gun instruction. Weather fine all day.	
VINNEZEELE	25/9/17		Weather continued fine. Routine the same as on previous day & the afternoon devoted to cleaning of equipment &c	
VINNEZEELE	26/9/17		Lieut. G. Smith reported for duty from England & Sgt. D. Macdonald promoted to 2nd Lieutenant.	
			Draft of one hundred & fifty six O/R arrived from Base.	
			Received orders to move the following day to ARNEKE area.	
			Eleven officers who are unfit for General Service struck off the strength of the Battalion	

Army Form C. 2118.

Instructions regarding War Diaries and Intelligence Summaries are contained in F. S. Regs., Part II. and the Staff Manual respectively. Title pages will be prepared in manuscript.

WAR DIARY
or
INTELLIGENCE SUMMARY.

(Erase heading not required.)

Place	Date	Hour	Summary of Events and Information	Remarks and references to Appendices
WINNEZEELE	27/9/17		Battalion moved out from WINNEZEELE at 10 am. & arrived at LEDRINGHEM at about 1.30 pm. Companies billeted in barns in different parts of the town, very scattered but accommodation good.	
LEDRINGHEM	28/9/17		Weather fine – In view of the draft which had just arrived the day was allocated to Coy. officers for re-organisation & for training under Coy arrangements.	
			In the afternoon a team from the draft played a Battalion team soccer. Result 4 to 1 in favour of the Battalion team	
			~~A rugby match was also played between our Regt. team & the 2nd Regiment. Result~~	
LEDRINGHEM	29/9/17.		Training under Company arrangements & reorganisation of platoons from 9 am. to 12 noon.	

A5834 Wt. W4973/M687 750,000 8/16 D. D. & L. Ltd. Forms/C.2118/

Instructions regarding War Diaries and Intelligence Summaries are contained in F. S. Regs., Part II. and the Staff Manual respectively. Title pages will be prepared in manuscript.

WAR DIARY
or
INTELLIGENCE SUMMARY.
(Erase heading not required.)

Army Form C. 2118.

Place	Date	Hour	Summary of Events and Information	Remarks and references to Appendices
LEDRINGHEM	29/9/17		In the afternoon we played rugby against a team from the 2nd Regt. after a good fast game the score was three points all. Draft of 16 O/R arrived. 2nd Lt. Thompson reported back from England for duty.	
LEDRINGHEM	30/9/17		Church parades. – weather lovely.	

4th. S.A. INFANTRY REGT. 30 SEP 1917 Ref. No. SOUTH AFRICAN SCOTTISH.

D. M. MacLeod ....Lieut. Colonel.
Commanding 4th. South African Infantry.

A5834 Wt. W4973/M687 750,000 8/16 D. D. & L. Ltd. Forms/C.2118/13.

Instructions regarding War Diaries and Intelligence Summaries are contained in F. S. Regs., Part II. and the Staff Manual respectively. Title pages will be prepared in manuscript.

WAR DIARY
or
INTELLIGENCE SUMMARY.
(Erase heading not required.)

Army Form C. 2118.

4 S African Bn

Vol 19

Place	Date	Hour	Summary of Events and Information	Remarks and references to Appendices
EDRINGHEM	1/10/17		Weather fine – Training from 8.45 am to 12.30 pm. Physical Drill Bayonet fighting, musketry & Close Order Drill. All Specialists trained in their own particular duties.	
			Inter-Company football in the afternoon.	
EDRINGHEM	2/10/17		The day was spent in bathing, companies having to march some four kilos to the Divisional baths at Arneke.	
			In the afternoon two inter-Company football matches were played both of which were good hard games.	
EDRINGHEM	3/10/17		Training from 8.45 am to 12.30 pm. Instruction in German machine guns, Lewis gun training, Artillery formations, Bayonet fighting & Physical training.	
			Draft of seventeen O/R arrived mostly B.E.F. men from Base.	

A5834 Wt. W4973 M687 750,000 8/16 D. D. & L. Ltd. Forms/C.2118/13.

Army Form C. 2118.

WAR DIARY
or
INTELLIGENCE SUMMARY.
(Erase heading not required.)

Instructions regarding War Diaries and Intelligence Summaries are contained in F. S. Regs., Part II. and the Staff Manual respectively. Title pages will be prepared in manuscript.

Place	Date	Hour	Summary of Events and Information	Remarks and references to Appendices
HOULLE	4/10/17		The Battalion moved by march route to HOULLE leaving at 8.a.m. arriving at their billets at about 4 p.m. Weather dull with hard rain after our arrival in HOULLE. Billets very scattered & rather crowded.	
HOULLE	5/10/17		Training on area allotted to us about six kilo's from billets from 12.30 p.m. to 6 p.m. Artillery formation by coys & by Battalion marching & Bayonet Fighting. Weather-fine but rather chilly.	
HOULLE	6/10/17		Training on EPERLEQUES training area from 12.30 p.m. to 6 p.m. Coys marched out independently & had dinner on training ground at 12 noon after which we practised Platoon & Coy attack formations with sectional rushes, Bayonet fighting & musketry & marched home at 6 p.m.	

A5834 Wt. W4973 M687 750,000 8/16 D. D. & L. Ltd. Forms/C.2118/13.

Army Form C. 2118.

WAR DIARY
or
INTELLIGENCE SUMMARY.
(Erase heading not required.)

Instructions regarding War Diaries and Intelligence Summaries are contained in F. S. Regs., Part II. and the Staff Manual respectively. Title pages will be prepared in manuscript.

Place	Date	Hour	Summary of Events and Information	Remarks and references to Appendices
HOULLE	7/10/17		The 5th Army musketry range was allotted to the Battalion but after marching out it rained so hard that no shooting could be done & after lunch we marched home & carried on with training in billets till 6pm.	
HOULLE	8/10/17		Weather fine but cloudy: Training from 11.30am. till 5.pm. on EPERLECQUES Area. Platoon & Coy attack, followed by Battalion attack under the Commanding Officer. Yukon pack carriers training from 9am. to 7pm.	

Instructions regarding War Diaries and Intelligence Summaries are contained in F. S. Regs., Part II. and the Staff Manual respectively. Title pages will be prepared in manuscript.

WAR DIARY
or
INTELLIGENCE SUMMARY.
(Erase heading not required.)

Army Form C. 2118.

Place	Date	Hour	Summary of Events and Information	Remarks and references to Appendices
HOULLE	9/10/17.		The Battalion made use of the 5th Army Musketry Range from 10 AM till 4 PM. The usual firing practices took place.	
HOULLE	10/10/17		Rev 3 AM. Fall in 4 AM. Battalion marched to Watten, a distance of about 6 Kilos, & entrained in good time under the able supervision of the Battalion Entraining Officer [illegible] Arrived at our destination Dirty Bucket Corner about 4 PM. This place is well named. We then marched to Brake Camp & were billeted in Huts.	
BRAKE CAMP	11/10/17		Orders received for Battalion to be prepared to move at a moment's notice. A working party of 200 OR. under Capt McCubbin embussed at 2-30 PM & debussed	

A5834 Wt. W4973 M687 750,000 8/16 D. D. & L. Ltd. Forms/C.2118/13.

Instructions regarding War Diaries and Intelligence Summaries are contained in F. S. Regs., Part II. and the Staff Manual respectively. Title pages will be prepared in manuscript.

WAR DIARY
or
INTELLIGENCE SUMMARY.
(Erase heading not required.)

Army Form C. 2118.

Place	Date	Hour	Summary of Events and Information	Remarks and references to Appendices
			in the St. Julien Area. They then proceeded & were engaged in carrying material to the front line. The party returned at 5:30 AM on the morning of the 12th.	
REIGERSBERG CAMP	12/10/17		The Battalion marched out from Brake Camp at 2.15 P.M. & proceeded to Reigersberg Camp, a distance of 7 Kilos. Rain fell heavily during the march & continued right through till the morning of the 13th. The Camp here consisted of a few Tents & Bivouacs made of tarpaulin sheets. Rather a muddy place. Assault & mobilization were issued about 7 P.M.	
REIGERSBERG CAMP	13/10/17		A cold miserable wet night was spent in this place but in spite of this the men were in good spirits. The Battalion	

A5834 Wt. W4973 M687 750,000 8/16 D. D. & L. Ltd. Forms/C.2118/13.

Army Form C. 2118.

WAR DIARY
or
INTELLIGENCE SUMMARY.
(Erase heading not required.)

Instructions regarding War Diaries and Intelligence Summaries are contained in F. S. Regs., Part II. and the Staff Manual respectively. Title pages will be prepared in manuscript.

Place	Date	Hour	Summary of Events and Information	Remarks and references to Appendices
			started moving by Companies at 5 minutes interval, about 4 P.M. the following Officers went into the line	

Headquarters	"A" Coy	"B" Coy	"C" Coy	"D" Coy
MAJOR HUNT (in command)	8/CAPT. GRIERSON	CAPT McCUBBIN	2/Lt ALLEN	8/Capt SMITH
2/Lt MACKENZIE (Act. Adjt.)	2/Lt SAUNDERS	2/Lt MALE	" THOMPSON	2/Lt MACDONALD
" MANSFIELD (INT. OFF)	" BELL	" DOUGLAS.	" de la COUR	" McINTOSH.
" NEILLE (SIGNAL OFF)				
Capt LAWRENCE (M.O.)				

WE made our way to the Front line via the French Boards known as Alberta Track. "B" Coy were relieving the various elements of the 26th & 27th Brigades in the Right Sector & "C" Coy in the left sector. On arrival at the line (which was about 11 PM.) the men who we were to relieve had, when they saw us in the distance, cleared out making the task of taking over as we had to find the front line for ourselves, a rather difficult matter owing to the terrible muddy state of the shell poached country.
"D" Company were in support of "B" Coy about 500 yards

A5834 Wt. W4973 M687 750,000 8/16 D. D. & L. Ltd. Forms/C.2118/13.

Army Form C. 2118.

WAR DIARY
or
INTELLIGENCE SUMMARY.
(Erase heading not required.)

Instructions regarding War Diaries and Intelligence Summaries are contained in F. S. Regs., Part II. and the Staff Manual respectively. Title pages will be prepared in manuscript.

Place	Date	Hour	Summary of Events and Information	Remarks and references to Appendices
			as one of the stiffest nights they have ever spent. The Duck Board Track ending about 600 yards from the Line, the remaining distance seemed like a horrible nightmare. The mud was simply appalling. Men would get stuck fast & 2 or 3 of their comrades would have to stop & pull them out. This caused the line to break & often connection was lost altogether. However the dogged determination of the men to get there eventually got us into the Line & the enemy assisted us greatly in our relief by keeping his Artillery & Machine Guns quiet. The day passed by quietly enough though good sport was given us sniping the enemy. In this respect he was fairly active but fortunately	

Army Form C. 2118.

WAR DIARY
or
INTELLIGENCE SUMMARY.
(Erase heading not required.)

Instructions regarding War Diaries and Intelligence Summaries are contained in F. S. Regs., Part II. and the Staff Manual respectively. Title pages will be prepared in manuscript.

Place	Date	Hour	Summary of Events and Information	Remarks and references to Appendices
			in rear + "D" Coy. is support of "C" Coy about the same	
			distance behind. The relief was reported complete about 11-30 PM	
			with the exception of an advanced Post at Shaft about	
			150 yards ahead, which could not be found.	
			Owing to the difficulty of keeping the Diary up to date	
			in the line the remaining 10 days was written up from	
			Diary's supplied from Company's at COUDEKERQUE-BRANCH.	
COUDEKERQUE-BRANCH			At dawn "C" Coy. relieved the Post at SHAFT + the Battalion	
			was now holding about 1000 yards of the Front line of	
	14/10/17		the famous YPRES SALIENT. The night of the 13th is	
			looked upon by the 2 Companies in the front line	

A5834 Wt. W4973/M687 750,000 8/16 D. D. & L. Ltd. Forms/C.2118/1

Army Form C. 2118.

Instructions regarding War Diaries and Intelligence Summaries are contained in F. S. Regs., Part II. and the Staff Manual respectively. Title pages will be prepared in manuscript.

WAR DIARY
or
INTELLIGENCE SUMMARY.
(Erase heading not required.)

Place	Date	Hour	Summary of Events and Information	Remarks and references to Appendices
			he never hit a target.	
	15/10/17		To-day sniping was fairly lively ~~action~~. The enemy again failed to score. One of our men hit a man who was up a tree & was sure he had killed an enemy Intelligence Officer or an F.O.O. Nothing less! About 4 am four Germans approached one of "C" Company's post &, failing to answer the challenge, one was shot through the chest, the other three disappearing. A report from SHAFT to the effect that four Germans approached them, two of whom were killed, the other two managing to get away. Enemy planes fairly active all day long, flying low. Engaged by our Lewis Guns & Rifle Fire. Artillery on both sides lively.	

A5834 Wt. W4973/M687 750,000 8/16 D. D. & L. Ltd. Forms/C.2118/13.

Army Form C. 2118.

WAR DIARY
or
INTELLIGENCE SUMMARY.
(Erase heading not required.)

Instructions regarding War Diaries and Intelligence Summaries are contained in F. S. Regs., Part II. and the Staff Manual respectively. Title pages will be prepared in manuscript.

Place	Date	Hour	Summary of Events and Information	Remarks and references to Appendices
17/10/17.			At CHEDDAR VILLA 2/Lt. K.R.Y. MACKENZIE the Acting Adjutant was reported a Casualty having been slightly gassed at HUBNER FARM. Having been sent to Hospital 2/Lt Douglas took over his duties. The day passed fairly quiet except for a few 5'9s which the enemy sent over in our direction. One shell landed in the Trench & unfortunately "D" Coy suffered to the extent of nine casualties. During the night the enemy was fairly active overhead. A few Bombs were dropped near us without doing any damage.	
18/10/17			The Brigade Headquarters having been shelled rather heavily at Artillery House they removed to CHEDDAR VILLA. This necessiated Battalion Headquarters moving to a new place. This we	

A5834 Wt. W4973/M687 750,000 8/16 D. D. & L. Ltd. Forms/C.2118/13.

Instructions regarding War Diaries and Intelligence Summaries are contained in F. S. Regs., Part II. and the Staff Manual respectively. Title pages will be prepared in manuscript.

WAR DIARY
or
INTELLIGENCE SUMMARY.
(Erase heading not required.)

Army Form C. 2118.

Place	Date	Hour	Summary of Events and Information	Remarks and references to Appendices
	16/10/17		For 2 days two Guides per platoon had been reporting to Batt Headquarters daily (which was at HUBNER FARM) for the purpose of ensuring a good relief. At 12 noon orders were received that the Battalion would be relieved to-night by 1st S.A.I. Our Artillery active all day Enemy Spasmodic Bursts. About 8.P.M. the 1st S.A.I. arrived & after handing over Trench Stores etc. we made our way down the Duck Board Track to CALIFORNIA DRIVE. The relief was assisted greatly to find out the route etc. by Tapes which were laid in various places. The Battalion was reported relieved about 10 P.M. Battalion Headquarters now shifted to CHEDDAR VILLA with the whole Battalion in an old German Line now known as CALIFORNIA DRIVE	

Instructions regarding War Diaries and Intelligence Summaries are contained in F. S. Regs., Part II. and the Staff Manual respectively. Title pages will be prepared in manuscript.

WAR DIARY
or
INTELLIGENCE SUMMARY.
(Erase heading not required.)

Army Form C. 2118.

Place	Date	Hour	Summary of Events and Information	Remarks and references to Appendices
			did, taking up a position in CALIFORNIA DRIVE. During the day & night the enemy shelled us rather heavily. Owing to this & the fact that two 8.2" How's were to be put in position near our position we thought it advisable to shift.	
	19/10/17		The Brigadier & Major Hunt went reconnoitring this morning & came to the conclusion that it would be better to shift further back to trenches named respectively CALIFORNIA TRENCH and CALABAN TRENCH. During the morning orders were received for 2 Companies to proceed to Irish Farm. "A" & "B" Coys were selected & moved to this new position about 10 A.M. The remainder of the Battalion, at about	

A5834 Wt. W4973/M687 750,000 8/16 D. D. & L. Ltd. Forms/C.2118/13.

Army Form C. 2118.

Instructions regarding War Diaries and Intelligence Summaries are contained in F. S. Regs., Part II. and the Staff Manual respectively. Title pages will be prepared in manuscript.

WAR DIARY
or
INTELLIGENCE SUMMARY.
(*Erase heading not required.*)

Place	Date	Hour	Summary of Events and Information	Remarks and references to Appendices
			2 P.M. moved to the trenches mentioned above. This Line was not as clean or dry as the one we had just left but owing to the fact that the enemy artillery left this line severely alone we thought it advisable to stay there. About 7 P.M. the relief, 11th Battalion Royal Scots, started arriving & at 8-30 relief was reported complete. The Battalion then made tracks for REIGERSBERG CAMP (the Camp we occupied for one night before going into the Line) & arrived about 11 P.M. Hot food was served to the men who were soon asleep, glad to be able to take their Boots off & get a good sleep after nearly a week in the most muddy part of the whole British Line.	
	20/10/17		Nothing eventual happened to-day. Rain fell heavily at intervals ~~during~~ making the Camp, which was already	

A5834 Wt. W4973/M687 750,000 8/16 D. D. & L. Ltd. Forms/C.2118/13.

Army Form C. 2118.

Instructions regarding War Diaries and Intelligence Summaries are contained in F. S. Regs., Part II. and the Staff Manual respectively. Title pages will be prepared in manuscript.

WAR DIARY
or
INTELLIGENCE SUMMARY.
(Erase heading not required.)

Place	Date	Hour	Summary of Events and Information	Remarks and references to Appendices
			very muddy, into a horrible mess.	
	21/10/17		A working party of 80 OR under the Command of Capt Smith left this morning for IRISH FARM to work for the Artillery.	
	22/10/17		Another party of 200 O.R. under Capt Grierson left Camp at 3-30 PM. & proceeded to St. Julien for the purpose of carrying Stokes Mortar Ammunition up to the front line. This party had a very rough time, the enemy putting up a very heavy barrage & unfortunately this party was right in the centre of it. However the work was done & we were lucky to suffer so few casualties. The party returned in batches, the last arriving at 1. A.M.	
	23/10/17		A party of 75 OR under 2/Lt Allen proceeded to the St. JULIEN area to work on a new Duck Board Track.	

WAR DIARY
or
INTELLIGENCE SUMMARY.
(*Erase heading not required.*)

Instructions regarding War Diaries and Intelligence Summaries are contained in F. S. Regs., Part II. and the Staff Manual respectively. Title pages will be prepared in manuscript.

Place	Date	Hour	Summary of Events and Information	Remarks and references to Appendices
	24/10/17		The Battalion moved at 10-30 AM to the WORMHOUDT AREA, a distance from NOUVEAU MOND, at some points, of only one mile. The party under Capt Smith reported back at this place also a draft of 2 Officers (2/Lts Barry & Jackson) & 128 O.R. Billets in this AREA were very scattered, the Battalion covering at least three Kilometres.	
	25/10/17		The Battalion proceeded by March Route to the GOUDEKERQUE BRANCH. The Battalion was the last unit of the Brigade to move & the route followed was via BERGUES — DUNKIRK MAIN ROAD. Started at 9 AM & halted for the midday meal at 12.45 PM. Started again at 1-45 PM & arrived at our destination about 3-30 P.M. the distance being nearly	

A5834 Wt. W4973/M687 750,000 8/16 D. D. & L. Ltd. Forms/C.2118/13.

Army Form C. 2118.

WAR DIARY
or
INTELLIGENCE SUMMARY.
(*Erase heading not required.*)

Instructions regarding War Diaries and Intelligence Summaries are contained in F. S. Regs., Part II. and the Staff Manual respectively. Title pages will be prepared in manuscript.

Place	Date	Hour	Summary of Events and Information	Remarks and references to Appendices
			The Battalion, less the working parties, left Camp at 1.15 PM & marched for about 1 Mile to a point where we were to Embus for the WORMHOUDT AREA. At this point the party under 2/Lt Allen reported back & at 3-30 P.M. the Battalion, less Capt. Smith's party, embussed, & arrived at NOUVEAU MONDE. All ranks were glad to get away from the YPRES SALIENT. The only good point in this part of the Line was the liberal issue of Rum which was at all times necessary.	
			Our total casualties from the 11/10/1917 till 22/10/17 were	

	OFF.	O.R.
KILLED	1	10.
WOUNDED	1	61.
MISSING	–	2.

In addition nearly 20 men were evacuated sick two of whom were suffering from Trench Feet.

A5834 Wt. W4973/M687 750,000 8/16 D. D. & L. Ltd. Forms/C.2118/13.

Instructions regarding War Diaries and Intelligence Summaries are contained in F. S. Regs., Part II. and the Staff Manual respectively. Title pages will be prepared in manuscript.

WAR DIARY
or
INTELLIGENCE SUMMARY.
(Erase heading not required.)

Army Form C. 2118.

Place	Date	Hour	Summary of Events and Information	Remarks and references to Appendices
			twelve miles	
	26/10/17		Our new Billets are rather good & all ranks are looking forward to a long rest Nothing of importance to record to-day.	
OUDREMERQUE BRIANCHIE	27/10/17		The Battalion spent the day in Billets. Re-organising & cleaning up being the chief items.	
do	28/10/17		Baths were alloted to the Regiment but had to be cancelled owing to a warning order being received from Brigade. Preparation being made for the move to a new sector to-morrow. About 10 PM. enemy aircraft fairly active, dropping Bombs, but up to the time of writing 10.15 PM. no casualties have been reported. Been a lovely day though somewhat chilly.	

Army Form C. 2118.

Instructions regarding War Diaries and Intelligence Summaries are contained in F. S. Regs., Part II. and the Staff Manual respectively. Title pages will be prepared in manuscript.

WAR DIARY
or
INTELLIGENCE SUMMARY.
(Erase heading not required.)

Place	Date	Hour	Summary of Events and Information	Remarks and references to Appendices
LA PANNE.	29/10/17.		The Battalion, having embussed about 2 Kilometres from Coudekerque Branche arrived here, after a journey of about 10-12 miles, at 1-30. We are holding a ~~line~~ line of posts, along the sea coast. The Town & the Billets are without doubt very good. Trying hard to snow this morning.	
LA PANNE.	30/10/17		Forenoon allotted to Companies for reorganising etc. Afternoon repairing & improving defensive system. Raining during afternoon.	
LA PANNE.	31/10/17		Companies "B" & "D" training from 9 to 12 o'clock. Draft of ~~2 Officers~~ & 111 O.R. arrived from Depot. Nice sunny day.	

[signature] Lieut. Colonel.
Commanding 4th. South African Infantry.

A5834 Wt. W4973/M687 750,000 8/16 D. D. & L. Ltd. Forms/C.2118/13.

Instructions regarding War Diaries and Intelligence Summaries are contained in F. S. Regs., Part II. and the Staff Manual respectively. Title pages will be prepared in manuscript.

or

INTELLIGENCE SUMMARY.

(*Erase heading not required.*)

Vol 20

Place	Date	Hour	Summary of Events and Information	Remarks and references to Appendices
LA PANNE BAINS	1/11/17		Baths at St. Idesbalde were alloted to the Regiment + 400 men were bathed. "D" Company carried out 3 practices on the Range. 5 rounds Grouping, 10 Application + 15 Rapid. The firing was good. 2 Officers + 155 OR were detached for work with the 2nd Australian Tunnelling Company. The Lewis Gun Officer was instructed to test 1000 rounds "R.L." + "J." + report thereon. The Divisional Band visited the Regt. + discoursed music during the afternoon. The day was fairly dry but very cloudy with an occasional drizzle of rain.	
LA PANNE BAINS	2/11/17		Inter Company reliefs took place + were reported complete at 10-20 A.M. "D" Coy relieving "A" Company. Baths at St. Idesbalde alloted to Regt. from 2-3 P.M. + 100 OR. of Draft recently arrived were put through. Weather cloudy but dry. Nothing of importance to report.	
LA PANNE BAINS	3/11/17		"A" Coy. did training during the forenoon. "D" Company in Left Sub Sector "C" Coy in Right Sub Sector. Fine clear day inland but misty at sea. Enemy aircraft active between 9 PM & 9.30 PM. Dropped about 12 Bombs in vicinity. Medical Officer inspected all ranks to-day.	

Army Form C. 2118.

WAR DIARY
or
INTELLIGENCE SUMMARY.
(Erase heading not required.)

Instructions regarding War Diaries and Intelligence Summaries are contained in F. S. Regs., Part II. and the Staff Manual respectively. Title pages will be prepared in manuscript.

Place	Date	Hour	Summary of Events and Information	Remarks and references to Appendices
La Panne Bains	4/11/17		The Brig-General visited the Camp this morning. 500 ORanks proceeded to the 1st S.A.F. Ambulance & underwent the treatment for Trench Feet. A Signal Balloon fell in the Sea opposite the Left Sub Sector. No Church Parade took place owing to the Trench Foot treatment. Excellent day.	
La Panne Bains	5/11/17		Belgian Baths allotted to Battalion & 550 O.R. were bathed. Remainder of Battalion underwent the Trench Foot treatment. Inter-Coy relief took place this afternoon. "A" Coy relieved "C" Coy in ~~Right~~ Right Sub Sector. Relief reported complete at 2-35 P.M. A Draft of 6 O.R. reported. The C.O. 2nd in command & Company Commanders of the relieving Belgian	Good day.
La Panne Bains	6/11/17		Battalion inspected the Coast Defence System this morning. Weather: Showery & rather cold in the morning. Afternoon brightened up.	

Instructions regarding War Diaries and Intelligence Summaries are contained in F. S. Regs., Part II. and the Staff Manual respectively. Title pages will be prepared in manuscript.

WAR DIARY
or
INTELLIGENCE SUMMARY.
(Erase heading not required.)

Army Form C. 2118.

Place	Date	Hour	Summary of Events and Information	Remarks and references to Appendices
Coxyde Bains	7/11/17		The 16th Infantry Batt. 6th Brigade 2nd Division (Belgians) started arriving in small parties about 9-30 am but the relief was not complete till 12-30 pm. We marched out from La Panne Bains at 1PM & arrived here about 2 PM. This is a small deserted village & occasionally get shelled. Weather was bad in the morning, rain falling heavily. In the afternoon it cleared somewhat, but at night the wind rose to what was practically a gale.	
Coxyde Bains	8/11/17		"A" "B" & "C" Companies were training from 9-12. Lt. Bowker reported this afternoon. Attached to Batt. for 1 months training. Wet & stormy day.	
Coxyde Bains	9/11/17		"C" Company moved out of Camp to be under the C.O. 3rd S.A. I. Regt. Strength 4 Off 178 O.Ranks. Eleven Gothas passed overhead & were scattered by Anti-Aircraft & Lewis Gun fire. Cold & rainy day.	

Instructions regarding War Diaries and Intelligence Summaries are contained in F. S. Regs., Part II. and the Staff Manual respectively. Title pages will be prepared in manuscript.

WAR DIARY
or
INTELLIGENCE SUMMARY.
(Erase heading not required.)

Army Form C. 2118.

Place	Date	Hour	Summary of Events and Information	Remarks and references to Appendices
MIDDLESEX CAMP	10/11/17		The Battalion, less "B" & "C" Coy arrived here about 10.45 AM. Leaving left Coxyde Bains at 10 AM. Working parties of 5 Off & 250 OR. reported to "F" Shorai Coy. R.E. & were engaged in carrying. They returned about 4 P.M. Wet day rather stormy. Camp is composed of Huts & Dug-outs scattered over a big area in the sand dunes.	
MIDDLESEX CAMP	11/11/17		Enemy aircraft flying overhead in fairly large numbers. Bathing took place at Yorkshire Camp between 2PM & 5 PM. when 300 OR were bathed. Raining day with an occasional burst of sunshine. Battalion less B & C Companies detached were training from 9 to 12 noon.	
MIDDLESEX CAMP	12/11/17		A Draft of 26 O.R. was arrived from Base. Nice day. Training carried out from 9 am till 12 noon. Nothing important to record. Baths in the Camp are available daily from 2PM to 5PM.	
MIDDLESEX CAMP	13/11/17		All Officers reconnoitred the Line to-day	

A5834 Wt. W4973 M687 750,000 8/16 D. D. & L. Ltd. Forms/C.2118/13.

Army Form C. 2118.

WAR DIARY
or
INTELLIGENCE SUMMARY.
(Erase heading not required.)

Instructions regarding War Diaries and Intelligence Summaries are contained in F. S. Regs., Part II. and the Staff Manual respectively. Title pages will be prepared in manuscript.

Place	Date	Hour	Summary of Events and Information	Remarks and references to Appendices
MIDDLESEX CAMP	14/11/17		Usual training took place between 9am & 12 noon. Working parties detailed to repair huts in Camp previous to handing over. Many E. Aircraft overhead in the forenoon. Nice sunny day inclined to be cold at night. About 11 PM. enemy shelled the vicinity of Camp.	
MIDDLESEX CAMP	15/11/17		Training as usual in the forenoon. About 1-30 am & again at 4-20 am the Enemy dropped a few shells in the Camp without however causing any damage	
MIDDLESEX CAMP	16/11/17		"A" Coy were relieved by the 3rd Regt. at 10-30 PM. The remainder of the Regt was relieved by the 141st R. Infantry Regt. French at 4-30 PM. We then proceeded to LA PANNE BAINS. Cloudy day. "B" Coy. rejoined from 2nd Australian Tunnelling Coy.	
LA PANNE	17/11/17		Foot inspection under Company arrangements. Lt Col D.M. MacLeod DSO being in command of XV Corps Reserve a reconnoitring party from the 2nd & 4th Regiments went over the defences. 10 Off. & 600 OR. went to Coxyde Bains & worked under the	

A3834 Wt. W4973 M687 750,000 8/16 D. D. & L. Ltd. Forms/C.2118/13.

Army Form C. 2118.

WAR DIARY
or
INTELLIGENCE SUMMARY.

(Erase heading not required.)

Instructions regarding War Diaries and Intelligence Summaries are contained in F. S. Regs., Part II. and the Staff Manual respectively. Title pages will be prepared in manuscript.

Place	Date	Hour	Summary of Events and Information	Remarks and references to Appendices
LAPANNE	18/11/17		Corps Cyclists. Fine day. Church Parades were held at 11-15 AM. "C" Company, who were attached to the 3rd S.A.D. in the line rejoined Unit this afternoon at 4-30 PM, Having had only 2 Casualities (wounded)	
			Dry but cloudy.	
GHYVELDE	19/11/17		Battalion moved from LAPANNE at 2.0 pm and proceeded by march Route to GHYVELDE. Arrived at GHYVELDE at 4.15 pm. Camped in Huts. Weather cold. Battalion marched well. no stragglers.	
Teteghem	20/11/17		Moved by march route to TETEGHEM. Left GHYVELDE at 10.30 AM arrived TETEGHEM 1.15 pm. no men fell out. Weather dull Battalion in Billets. Scattered over area. Billets taken over in very filthy Condition. Same reported to B.H.Q. QM Stores lorry delayed by breakdown.	

A5834 Wt. W4973 M687 750,000 8/16 D. D. & L. Ltd. Forms/C.2118/13.

Instructions regarding War Diaries and Intelligence Summaries are contained in F. S. Regs., Part II. and the Staff Manual respectively. Title pages will be prepared in manuscript.

WAR DIARY
or
INTELLIGENCE SUMMARY.
(Erase heading not required.)

Army Form C. 2118.

Place	Date	Hour	Summary of Events and Information	Remarks and references to Appendices
ESQUELBECQ	21/11/17		Battalion moved at 7.55 am from TETEGHEM to ESQUELBECQ Distance approx: 12 miles, weather good for marching & men marched very well, arrived and billeted by 2.30 pm. Raining heavily Early morning, but cleared before marching out.	
LA REICLE	22/11/17		Battalion moved at 10 am from ESQUELBECQ to LA REICLE (main road, WORMHOUDT – CASSEL) arrived 11.45 am. approx distance 3 to 4 miles. Billets inadequate & very wet & muddy. weather dull but no rain. Map ref Sheet 27 I 17 d central. Marched in 23 officers & 789 and 4 off & 2 O/R attached. Company Billets very scattered.	
WARDRECQUES.	23/11/17		Battalion moved at 9.15 am from LAREICLE to WARDRECQUES. Distance approx 15 miles. arrived at 4.0 pm. No Stragglers. Billets very good & clean weather very fine. Sunshine nearly all day. (Map Ref. Hazebrouck 5A E 4.2.7.)	

A5834 Wt. W4973/M687 750,000 8/16 D. D. & L. Ltd. Forms/C.2118/13.

Instructions regarding War Diaries and Intelligence Summaries are contained in F. S. Regs., Part II. and the Staff Manual respectively. Title pages will be prepared in manuscript.

WAR DIARY
or
INTELLIGENCE SUMMARY.
(Erase heading not required.)

Army Form C. 2118.

Place	Date	Hour	Summary of Events and Information	Remarks and references to Appendices
ASSINGHEM	24/11/17		Battalion moved from WARDRECQUES at 10.0 AM by March Route to ASSINGHEM (MAP HAZEBROUCKE B4 82) distance approx: 15 miles weather inclined to be showery, but generally fine for marching. Men marched well & there were no stragglers. Billets central & fairly good. G.O.C. Division paid a call just after battalion were billeted. Battalion marched in at 4 0 pm.	
RENTY	25/11/17		Battalion moved at 11.30 am from ASSINGHEM and arrived at RENTY at 3.45 pm. Men marched well & there were no stragglers. Heavy sleet storm during march. Billets bad & inadequate. Re-arrangement necessary, no sanitary arrangements. Major Hunt returned from leave & brought draft of 87 O/R. Distance approx 8-9 miles.	
RENTY	26/11/17		Wet morning: Reorganising Platoons &c. Rearrangment of Billets.	

A9834 Wt. W4973 M687 750,000 8/16 D. D. & L. Ltd. Forms/C.2118/13.

Instructions regarding War Diaries and Intelligence Summaries are contained in F. S. Regs., Part II. and the Staff Manual respectively. Title pages will be prepared in manuscript.

WAR DIARY
or
INTELLIGENCE SUMMARY.
(Erase heading not required.)

Army Form C. 2118.

Place	Date	Hour	Summary of Events and Information	Remarks and references to Appendices
RENTY	27/11/17		Wet Morning. Training in Billets under Company arrangements. Commanding Officer & Adjt to Conference at BHQ.	
RENTY	28/11/17		Fine day. Training under Company arrangements. 8 O/Rs arrived.	
RENTY	29/11/17		Fine weather. Training as per programme from 9 - to 1 pm Presentation of Parchment Certificates to Privates PERRIE, O'BYRNE & DAMANT. C.O. & Lewis Gun Officer to Lewis Gun Demonstration at LE TOQUET. Brig-General visited Billets. STANDREWS day greetings received from 26th Brigade. (in GAELIC) Regt played new draft at Ass: Football. Drawn Game.	
RENTY	30/11/17		Dull morning - Battalion training as per programme issued. Guest night at Mess of Brig Gen & Staff visited. Warning order to move received.	

D. J. Hunt Major
for Lieut. Colonel.
Commanding 4th. South African Infantry.

A5834 Wt. W4973/M687 750,000 8/16 D. D. & L. Ltd. Forms/C.2118/13.

Instructions regarding War Diaries and Intelligence Summaries are contained in F. S. Regs., Part II. and the Staff Manual respectively. Title pages will be prepared in manuscript.

WAR DIARY
or
INTELLIGENCE SUMMARY.
(Erase heading not required.)

Army Form C. 2118.

4 S A Infy Bn

Sept 21

Place	Date	Hour	Summary of Events and Information	Remarks and references to Appendices
EPES	1/12/17		Left Henty this morning at 9 am & arrived at EPES about 5-45 PM after a long march. No lorries were available & Blankets had to be left behind.	
ANVIN	2/12/17		Left EPES for ANVIN to entrain for PERONNE. Entrained at ANVIN about 12-30 am 3/12/17. Lorries with Blankets turned up	
PERONNE	3/12/17		Arrived at PERONNE at mid day. Had Dinner near the station then left for Don Camp arriving there at 4 PM.	
DON CAMP	4/12/17		Left DON CAMP for FINS at 12 mid day, arriving there 3-15 PM. The Regiment left FINS at 4PM for the Firing Line	
LINE	5/12/17		The Battalion holding a 3 Company frontage in the GOUZEAUCOURT AREA. Enemy artillery active on Frontline and rear areas.	

A5834 Wt. W4973 M687 750,000 8/16 D. D. & L. Ltd. Forms/C.2118/13.

Instructions regarding War Diaries and Intelligence Summaries are contained in F. S. Regs., Part II. and the Staff Manual respectively. Title pages will be prepared in manuscript.

WAR DIARY
or
INTELLIGENCE SUMMARY.

(*Erase heading not required.*)

Army Form C. 2118.

Place	Date	Hour	Summary of Events and Information	Remarks and references to Appendices
LINE.	6/12/17		Fine weather prevails. Enemy artillery active all day. Trenches in fair condition	
LINE	7/12/17		Weather still holds good. Both artilleries still active. Suffered a few casualties during the last few days. Men beginning to report sick.	
LINE	8/12/17		Dull day & fairly cold. Firing lively from both sides. Going to get relieved to-night by 3rd S.A.I.	
LINE	9/12/17		Weather ~~not~~ bad. Slight fall of rain. Upon relief took up position in Support Line with HQRS in Sunken Road near Owen X.	
LINE	10/12/17		Left Support Line & went into Hutments at L2 Camp W.3.C.	
L2 Camp	11/12/17		Rested in Hutments. great attention was paid to men's feet which were in fairly bad condition.	

A5834 Wt. W4973/M687 750,000 8/16 D. D. & L. Ltd. Forms/C.2118/13.

Instructions regarding War Diaries and Intelligence Summaries are contained in F. S. Regs., Part II. and the Staff Manual respectively. Title pages will be prepared in manuscript.

WAR DIARY
or
INTELLIGENCE SUMMARY.
(Erase heading not required.)

Army Form C. 2118.

Place	Date	Hour	Summary of Events and Information	Remarks and references to Appendices
LINE	12/12/17		Left Hutments this afternoon at 4-15 PM and relieved the 3rd S.A.I. in the Line. Relief reported complete at about 8-10 PM.	
LINE	13/12/17		Sector is now comparitively quiet from what it was when in last time. A lot of work was undertaken.	
LINE	14/12/17		Good progress is being made with work on hand. Trenches a bit wet & men's feet beginning to get sore.	
LINE	15/12/17		To be relieved to-night by 3rd S.A.I. Artillery on both sides have been fairly quiet this time. M. Guns also quiet only occasional bursts. Sniping becoming active.	
SUPPORT LINE	16/12/17		Two Companies are now in Support Line & two in Reserve. B & C. Coy being in Reserve with A and B in Support.	

A5834 Wt. W4073/M687 750,000 8/16 D. D. & L. Ltd. Forms/C.2118/13.

Army Form C. 2118.

WAR DIARY
or
INTELLIGENCE SUMMARY.
(Erase heading not required.)

Instructions regarding War Diaries and Intelligence Summaries are contained in F. S. Regs., Part II. and the Staff Manual respectively. Title pages will be prepared in manuscript.

Place	Date	Hour	Summary of Events and Information	Remarks and references to Appendices
SUPPORT LINE	17/12/17		Preparations were made for men's feet to be rubbed to-day and this was carried out. Nothing eventful to report.	
SUPPORT LINE	18/12/17		Weather is fairly good but cold. Enemy aircraft have been slightly active during the last few days. Nothing of importance to record.	
LINE	19/12/17		Preparing to move forward to-night again to relieve the 3rd S.A.I. Men are not feeling very fit.	
LINE	20/12/17		Relief complete of the 3rd S.A.I. about 8-30 P.M. A lot of work has again been started + hope to have all men under shelter before going out again. This is now becoming a fairly quiet sector. Battalion Intelligence Officer was killed to-day in No MANS LAND.	
LINE	21/12/17		Visibility was ~~again~~ very poor to-day. Large wiring parties were wiring the front line. Nothing important happened. Sniping fairly active.	

A5834 Wt. W4073/M687 750,000 8/16 D. D. & L. Ltd. Forms/C.2118/13.

Instructions regarding War Diaries and Intelligence Summaries are contained in F. S. Regs., Part II. and the Staff Manual respectively. Title pages will be prepared in manuscript.

WAR DIARY
or
INTELLIGENCE SUMMARY.
(Erase heading not required.)

Army Form C. 2118.

Place	Date	Hour	Summary of Events and Information	Remarks and references to Appendices
LINE	22/12/17.		Snipers from both sides active. Artillery (enemy) active. M. Guns spasmodic bursts. Very cold. Men working hard to keep warm.	
HUTMENTS W.3C.	23/12/17		We are being relieved to-night by the 3rd S.A.I. & proceeding to Brigade reserve. Both artilleries fairly active. Bitterly cold day and fairly strong wind blowing.	
HUTMENTS	24/12/17		Men were allowed to rest most of the day as they were feeling done up. Preparations were made to give the Regiment as good a Xmas Dinner as possible.	
HUTMENTS	25/12/17		This was a real old-fashioned Xmas day. Nice and clear & snow lying deep on the ground. All men had a bath and a clean change of clothing. A fairly good Dinner under existing circumstances was put up.	

A5834 Wt. W4973 M687 750,000 8/16 D. D. & L. Ltd. Forms/C.2118/13.

Instructions regarding War Diaries and Intelligence Summaries are contained in F. S. Regs., Part II. and the Staff Manual respectively. Title pages will be prepared in manuscript.

WAR DIARY
or
INTELLIGENCE SUMMARY.

(*Erase heading not required.*)

Army Form C. 2118.

Place	Date	Hour	Summary of Events and Information	Remarks and references to Appendices
HUTMENTS	26/12/17		No work was carried out to-day. Every man in Camp has his feet treated to-day. Very little work was carried out owing to this fact but two huts were half completed for Bomb protection	
HUTMENTS	27/12/17		A good deal of work was carried out in Camp to-day. Very hard work digging owing to frost but excellent progress was made. A bitterly cold day. Nothing important happened. Relieving 3rd S.A.I. in the Line to-night	
LINE	28/12/17		Relief of 3rd S.A.I. was completed at 8-25 P.M. last night. Men started work on shelters & wiring etc. Fairly quiet to-day.	

A5834 Wt. W4973 M687 750,000 8/16 D. D. & L. Ltd. Forms/C.2118/13.

Army Form C. 2118.

WAR DIARY
or
INTELLIGENCE SUMMARY.
(Erase heading not required.)

Inst[illegible]ions regarding War Diaries and Intelligence Summaries are contained in F. S. Regs., Part II. and the Staff Manual respectively. Title pages will be prepared in manuscript.

Place	Date	Hour	Summary of Events and Information	Remarks and references to Appendices
LINE	29/12/17		A clear bright day but very cold. Enemy artillery very active all day. Enemy planes slightly active. A good deal of work was carried out.	
LINE.	30/12/17		Heavy barrage dropped on our left this morning. Enemy raided A+S. Hdrs Sap Head + suffered severely. Gouzeaucourt was heavily shelled with heavies + Gas. Made out operation order for move to support.	
SUPPORT LINE	31/12/17		Trenches were cleaned up + everything put in order pending the relief to-night by the 3rd S. A. I who have been out resting. Relief complete at 1-15 am 1st inst. During the early part of the month our casualties were fairly heavy. The following	

A3834 Wt. W4973 M687 750,000 8/16 D. D. & L. Ltd. Forms/C.2118/13.

Instructions regarding War Diaries and Intelligence Summaries are contained in F. S. Regs., Part II. and the Staff Manual respectively. Title pages will be prepared in manuscript.

WAR DIARY
or
INTELLIGENCE SUMMARY.
(Erase heading not required.)

Army Form C. 2118.

Place	Date	Hour	Summary of Events and Information	Remarks and references to Appendices
			being the total for the month	
				Officers	O. Ranks
			KILLED 1 18	
			WOUNDED 1 84	
			MISSING One Other Rank.	
			In addition the Regiment has suffered rather severely from a health point having had app. 260 admissions to hospital during the month. 20 cases of Trench Feet have also occurred.	
			[illegible signature]	
			MAJOR	
			COMMANDING 4th S.A.I.	

9TH (SCOTTISH DIVISION)

SOUTH AFRICAN INFY BDE

4TH STH AFRICAN INFY REGT

JAN - FEB 1918

To 66 DIV 1918 SEPT

9th DIV

So African Bde

4th Bn So. African Inf Reg.

Jan - Feb 1918

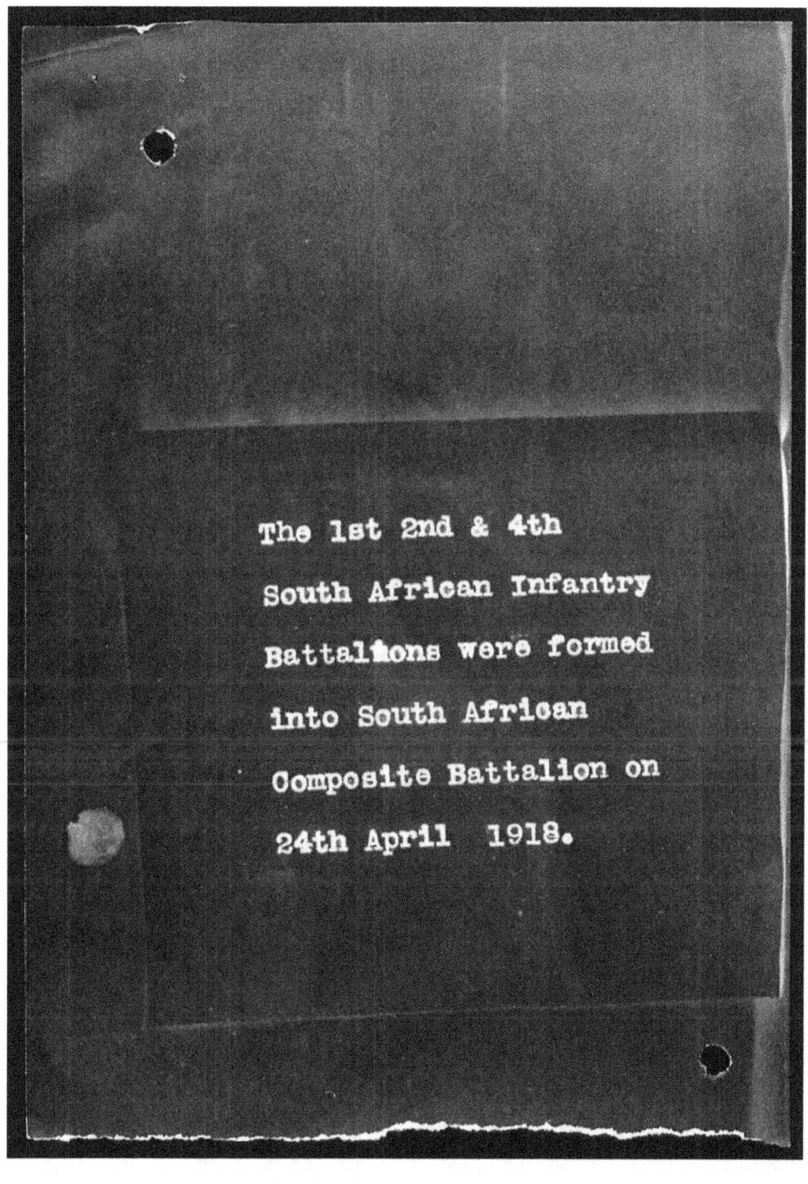

The 1st 2nd & 4th
South African Infantry
Battalions were formed
into South African
Composite Battalion on
24th April 1918.

Instructions regarding War Diaries and Intelligence Summaries are contained in F. S. Regs., Part II. and the Staff Manual respectively. Title pages will be prepared in manuscript.

WAR DIARY
or
INTELLIGENCE SUMMARY.
(Erase heading not required.)

Army Form C. 2118.

4th S.A.I. JANUARY 1918 22

Place	Date	Hour	Summary of Events and Information	Remarks and references to Appendices
SUPPORT LINE	1/1/18	9PM	We reported relief complete at 1.15 am. Since last in Support Line the disposition of the Battalion has been changed. A. Coy are in right support with "C" Coy in left support. The reserve line is held by two Companies with "B" on the left and "D" Coy on the right. The New Year came in without any unusual display from either side. Two Companies were detailed for carrying wire and pickets up to the Left & Right Sector. Quiet all day. Weather good with a nice dry frost.	
SUPPORT LINE	2/1/18	9PM	Working parties consisting of two Companies were out during the night wiring. In all 65 coils were put down. 51 on Right Sub Sector and 14 on Left Sub-sector. 20 O.R. were detailed to carry R. E. material. Both Artilleries active at periods. Weather during early part of day. Later it started to thaw & towards evening a slight drizzle commenced.	

Army Form C. 2118.

Instructions regarding War Diaries and Intelligence Summaries are contained in F. S. Regs., Part II. and the Staff Manual respectively. Title pages will be prepared in manuscript.

WAR DIARY
or
INTELLIGENCE SUMMARY.
(*Erase heading not required.*)

4th S.A.I. JANUARY - 1918

Place	Date	Hour	Summary of Events and Information	Remarks and references to Appendices
SUPPORT LINE	3/1/18	10PM	During the morning the Right Support + Right Reserve Line were fairly heavily shelled. Artilleries on both sides were fairly active. Both aircrafts were active during the day. About 9PM the enemy started sending over Gas Shells. A fairly large number were sent over but fortunately no casualties occurred as the men were warned in time. Nice clear day. Slight frost.	
LINE	4/1/18	11-30 PM	About 3-30 am the enemy sent over a few more Gas Shells. Day has been fairly quiet. The Battalion is moving up to the Line again, being relieved by the 1st S.A.I.. Relief of the 3rd S.A.I. by us was completed at 11-45 PM. Slight aerial activity on both sides. Nice clear day but somewhat cold.	

Instructions regarding War Diaries and Intelligence Summaries are contained in F. S. Regs., Part II. and the Staff Manual respectively. Title pages will be prepared in manuscript.

WAR DIARY
or
INTELLIGENCE SUMMARY.
(*Erase heading not required.*)

Army Form C. 2118.

4th S.A.I. JANUARY-1918

Place	Date	Hour	Summary of Events and Information	Remarks and references to Appendices
LINE	5/1/18	10-40PM	Observation difficult to-day owing to misty weather. Situation quiet throughout the day. Dropped two shells in the Quarry, fortunately not causing any casualties. Nothing important to record.	
LINE	6/1/18	11-20PM	Cold day with mist hanging around. Rain during early part of night. Four E.A. crossed our line about 4 am. & bombed behind our Line. An uneventful day was passed.	
LINE	7/1/18	10-45PM	Rained practically all day. The consequence being that the thaw caused the Trenches to become, in some places, almost impassible. At 4-30PM a concentration shoot took place on Cemetery. Enemy retaliated somewhat, causing a few casualties. 2/Lt STRUBEN and 2/Lt REYNOLDS were wounded. In addition 6 OR Killed 20 OR Wounded	

A5834 Wt W4973/M687 750,000 8/16 D. D. & L. Ltd. Forms/C.2118/13.

Instructions regarding War Diaries and Intelligence Summaries are contained in F. S. Regs., Part II. and the Staff Manual respectively. Title pages will be prepared in manuscript.

WAR DIARY
or
INTELLIGENCE SUMMARY.
(Erase heading not required.)

Army Form C. 2118.

4th S. A. I. — January 1918

Place	Date	Hour	Summary of Events and Information	Remarks and references to Appendices
FINS	8/1/18	11-30PM	Snow fell heavily this morning. Visibility very bad. Both Artilleries quiet. Aircraft nil. Fairly quiet day. Battalion relieved by BLWSH (3rd Regt). Relief complete at 11-30PM. Arrived at FINS and became Battalion in Brigade Reserve.	
FINS	9/1/18		Each Company did two hours work on Huts (Anti-Bomb protection). All ranks had a hot bath and a change of clothing. Snow fell during the morning. Towards evening the thaw set in with a slight showers of rain.	
FINS	10/1/18		Work was carried on during the day on improving Huts. Each hut was floored with Felt + general improvement carried on throughout; Major C.M. BROWNE M.C.	

Instructions regarding War Diaries and Intelligence Summaries are contained in F. S. Regs., Part II. and the Staff Manual respectively. Title pages will be prepared in manuscript.

WAR DIARY
or
INTELLIGENCE SUMMARY.
(Erase heading not required.)

Army Form C. 2118.

4th S.A.I. JANUARY 1918

Place	Date	Hour	Summary of Events and Information	Remarks and references to Appendices
			reported from the U.K. for duty. Still thawing & camp very muddy.	
FINS	11/1/18		All ranks allowed to rest and clean up in view of the impending move to-morrow to MOISLAINS for ten days rest. Major C.M. BROWNE M.C. took over command of the Regiment vice Major D.R. HUNT.	
MOISLAINS	12/1/18		Major D.R. Hunt having proceeded to England on Special Duty is struck off the strength of the Regiment. The Battalion proceeded by march route to MOISLAINS leaving FINS at 10 am and arrived here at 2-30 PM. Billeted in Nissen and Adrian Huts.	
MOISLAINS	13/1/18		The Battalion paraded to-day at 9-30 am and trained until 12-30 PM. In the afternoon a certain ammount of recreational training took place	

A5834 Wt. W4973/M687 750,000 8/16 D. D. & L. Ltd. Forms/C.2118/13.

Instructions regarding War Diaries and Intelligence Summaries are contained in F. S. Regs., Part II. and the Staff Manual respectively. Title pages will be prepared in manuscript.

Army Form C. 2118.

WAR DIARY
or
INTELLIGENCE SUMMARY.
(Erase heading not required.)

4th S. A. I. JANUARY - 1918

Place	Date	Hour	Summary of Events and Information	Remarks and references to Appendices
			Capt. J. McC. Mitchell arrived from U.K. and is taken on the strength.	
MOISLAINS	14/1/18		Training took place from 9-30 am till 12-30 PM. Recreational training took place during the afternoon. The Regimental Soccer Team played the VII Corps Rest Station & beat them by 3 goals to Nil.	
MOISLANS	15/1/18		TRAINING from 9. A. M to 12-30 p.m. ~~With~~ In afternoon Recreational training carried on for an hour & then stopped owing to heavy rain. Started a Lewis Gun instructional class for 32 men. Whale oiling under supervision from 5 to 5.30 p.m.	
MOISLANS	16/1/18		Training from 9 A M to 12.30 p.m.; mostly in huts due to heavy rain. No recreational training for same reason. Hut accommodation improved with assistance of a few R.E. stoves rebuilt, Beds repaired & floors bricked. Very stormy & violent winds all night. Whale oiling as 15th.	

A5834 Wt. W4973/M687 750,000 8/16 D. D. & L. Ltd. Forms/C.2118/13.

Army Form C. 2118.

WAR DIARY
or
INTELLIGENCE SUMMARY.
(Erase heading not required.)

Instructions regarding War Diaries and Intelligence Summaries are contained in F. S. Regs., Part II. and the Staff Manual respectively. Title pages will be prepared in manuscript. 4th S.A.I.

JANUARY - 1918

Place	Date	Hour	Summary of Events and Information	Remarks and references to Appendices
MOISLANS	17/1/18		Training in Huts from 9 A.M. to 12-30 p.m. Huts too crowded & dark for good work. Improvement of Huts continued. No recreational training. Weather bad. Whaleoiling as 16th.	
MOISLANS	18/1/18		TRAINING from 9. to 12.30 p.m. in the open:- MUSKETRY, Bayonet fighting close order drill, Bombing & March Past. No recreational training in afternoon due to bad weather. Improvement of huts continued. Whaleoiling as 17th.	
MOISLANS	19/1/18		Furnished Working party 5 officers & 250 O.R. for work on corps line. Left at 7 a.m. and back at 4-45 p.m. Lewis Gun class at work. Also improving camp bricking floors of huts, mending bunks &c. Fine mild day. rain only in evening.	

Instructions regarding War Diaries and Intelligence Summaries are contained in F. S. Regs., Part II. and the Staff Manual respectively. Title pages will be prepared in manuscript.

WAR DIARY
or
INTELLIGENCE SUMMARY.
(Erase heading not required.)

Army Form C. 2118.

4th S A I — JANUARY - 1918

Place	Date	Hour	Summary of Events and Information	Remarks and references to Appendices
MOISLANS	20/1/18		Furnished Working party 5 officers & 250 O.R. for work on Corps line. Left at 7 a.m., returned to camp p.m. Also found Wkg party of 1 N.C.O. and 12 men for fatigue to Div Train. Lewis Gun class on instruction in morning and on digging trench at musketry range. Mild weather	
MOISLANS	21/1/18		Furnished working party of 3 officers & 150 O.R. for work on Corps line & a party of 13 O.R. to 9th Divl Train. Rest training from 9 to 12.30 p.m. Musketry - Artillery formation - Bayonet fighting - Battalion Drill - Extended order Drill. Mild weather but showery.	
MOISLANS	22/1/18		1 N.C.O. & 12 men on working party with 9th DIVN train. Rest of Battalion training - Musketry - Antigas Drill - Bayonet fighting - Extended order drill - Artillery formation - Mild weather but showery.	

Instructions regarding War Diaries and Intelligence Summaries are contained in F. S. Regs., Part II. and the Staff Manual respectively. Title pages will be prepared in manuscript.

WAR DIARY
or
INTELLIGENCE SUMMARY.
(Erase heading not required.)

Army Form C. 2118.

4th S.A.I. JANUARY-1918

Place	Date	Hour	Summary of Events and Information	Remarks and references to Appendices
MOISLANS	23/1/18		WORKING party of 1 N.C.O. and 12 O.R with 9th DIVN TRAIN TRAINING 9 A.M. to 12.30 A.M:- Bayonet fighting - MUSKETRY. ARTILLERY FORMATION Antigas drill & march past - Reconnoitring party of 5 officers visited front line - Right sub sector of Left Brigade front in morning. at 8 p.m. Details of relief explained to officers & platoon commanders	
MOISLANS	24/1/18		Advance parties of 1 officer & 1 NCO per Coy & H.Q. to line at 9 A.M. to take over stores Battalion fell in at 2 p.m & entrained at 3 p.m. at D20d34. All details detrained half way & proceeded to detail camp at SOREL-LE-GRAND. Battalion detrained at TYRE dump by 4.55 p.m. 1st platoon moved at 5 p.m, and last platoon left detraining point at 5.40 p.m. 9th Seaforth guides at Q35c9510. Relief complete at 8 p.m. We relieved the 7th Seaforths. A good relief. Furnished Dugout platoon 1 officer & 36 O.R to BDE & fatigue 1 off & 26 O.R. to 178th Tunnellers	Food Transport gassed on road home

A5834 Wt. W4973/M687 750,000 8/16 D. D. & L. Ltd. Forms/C.2118/13.

Instructions regarding War Diaries and Intelligence Summaries are contained in F. S. Regs., Part II. and the Staff Manual respectively. Title pages will be prepared in manuscript.

WAR DIARY
or
INTELLIGENCE SUMMARY.
(Erase heading not required.)

Army Form C. 2118.

4th S. A. I.

JANUARY - 1918

Place	Date	Hour	Summary of Events and Information	Remarks and references to Appendices
RT Sub Sector GOUZEAUCOURT	25/1/18		Misty morning - Visibility better in afternoon. Battalion holds front line from R.31 D 50-35 to R 26 C 50-30 with Batt H.Q. at Q 36 D 64-71 - Gauche Wood Map. Two companies in front line each of three platoons - Two platoons in posts & one platoon in support. One company for counter attack at Station - one company for Garrison of village. Two platoons near Batt H.Q. and one platoon in sunken road app R25C central. Village shelled at intervals all day, also vicinity of Station. Village heavily shelled from 5.20 p.m to 5.35 p.m. Two of our Transport were casualties. Rations dumped at Q 36 B 90.05.	

Instructions regarding War Diaries and Intelligence Summaries are contained in F. S. Regs., Part II. and the Staff Manual respectively. Title pages will be prepared in manuscript.

WAR DIARY
or
INTELLIGENCE SUMMARY.
(Erase heading not required.)

Army Form C. 2118.

4th S.A.I. JANUARY-1918

Place	Date	Hour	Summary of Events and Information	Remarks and references to Appendices
Rt Sub Sector GOUZEAUCOURT	26/1/18		Misty weather all day. Visibility poor. Enemy very quiet all day. Work improving trenches & carrying parties. Two listening posts sent out at night and wire examined & reported on by Intelligence officer. Intercompany relief. B Coy to Rt front company. A to Village garrison Coy. C to left front company. D to Station as counterattacking coy. Relieved late due to carrying parties & completed at 12.M.N	
Rt Sub Sector GOUZEAUCOURT	27/1/18		Misty all day - visibility poor. Weather mild. Work consisting principally in repairing front trenches, furnishing carrying parties, & salvaging work. Advance parties left at 8 A.M. to take over Support line from 3rd S.A.I. Guides from [illegible] for relief left & met platoons of 3rd S.A.I at Q35 B87 at 8.30pm. Relief complete at 10-45 pm. Relief complete at Support line at 12. M.N. Batt H.Q at Q23 C63. Battalion holds line app Q23 C63 to app Q28 D91.	

A5834 Wt. W4973/M687 750,000 8/16 D. D. & L. Ltd. Forms/C.2118/13.

Instructions regarding War Diaries and Intelligence Summaries are contained in F. S. Regs., Part II. and the Staff Manual respectively. Title pages will be prepared in manuscript.

WAR DIARY
or
INTELLIGENCE SUMMARY.
(*Erase heading not required.*)

Army Form C. 2118.

4th S.A.I. JANUARY 1918

Place	Date	Hour	Summary of Events and Information	Remarks and references to Appendices
Supports map 57C Q23c63	29/1/18		Parties salvaging timber for repairing shelters. Thirty men also working for R.E. Salvaged & erected a 100 gallon tank at Dead man's corner. Q23c63. In evening found a party for RE in front line at GOUZEAUCOURT. Slight frost in morning - a fine day - Visibility good. Lt. Col. McLeod reassumed command on return from Leave	
			Slight frost in morning - fine day - Visibility good.	
Supports map 57C 23c63.	30/1/18		Fatigue parties out from all companies salvaging stores. Same returned to Q.M. store for salvage. Dug two supporting points, salvaged Timber, made a new Bomb store, made a new Drying Room. Some hostile sneezing gas in vicinity of Batt H.Q. Practised Stand to in trenches to be lived.	

A5834 Wt. W4973/M687 750,000 8/16 D. D. & L. Ltd. Forms/C.2118/13.

Instructions regarding War Diaries and Intelligence Summaries are contained in F. S. Regs., Part II. and the Staff Manual respectively. Title pages will be prepared in manuscript.

WAR DIARY
or
INTELLIGENCE SUMMARY.
(Erase heading not required.)

Army Form C. 2118.

4th S. A. I. JANUARY - 1918

Place	Date	Hour	Summary of Events and Information	Remarks and references to Appendices
Supports Map 57c Q23c63	31/1/18		Frost in morning - Visibility poor all day. All companies cleaned up. Capt McCuthun inspected Batt HQ. & all clean. Battalion relieved by 1/6th Cheshire Battalion of 118th Brigade. Our guides met the incoming battalion on Fins Gouzeaucourt Road east of W3 central. Relief complete 8.45 pm. On relief the battalion moved to hutments at SOREL LE GRAND	
			D M MacLeod Lt. Col Commanding 4th South African Infy (South African Scottish)	

A5834 Wt. W4973/M687 750,000 8/16 D. D. & L. Ltd. Forms/C.2118/13.

ARMS, CLOTHING and EQUIPMENT (Cont'd).

Every man will carry two Mills Hand grenades, and one ground flare in his breast and side pockets. Bombing platoons will carry additional grenades in the carriers provided.

Every man will carry three sandbags, one over each shoulder and one as a cover to his rifle.

Each section and platoon Commander will carry Artillery flags.

Every Officer and N.C.O. will carry two Very Lights, green and white.

Rifle grenadiers will each carry eight rifle grenades.

Great coats will be worn over equipment until shortly before Zero hour when they will be dumped.

Companies will take forward their full equipment of wire cutters, Very pistols, etc.

20. CARRYING PARTIES.

The carrying sections of each Company will carry the following :-

4 boxes of S.A.A.
4 boxes of Rifle Grenades.

On arrival at the blue line Company dumps are to be formed and carrying sections will return for further stores as required.

21. RATIONS.

One day's rations will be carried in addition to the iron rations. All water bottles will be full.

Dawson Christian

Lieut. Colonel.
Commanding, 4th. S.A.I.

Instructions regarding War Diaries and Intelligence Summaries are contained in F. S. Regs., Part II. and the Staff Manual respectively. Title pages will be prepared in manuscript.

WAR DIARY
or
INTELLIGENCE SUMMARY.

(*Erase heading not required.*)

Army Form C. 2118.

Vol 23

4th South African Infantry

February 1918

Place	Date	Hour	Summary of Events and Information	Remarks and references to Appendices
REL LE AND	1/2/18		Moved from Sorel Le Grand at 8.30 A.M. Entrained at Station AX13 V.18.a.1.2 Left at 10 A.M approx: reaching PERONNE about 12 NOON. Had the field kitchens there & had tea. Entrained at Peronne Station at 1.30 p.m. Left at 2 p.m. Detrained at LE PLATEAU on MARICOURT-BRAY Road at 3.20. Moved at 3.40 p.m to SUZANNE & billetted at 5 p.m in hutments. A bitterly cold day all day.	
SUZANNE	2/2/18		Men cleaning equipment all day, & getting quarters comfortable. Collected wood for issue to the troops.	
SUZANNE	3/2/18		Frost in morning & afternoon. Church parades. Collecting firewood - Getting bunks into the huts.	
SUZANNE	4/2/18		Mild weather. Battalion training from 9 to 12.30 p.m. Physical Drill - Saluting - Musketry Instruction - Bayonet fighting. Throwing Dummy Bombs - . Hutments being bunked & duckboarded.	

A5834 Wt. W4973/M687 750,000 8/16 D. D. & L. Ltd. Forms/C.2118/13.

Army Form C. 2118.

Instructions regarding War Diaries and Intelligence Summaries are contained in F. S. Regs., Part II. and the Staff Manual respectively. Title pages will be prepared in manuscript.

WAR DIARY
or
INTELLIGENCE SUMMARY.
(Erase heading not required.)

4 S.A.I. February 1918.

Place	Date	Hour	Summary of Events and Information	Remarks and references to Appendices
SUZANNE	5/2/18		All coys on Working parties making a Rifle Range and Bayonet assault course A & B 8-30 to 12-30 C & D from 12.30 to 4-30. All companies bathed at S.A.M.C. baths.	
SUZANNE	6/2/18		All coys on Working parties. A.B & C on Rifle Range & Bayonet assault course from 8.30 to 10.30 A.M. D coy carried bundles for huts. In afternoon all companies training from 2 to 4.10 p.m. General Congreve came round inspecting. Very fine mild day.	
SUZANNE	7/2/18		Training and working parties. Played A.S.C. in afternoon won by 3 goals to 1.	

Instructions regarding War Diaries and Intelligence Summaries are contained in F. S. Regs., Part II and the Staff Manual respectively. Title pages will be prepared in manuscript.

WAR DIARY
or
INTELLIGENCE SUMMARY.
(*Erase heading not required.*)

Army Form C. 2118.

4th S.A.I. February 1918

Place	Date	Hour	Summary of Events and Information	Remarks and references to Appendices
SUZANNE	8/2/18		Two Coys on range. Grouping & application. A at 8.15 am B at 12.30 pm. C & D companies Throwing Live Bombs – Physical Training – Company Drill from 8 to 11 a.m. All companies on anti aircraft protection round the huts. Some rain during the day otherwise mild. Lectures to Officers & N.C.O.s	
SUZANNE	9/2/18		C & D Coys on range – MUSKETRY and Application. A & B coys a two hours route march. All coys on anti-aircraft protection round Huts. "Thistles" performed in the evening. Fine day but cold wind. Played 9th D.S.C. won 3–0	
SUZANNE	10/2/18		In morning C.O. addressed the battalion re the breaking up 3rd S.A.I and announced there would be an intercompany competition on 16-2-18 to decide which original company battalion should be eliminated to allow of the 3rd regt reinforcement coming in as a complete company. Headquarters fired grouping and application from 9 to 12.30 noon. All Coy Lewis gunners carried out target practice with ball ammunition from 2 to 4 p.m. The remainder of the battalion had an intersection rifle competition	

(B5834) Wt. W4973 M687 750,000 8/16 D. D. & L. Ltd. Forms/C.2118/1.

Instructions regarding War Diaries and Intelligence Summaries are contained in F. S. Regs., Part II. and the Staff Manual respectively. Title pages will be prepared in manuscript.

or

INTELLIGENCE SUMMARY.

(Erase heading not required.)

4 A.I. February 1918.

Place	Date	Hour	Summary of Events and Information	Remarks and references to Appendices
	10/2/18		for which prizes were given. No 11 platoon C Coy turned out the best section. Also an individual competition (Bobbing jimmy), 91 men competed. Excellent weather - mild	
SUZANNE	11/2/18		Training A.B & C coys did field firing practices by companies in addition together with C Coy carried on with general training & construction of anti-aircraft protection of the huts. Good weather. Played A.S.C & won by 3-nil	
SUZANNE	12/2/18		D Coy did field firing. A, B and C Coys fired 5 rounds application X, 15 rounds rapid, and experiments of fire practices. General training and anti aircraft protection of huts. Weather good, but very misty in morning	
SUZANNE	13/2/18		Wet - Companies constructing anti-aircraft protection for huts.	

A5834 Wt. W4973 M687 750,000 8/16 D. D. & L. Ltd. Forms/C.2118/13.

Instructions regarding War Diaries and Intelligence Summaries are contained in F. S. Regs., Part II. and the Staff Manual respectively. Title pages will be prepared in manuscript.

WAR DIARY
or
INTELLIGENCE SUMMARY.
(Erase heading not required.)

Army Form C. 2118.

4th S.A.I. February 1918.

Place	Date	Hour	Summary of Events and Information	Remarks and references to Appendices
SUZANNE	14/2/18		C and D coys fired 5 rounds application & 15 rounds rapid fire. Rest of battalion general training & all coys making anti aircraft protection of huts. Weather mild	
SUZANNE	15/2/18		8 officers and 187 O.R. 3rd Regiment marched in and were taken on strength as from 16-2-18. The 1st S.A.I & 2nd S.A.I were using all the ranges. Battalion on general training. All companies in afternoon getting ready for competition.	
SUZANNE	16/2/18		Inter company competition for the elimination of one of the Companies to allow of the 3rd Regt reinforcement joining the battalion as a company. The following acted as judges:- Inspection Brig. Gen Dawson 1st S.A.I. B12 Drill - Lt Col. [illegible] Christian 2nd S.A.I Musketry 2/Lt T. Bancroft 2nd S.A.I Gas - Lt. Watson - 9th Division Gas Officer	

A5834 Wt. W4973 M687 750,000 8/16 D. D. & L. Ltd. Forms/C.2118/13.

WAR DIARY
or
INTELLIGENCE SUMMARY.
(Erase heading not required.)

Army Form C. 2118.

Instructions regarding War Diaries and Intelligence Summaries are contained in F. S. Regs., Part II. and the Staff Manual respectively. Title pages will be prepared in manuscript.

4th S.A.I — February 1918.

Place	Date	Hour	Summary of Events and Information	Remarks and references to Appendices
SUZANNE	16/2/18		General Knowledge – Major F.E. Cochran – 1st S.A.I. Bde	
			Lewis Gun Drill – 2nd Lt F. Bell 2nd S.A.I	
			Map Reading – Lt. F. Burton – 1st S.A.I Bde.	
			Signalling do. do.	
			Inspection of Billets – Major Hunter – 5th Camerons.	

Result of Competition

Items of Competition	Maximum Marks	A Coy Marks	B Coy Marks	C Coy Marks	D Coy Marks
Inspection of Company	200	153	141	146.5	157
Drill	100	71	86	78	80
Musketry	150	81	80	82.5	80
Gas	100	80	92.5	85	90
General Knowledge	100	58	70	74	74
Lewis Gun Drill	100	75	80	80	92
Map Reading	50	45	47	44	47
Signalling	50	46	45	42	47
Inspection of Billets	150	120	115.5	124	137
Totals	1000	729	757	756	804

A5834 Wt. W4973 M687 750,000 8/16 D. D. & L. Ltd. Forms/C.2118/13.

Instructions regarding War Diaries and Intelligence Summaries are contained in F. S. Regs., Part II. and the Staff Manual respectively. Title pages will be prepared in manuscript.

WAR DIARY
or
INTELLIGENCE SUMMARY.

(Erase heading not required.)

Army Form C. 2118.

4th S.A.I. February 1918.

Place	Date	Hour	Summary of Events and Information	Remarks and references to Appendices
SUZANNE	16/2/18		The result of the competition decided that "A" company should fall out & be drafted one platoon to each of the three other companies. Weather very fine but bitterly cold & frosty.	
SUZANNE	17/2		The Battalion paraded at 8.20 and at 8.30 a.m. marched to Delville Wood. Halted by the side of the Road a few hundred yards short of Longueval for midday meal. At 1 p.m. the S.A. Brigade formed up in square in Delville Wood for a memorial service, facing a cross erected by Brigade. After the service General Lukin, commanding the Division, presented ribbons to men of the Brigade who had recently got awarded decorations. The Brigade then marched past in column of route. The Battalion collected stones & each man deposited a stone round a cross erected by the Battalion to the memory of those of the Battalion who fell in July 1916. Afterwards marched back to camp	The cross made by Pioneer 5th [?] Regt Royal [?] made [?] reference of cross (S.A. Scottish) Trench map LONGUEVAL 57c S.W.3 S.18.C.20.95.

A3834 Wt. W4973 M687 750,000 8/16 D. D. & L. Ltd. Forms/C.2118/13.

Instructions regarding War Diaries and Intelligence Summaries are contained in F. S. Regs., Part II. and the Staff Manual respectively. Title pages will be prepared in manuscript.

WAR DIARY
or
INTELLIGENCE SUMMARY.
(Erase heading not required.)

Army Form C. 2118.

4th S. A. I. — February 1918

Place	Date	Hour	Summary of Events and Information	Remarks and references to Appendices
SUZANNE	17/2/18		via Montauban and Maricourt, at Maricourt filed past the late Colonel Jones's grave. Back to camp about 5 pm. Weather cold but very fine.	
SUZANNE	18/2/18		All Companies at Musketry, practising for A.R.A competition with selection of best company to result therefrom. Also constructing Anti-aircraft defences. Very cold but fine	
SUZANNE	19/2/18		The 3rd Regiment company took over the place of A Company in the Battalion. One platoon each of the old A Coy going to B. C & D companies respectively. The Battalion is again as from date organized with four platoons per company after for some time having had only three platoons per company. Training as usual - Field firing - company [illegible]	

A5834 Wt. W4973 M687 750,000 8/16 D. D. & L. Ltd. Forms/C.2118/13.

Army Form C. 2118.

Instructions regarding War Diaries and Intelligence Summaries are contained in F. S. Regs., Part II. and the Staff Manual respectively. Title pages will be prepared in manuscript.

WAR DIARY
or
INTELLIGENCE SUMMARY.
(Erase heading not required.)

4th S.A.I. — February 1918.

Place	Date	Hour	Summary of Events and Information	Remarks and references to Appendices
SUZANNE	20/2/18		Training - All companies on the range 5 Rounds application and 15 Rounds Rapid: [illegible] the whole regiment. Had a running competition.	
SUZANNE	21/2/18		Training - Platoon Training and Field Firing	
SUZANNE	22/2/18		Training of [illegible] by companies in morning. In afternoon played the 5th Camerons in semi-final for Furze cup & lost 5-1.	
SUZANNE	23/2/18		Training. Two companies in the attack & two watching them revised the companies; carried out with live ammunition & grenades. Had four Lewis guns and four Stokes Mortars cooperating. On the whole well carried out. Section leaders and Lewis gunners showed initiative. Boxing in evening.	

Instructions regarding War Diaries and Intelligence Summaries are contained in F. S. Regs., Part II. and the Staff Manual respectively. Title pages will be prepared in manuscript.

WAR DIARY
or
INTELLIGENCE SUMMARY.
(Erase heading not required.)

Army Form C. 2118.

4th S.A.I. February 1918

Place	Date	Hour	Summary of Events and Information	Remarks and references to Appendices
SUZANNE	24/2/18		Church parades. Mild weather	
SUZANNE	25/2/18		The battalion practised Artillery formations from Columns of route opening out to attack. Well carried out without noise. Rain interfered with training after same. In afternoon 2nd in command of companies carried out a reconnaissance of ground for Brigade scheme on 26th. Mild weather but wet & chilly	
SUZANNE	26/2/18		No 11 Platoon of "C" Coy 4th S.A.I won the Divisional A.R.A competition. South African Scottish scored 292 points 6th K.O.S.B.S scored 271 do. 7th Seaforths scored 201 do. beating the 26th & 27th Brigade representative teams as above. The battalion carried out a Brigade Tactical scheme the general scheme being it was a counterattack to drive the Germans out of our lines!	

A5834 Wt. W4973/M687 750,000 8/16 D. D. & L. Ltd. Forms/C.2118/12.

Army Form C. 2118.

WAR DIARY
or
INTELLIGENCE SUMMARY.
(Erase heading not required.)

Instructions regarding War Diaries and Intelligence Summaries are contained in F. S. Regs., Part II. and the Staff Manual respectively. Title pages will be prepared in manuscript.

4th S.A.I. February 1918

Place	Date	Hour	Summary of Events and Information	Remarks and references to Appendices
SUZANNE	27/2/18		Training as a Battalion. Practised consolidation in depth, then advanced in artillery formation of sections through Suzanne & changing direction half right attacked two objectives on the Lump from system using ball S.A.A. Lewis guns & Stokes mortars co-operated	
SUZANNE	28/2/18		Training - consolidated shell holes. then watched the 2nd Regt in attack practice, & counter attacked on flank.	
			Ration strength of regt at date 37 officers 905 O.R.	
			Paper strength do do 53 officers 1055 O.R.	

[signature] Lt Col Commdg
4th S.A.I.

A5834 Wt. W4973/M687 750,000 8/16 D. D. & L. Ltd. Forms/C.2118/13.

www.ingramcontent.com/pod-product-compliance
Lightning Source LLC
Chambersburg PA
CBHW080913230426
43667CB00015B/2668